Thucydides

On Justice, Power, and Human Nature

Thucydides

On Justice, Power, and Human Nature

Selections from
The History of the Peloponnesian War

Edited and Translated by
PAUL WOODRUFF

Hackett Publishing Company
Indianapolis/Cambridge

For
T.F.R.G. Braun
Teacher and Friend

Copyright © 1993 by Hackett Publishing Company, Inc.

All rights reserved

Printed in the United States of America

17 16 15 14   7 8 9 10

Cover and text design by Dan Kirklin

For further information, please address

Hackett Publishing Company, Inc.
P.O. Box 44937
Indianapolis, Indiana 46244-0937
www.hackettpublishing.com

Library of Congress Cataloging in Publication Data

Thucydides.
   [History of the Peloponnesian War. English. Selections]
   On justice, power, and human nature: the essence of Thucydides' History of the Peloponnesian War/Thucydides; edited and translated by Paul Woodruff
   p. c.m.
   Includes bibliographical references.
   ISBN 0-87220-169-4. – ISBN 0-87220-168-6 (pbk.)
   1. Thucydides—Political and social views. 2. Thucydides. History of the Peloponnesian War. 3. Greece—History—Peloponnesian War, 431–404 B.C. I. Woodruff, Paul, 1943– . II. Title. III. Title: Thucydides on justice, power, and human nature.
DF229.T55W66 1993
938'.007202—dc20
                                        93–29617
                                            CIP

ISBN-13: 978-0-87220-169-9 (cloth)
ISBN-13: 978-0-87220-168-2 (pbk.)

Contents

Preface	vii
Introduction	ix
Bibliographical Notes	xxxiii
Maps	xxxvi

Thucydides
On Justice, Power, and Human Nature

1. **Early History and Method**   1
   a. Thucydides' preface [i.1]   1
   b. The archaeology [i.2–20]   2
   c. On historical method [i.21–22]   12

2. **Origins of the War**   15
   a. Thucydides' explanation for the war [i.23]   15
   b. Debate at Sparta in 432 [i.66–88]   16
   c. Meeting of the Peloponnesian League in 431 [Summary of i.118–24]   30
   d. Pericles' war speech [i.140–46]   31
   e. The war begins with an attack on Plataea [ii.1–8]   36

3. Pericles and the Plague — 39
a. The Funeral Oration of Pericles [ii.35–46] — 39
b. The plague: human nature laid bare by a natural disaster [ii.47–54] — 46
c. Military operations of 430 [ii.55–58] — 51
d. Pericles' last speech [ii. 59–64] — 52
e. Thucydides' judgment of Pericles [ii.65] — 56

4. Justice and power: Plataea and Mytilene — 59
a. Further events of 430 [ii.66–70] — 59
b. The siege of Plataea [ii.71–78] — 62
c. The Mytilenean debate [iii. 37–51] — 66
d. The Plataean debate [iii.52–68] — 76

5. Human Nature Laid Bare in Civil War — 89
a. The civil war in Corcyra [iii.81.2–85] — 89
b. The end of the Corcyrean insurgents [iv.47.3–48] — 94

6. Justice and Power: Acanthus and Melos — 97
a. The Spartans at Acanthus [iv.84.2–87] — 97
b. Events leading to the Peace of Nicias [Summary] — 100
c. The Melian dialogue [v.84–116] — 102

7. The Sicilian Expedition — 111
a. Sicilian antiquities, [Summary of vi.2–6] — 111
b. Debate at Athens [vi.8–26] — 112
c. Launching the expedition [Summary of vi.27–105] — 123
d. Defeat of the expedition [vii.1–viii.1, Summary and Translation] — 129

8. Aftermath of the Sicilian Expedition [Summary] — 155

Dates — 161
Glossary — 163
Index — 171

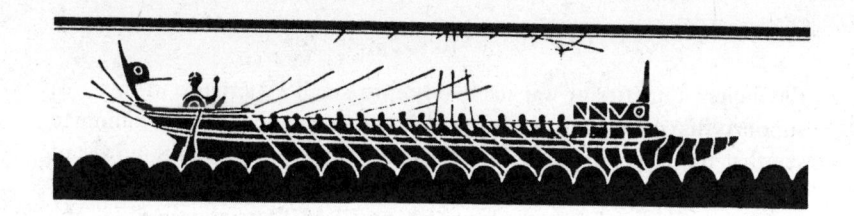

Preface

The aim of this book is to make the best known parts of Thucydides' *History* available to readers who are not scholars and do not want to get lost in the intricacies of Greek history or geography. Here is the basic narrative of the Peloponnesian War down to the Athenian disaster in Sicily. Here too are the famous speeches and debates, along with the vivid set-piece descriptions of the plague and the civil war and the gripping stories of the fall of Plataea and the loss of the Sicilian Expedition. All this is not enough, of course. If you like Thucydides you will want to read the entire book for its artful construction and for the many fine passages I have had to omit. Thucydides keeps his authorial voice quiet in the *History*, and the best way to detect his strategy is in the structure of the work. In these selections, then, I have done my best to indicate the shape of the surroundings for each passage.

I first knew Thucydides mainly as a source for Greek history, and a particularly difficult one at that. He not only left frequent seductive traps for the unwary scholar, but he littered his pages with obstacles in the form of long speeches in the hardest Greek prose I had ever seen. It was only after I began teaching him in philosophy classes (at the suggestion of my colleague Joe Horn) that I began to see what a brilliant mind was at work in his *History*. Then I recalled what I had learned from wonderful teachers—the dazzling lectures of G.E.M. de Ste. Croix and the warm tutorials of T.F.R.G. Braun, to whom this book is respectfully dedicated. I would like to say that they are not to blame for any errors I may have made, but I cannot deny that they have influenced my work deeply. I should mention one other teacher: "War is a violent teacher," writes Thucydides, personifying an abstraction as he so often does, meaning that men at war take on the violent qualities of war itself. My own small experience in this area supports his conclusion. On the positive side, however, I am also coming to see that military experience has allowed me to appreciate the power of Thucydides' descriptions as I never could before.

My translation is an unashamed betrayal of Thucydides: where the Greek is obscure, I have tried to be clear. In this I have concentrated on the abstract concepts that pepper the text—justice, power, human nature, and fear. At the same time I have tried to bring into English the toughness of the original, which has been obscured by the flabby but accurate translations now in use. My work began out of a love affair with Hobbes's translation for its simplicity and directness, and much of Hobbes remains.

Dates are always B.C.E. (Before the Common Era). Proper names, technical terms, and Greek words are explained in the glossary. References to Thucydides' text are in boldface when they guide the reader to passages included in this volume. References to notes in commentaries are by last name of author. Summaries and introductory sections are in *italics*; the translation is in roman.

In correcting my translation I am indebted to Mark Gifford, Michael Gagarin, David Dean-Jones, and various anonymous readers for the publisher. To these, many thanks. I must also thank Peter Green for helpful conversations about Thucydides, and confess one special debt: the title of this volume was proposed by Mark Gifford.

I am also grateful to Shirley Hull, Heidi Hall, Julie Baxter, and Mary Nix for assistance in typing the manuscript, and I must thank the Cambridge University Press for their kind permission to use substantial passages that I first translated for a work they commissioned, *Early Greek Political Theory from Homer to the Sophists* (forthcoming), which I edited with Michael Gagarin. The passages include all or parts of the following sections: i.1, 20–23, 70, 75–77; ii.35–46, 52–53, 60, 63, 65; iii.37–48, 81–84; v.84–116; vi.18, 39, 89; viii, 48, 64, 68, 89, 97.

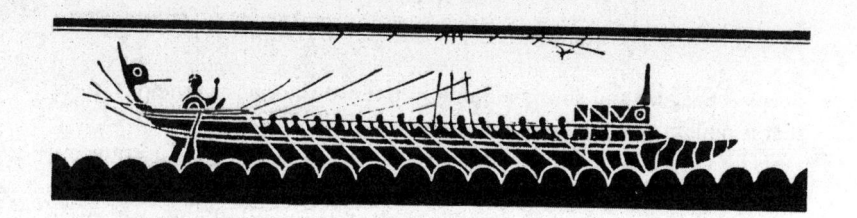

Introduction

The Author

Who is like Thucydides? He reminds us of modern historical scholars when he sweeps myth away from old stories (**i.20**, **vi.54**); but few historians are so artful in their selection and organization of material or so quiet about conflicting sources. In some ways Thucydides resembles a writer of historical fiction, and the tragic poets who began that sort of work in Greece probably taught him a great deal. Cornford called him "the artist who was no longer an actor," who "could discern the large outlines shaping all that misery and suffering into the thing of beauty and awe which we call tragedy" (1907: 250). Indeed, the influence of tragedy explains many elements in the *History*; but all in all the book is less like tragedy than it is like history: the absence of verse, of choruses, and, most important, of anything resembling reverence for the divine leaves it far from tragedy, which was written, after all, to be performed at a religious observance, and to linger in the mind as only verse can do. True, tragedy is driven by a sense of inevitable outcome, and Thucydides' story unfolds with a necessity to which he frequently calls our attention. But Thucydidean necessity (*anankē*) is not fate, and it has nothing to do with the gods. The style of the *History*, too, is remote from poetry. Thucydides is no tragedian.

Much of the *History* consists of paired speeches, and these recall the sophists who taught men to argue both sides of a question. No doubt this too left a mark on Thucydides (as it did on his poetic counterpart Euripides), so that he is more like a sophist than he is like any other writer, at least in the most famous parts of the *History*. This comparison applies only to form, however, for while the sophists do not seem to care which side is right in their fictional examples, Thucydides, in his real ones, is deeply engaged, and shows a moral outrage at the catastrophe of Greece that is no less obvious for being understated.

Is he a moral philosopher, then? He had a philosopher's education and was concerned, as philosophers are, to detect the real beneath the apparent. Jaeger, Strauss, and Grene all treat him as a political philosopher. In his political views he is like Plato in some ways and Aristotle in others. Like Plato he finds demagoguery antithetical to any serious thought of justice. Like both of them he is distrustful of out-and-out democracy, and like Aristotle he seems to favor a mixed constitution. He is far beyond any other ancient thinker, however, in his understanding of the ways of power in the real world. His work calls for comparison with that of Machiavelli and Hobbes, but he rarely instructs as they do. Hobbes put it best: "Digressions for instruction's cause, and other such open conveyances of precepts (which is the philosopher's part), he never useth; as having so clearly set before men's eyes the ways and events of good and evil counsels, that the narration itself doth secretly instruct the reader, and more effectually than can possibly be done by precept."[1]

Thucydides is not a philosopher, however. His subject is the history of the Peloponnesian War; and although he believes that this exemplifies general truths about human nature he never develops an explicit theory, never directly engages with philosophers in debate, and never pauses to explain his method in any detail. To be a philosopher is, at least, to take part in the running debate philosophers have with each other; and Thucydides does not do that.

Well, who *is* like Thucydides? No one, of course. He is unique and inimitable. He is a historian, and his *History of the Peloponnesian War* is our only source of information for much of the material it covers, but it is also a highly imaginative piece of work, energized by its author's concern for personal and political morality, and crafted to display his mastery of rhetorical style.

Of the life of Thucydides we know little beyond what he tells us. He was the son of an Athenian named Olorus, whose wealth came from gold mines in Thrace, in northern Greece; and was evidently related to Cimon, a successful Athenian general in the wars against Persia, since he was buried in Cimon's family tomb. We know that he was elected general in 424,[2] and that he lived long enough after 404, when the war ended, to reflect on that end in his unfinished *History*. Scholars infer, therefore, that he was a fairly

---

1. From Hobbes' Introduction (Molesworth Vol VII, p xxii; Schlatter 1975:18).
2. All dates in this volume are B.C.E.

young general, and put his birth between 460 and 455.

As general he was in charge of forces in northern Greece in 424, a year in which the Spartans were operating in that theater. The strategic city of Amphipolis was their chief target, and they succeeded in taking it away from the Athenians. Thucydides, who had been responsible for the defense, was punished by exile until the end of the war. Much of the twenty years he spent at his home in Thrace, but he also visited the Peloponnesus (probably including Sparta) and may also have travelled to Syracuse. After the war, he visited Athens and then returned to Thrace to try to finish writing the *History*. He died before revising Book VIII, with seven years of his story left to tell. He was buried at Athens in the tomb of Cimon's family. This far we are on fairly firm ground, but everything else we are told about Thucydides comes from biographies written centuries after his death. The story that he died by violence, for example, must be treated as legend.

Of his education we can only surmise that he learned much from the sophists who were beginning to be popular in Athens during his youth. Legend has it that he studied with the sophist-politician Antiphon, whom we know he greatly admired (**viii.68**), and with the philosopher Anaxagoras, about whom he says nothing. Probably, however, he learned most from Protagoras, but no teacher could take the credit for Thucydides. His style of writing is uniquely his own, and he must be counted as one of the most original prose stylists of the Greek or any language. As a thinker he has an extraordinary ability to produce the intellectual equivalent of counterpoint. Many themes are sounded in the *History* as its author explores both sides of complex issues. The most insistent of these is the necessity that falls on those who try to manage an empire: empires cannot remain stagnant; they must grow, and the managers of empire must pursue growth and keep order with a businesslike disregard for the moral principles they would otherwise hold dear. The tragic center of Thucydides' tale is a city that found itself compelled to wage an atrocious war, with dismal consequences for itself and its allies. It is a sad and a cautionary tale, brilliantly told, with unforgettable moments of irony.

The Combatants

The war that gives Thucydides' *History* its plot and narrative line was a classic confrontation between the sea power of Athens and the land power of Sparta (or Lacedaemon), complicated by political, cultural, and commercial rivalries. Greece was far from unified at the time, but consisted of a multitude of city-states of various sizes and, in some areas, tribal groups settled in villages. All spoke one dialect or another of Greek, and all shared a common heritage in religion and poetry. They had a distinct sense that they were Greek and everyone else was foreign (*barbaros*). Athens, Sparta, and others had joined hands under Spartan leadership to drive the Persian armies from Greek soil fifty years before the war of which Thucydides writes.

The principal differences between Sparta and Athens at the time of the war were these: (1) The Spartans had an ancient constitution, of which they were very proud, which combined elements of monarchy, aristocracy, and democracy. Its stability was the envy of Greece. Athens, on the other hand, had been through more than a century of political upheavals and emerged with a spanking new democracy.[3] (2) Sparta, isolated in the center of the Peloponnesus, was a bastion of resistance to cultural change, while Athens welcomed all sorts of innovation and became a home to what is called the new learning. This difference was further sharpened by a minor language barrier: the two cities spoke different dialects of Greek. They were divided also along ethnic lines; as Ionians, the Athenians had very different customs and traditions from Dorians, such as the Spartans, Corinthians, and Syracusans. (3) Sparta controlled its own fertile district, known as Laconia, as well as the conquered territory of Messenia. These made Sparta self-sufficient in terms of food. Athens, on the other hand, had too little farm land to support its large population and had virtually no forests; it depended on commerce to supply food for its people and timber for its shipbuilding. (4) Sparta was relatively poor in money and was not enriched by the voluntary alliance that it led. Athens controlled rich silver mines and some of its citizens owned gold mines in Thrace. It was a thriving commercial center and, to make it still richer, ruled an empire from which it collected payments. It was these that financed the Parthenon and the other grand buildings of the period.

Sparta
Spartan government was much admired by conservatives all over the Greek world. Sparta ruled an agricultural domain worked by a conquered people (the *helots*) who outnumbered the Spartans and were liable to rebel if Sparta showed any weakness. To meet this challenge, the Spartans developed a superb military machine and a system of government that was a

---

3. The concept of democracy in ancient Greece is best illustrated by the constitution of Athens, which was designed to distribute power among the citizens as equally as possible.

model of stability. Military leadership was in the hands of two hereditary kings. The Spartan Assembly was open to all citizens, but they did not all have the right to make speeches there. The Spartan Council of Elders (*Gerousia*) consisted of the two kings and twenty-eight well-born citizens who were elected for life. There were five officials known as *Ephors* ("Overseers") who were elected for one-year terms by the Assembly and whose duties included the judiciary. Citizenship was limited to freeborn males who owned landed estates of a certain size; at the time of the war there were fewer than four thousand citizens of military age. Spartan armies were the most feared in all Greece, owing to their discipline and training, but Sparta depended heavily for manpower on her allies.

Since the sixth century, Sparta had been developing a system of alliances—known as the Peloponnesian League—with the mainly Dorian cities of the Peloponnesus. The Spartans did not collect payments from their allies, as the Athenians did, but relied on them for direct military assistance and rewarded them by bolstering their traditional oligarchical governments against attempts by the people to seize power.[4]

Athens

The hallmark of democratic Athens was the freedom of its citizens, especially the freedom to speak their mind in the Assembly, and the city vibrated with opportunities that scandalized such conservatives as Plato.[5] The Assembly in Athens was a legislative body open to all citizens, any of whom could address the Assembly. Because the Assembly could be swayed by any effective speaker, some men rose to power without winning elected office, the most famous example in our period being Cleon. Such men were called demagogues. There was also a Council (*boulē*), consisting of five hundred citizens selected by lot, which prepared business for the Assembly. The use of the lottery for the Council and other offices presupposed the democratic principle that all citizens were qualified to assist in government. Generals, however, were elected, and could have considerable influence. All officials faced formal scrutiny on leaving office, so that they could be punished for corruption or malfeasance while in office. The popular courts consisted of large panels of up to 501 judges, who were ordinary citizens who had shown up to collect their day's pay for court duty. Such a large panel, it was thought, could not be bribed or otherwise

---

4. Oligarchies were governments controlled by small numbers of men who were rich and usually well born.

5. See Plato, *Republic* VIII 557B ff., 562D ff., 564D.

influenced unfairly. There was no judge or judiciary set above these panels, and their decisions were final. Pay for court duty meant that poor citizens could afford to take part.

Power in Athens was held by the citizens, and policy shifted quickly to suit their wishes. By Greek standards (and by most standards in history) this was extreme democracy, even though citizenship was limited to adult males whose parents were citizens. Women, slaves, and a large population of resident aliens (called *metics*) were excluded. Readers who are inclined to scoff at this should consider that democracy in the United States was not more inclusive than this until well into the nineteenth century.

In fact, citizenship was open to a much wider class in Athens than in Sparta. Rich or poor, if you could prove Athenian descent, you were a citizen of Athens. This too shocked the conservatives: day-laborers, with no landed estates at all, could pass judgment on the richest men of the city. At the start of the war there were more than forty thousand citizens in Athens, of whom twenty-one thousand could afford to serve as the heavily armed infantry known as hoplites. (Soldiers were required to buy their own equipment.) Resident aliens could contribute about eight thousand more men of the hoplite class.

After the Persian Wars, Athens ruled the sea as head of an alliance—the Delian League—of Greek cities against what remained of Persian rule over Greeks in Asia Minor. Athenian sea power brought commercial ascendancy, and the Delian League became an empire of island and coastal cities. Although Athens referred to these cities as her allies, Thucydides considered them to be virtually enslaved by Athens, and this was the view of the Peloponnesians. In fact, Athens shared interests with the democratic elements in many of the cities touched by its influence, while the Spartans found most in common with oligarchical regimes. Was the Athenian Empire truly oppressive? On the positive side, Athens kept the Aegean Sea safe for its island allies by stamping out piracy and keeping the Persians at bay; it also frequently defended the democratic elements of its allies against oligarchic takeovers. On the negative side, if any of the allies turned away from Athens, or ceased making payments, Athens put them down brutally.

Thucydides tells us that the empire was unpopular (ii.8, i. 99), but gives us a hint that it was not unpopular with the democrats of the subject cities (iii.47, cf. viii.48); he also supplies evidence that the empire was more popular with its subjects than the Peloponnesians expected. Athens had been exploiting dissension in the cities it dealt with for a long time, probably siding with democrats against oligarchs (iii.62), and in this way cultivated the loyalty of at least one faction in many of the cities that came into the empire. When a Spartan general reached the member cities of northern Greece in 424, he was surprised to see how little enthusiasm there was for the freedom he claimed to have brought them (iv.85); when the Sicilians offered safety to troops from the empire in 413, only a few chose to leave the Athenians to face defeat alone (vii.82); and when a number of allies rebelled in the moment of Athens' greatest weakness, after the Sicilian disaster, a surprising number remained loyal to Athens. All of these incidents took place after Athens had required higher payments to support the war, so it is likely that the Athenians were even more popular with their empire at the onset of hostilities. Thucydides is not deliberately trying to deceive us, however. The empire had never been popular with the rich and well born of the subject cities, and these were the people who mattered most to him.

The New Learning

The cultural difference between the combatants is the one that most interests Thucydides (i.70, i.84). Their educational system helped the Spartans field the most disciplined and effective army in all of Greece, but it also helped them to resist the intellectual and artistic revolution of the fifth century. No ruins of great buildings adorn the site of Sparta, no festive vases survive as great art in the museums. Sophists and other representatives of innovation were excluded during our period, and the great age of Spartan poetry—Tyrtaeus, Alcman, Terpander—was long gone.

The new learning was not born in Athens, but it was welcomed there by Pericles, who was the most effective leader of the democracy. It was mainly of interest to those who could afford the luxury of adult education and in itself was neither liberal nor conservative, but appealed equally to democrats like Pericles and oligarchs like Antiphon. Most ordinary Athenians were shocked by it, however, and it was gleefully satirized in a play of Aristophanes, *The Clouds*, which brings out its main elements: natural science and rhetoric, both pursued with a critical spirit that was not hindered by reverence for traditional beliefs or morality. A third element was anthropology, which began in this period as the study of human progress. Leaving myths of the golden age to one side, the early social scientists saw technology and social organization as improvements on primitive conditions.[6]

[6] For a review of early Greek anthropology see Guthrie (1971: 60–84). The main figures in this development are Democritus and Protagoras. Thucydides' *Archaeology* (which Guthrie ignores in this context) not only is indebted to their sort of work, but goes further in introducing empirical method to the subject.

Travelling teachers known as sophists were the main carriers of this new learning from city to city, but we should keep in mind that all men of learning were called sophists at the time. It was Plato who limited the use of the term to the more radical thinkers and gave it its pejorative tone. Thucydides' contact with the sophists gave him his interests in rhetoric, in human progress, and in the natural explanation of events; but he survived this education without losing his commitment to traditional morality.

Background of the War

Athens had been a city-state of minor significance until the middle of the sixth century, when growing commerce and a sharp change in government thrust it into the mainstream. The change in government was the institution of one-man rule—what the Greeks came to call a tyranny. The tyrant was Pisistratus, who, with his sons Hippias and Hipparchus, ruled Athens successfully for a large part of the century. Before Pisistratus, a statesman named Solon had attempted to patch up a compromise between the various class interests in Athens. The compromise failed (hence Pisistratus), but some of Solon's devices survived to be the foundation of democracy. In 510, Sparta put down the tyranny in Athens, unintentionally setting the stage for political evolution there. Some elements of democracy were in place by 500, but the whole was not functioning until about 461, when Pericles' spectacular career in politics got its start.

Meanwhile, the Greek cities along the coast of Asia Minor had been important centers of Greek commercial and cultural life, but they were brought under the Persian Empire by the sword of Cyrus the Great in 546. In 499, a number of these cities rebelled against the Persians but were roundly defeated, and in 494, Miletus, the gem of the Asiatic Greek cities, was brought down. At this point the Persians evidently realized they could not rule Asia Minor safely unless they controlled all of the Greeks around the Aegean. In 490, King Darius launched a naval expedition against mainland Greece. This was defeated by Athens in the famous battle of Marathon.

Ten years later a new Persian king, Xerxes, tried to conquer Greece with a much larger force. This time Athens could not face the enemy alone. With foresight it had equipped a substantial fleet that carried its women and children to safety and returned to join the allied Greek fleet that defeated the Persian ships at Salamis. The Persian army remained through the following year, to be defeated by a Spartan-led Greek army at the battle of Plataea (479). The victorious army was the product of an alliance of

Introduction

Greek cities, including Athens and its tiny neighbor Plataea. At the time, no one would have thought to question the right of the Spartans to lead such an effort. Both Sparta and Athens deserved to be proud of the victory. Without Spartan forces and leadership, the Greeks would not have won at Plataea; but absent the pluck and ingenuity of the Athenians at Salamis, the Persians would have been able to carry the war into the Peloponnesus by sea, divide the Greeks, and defeat them.

Soon after the Battle of Plataea the Spartans turned to matters closer to their home, and a number of Greek cities asked Athens to lead them against Persia. The alliance was cemented in 477 as the Delian League, with its center on the small sacred island of Delos, and the Greeks began a protracted mopping up of the remnants of Persian power around the Aegean Sea. Increasingly, as the years passed, the League took on the look of an empire. Athens was in charge from the start, of course, as the acknowledged leader in naval warfare. The allied cities turned most of the work over to Athens and agreed for their part to pay their share of the expenses of the League into the treasury at Delos. When the treasury was moved to Athens in 454, there could no longer be any doubt about the matter: the league was an empire, the contributions were enforced, and the leader of the league was its master.

Popular or not, the Athenian Empire grew by fits and starts, with some reverses, throughout the middle of the fifth century. During this period it came into conflict with Sparta and its allies on several occasions. The Thirty Years' Peace of 446 between Athens and Sparta was to last only fourteen years, and in 431 the Peloponnesian War began, as Sparta went to war against the growth of the Athenian Empire.

Brief History of the War

The first phase of the war began in 431 and lasted ten years. Although the Athenians met with some reverses, they were victorious on the whole, and the Peace of Nicias that followed (421–14) was favorable to Athenian interests. Pericles' original strategy in the war had been to avoid fighting the Spartans on land, and so to leave them free to waste and pillage Attica. Holed up in the city, with access to the sea protected by the long walls that led to their seaport at the Piraeus, the Athenians withstood year after year of Spartan raids in harvest season. The second year was disastrous: plague broke out in the city in 430, exacerbated by the overcrowding of refugees from the farmland outside the walls. A year later, weakened by the plague, Pericles himself died, a victim of the consequences of his own policy. Still,

Athens held out. Pericles' plan, which the Athenians followed at first all too closely, guaranteed a protracted war, costly to both sides, with no clear resolution. As long as Athens conceded the land to Sparta, and Sparta the sea to Athens, there was no hope of either side's bringing the war to an end. And, indeed, it was not until much later, in the second phase of the war, that Sparta built a navy with Persian gold and was able to threaten Athens with defeat at sea.

In 428 Mytilene rebelled against the Athenian Empire, along with most of the island of Lesbos. As a large city with its own independent fleet, Mytilene was too valuable to lose, so Athens sent a substantial force to bring the island city back into the fold. In 427, after a long siege, democrats in Mytilene sued for peace. Many Athenians wanted to make an example of Mytilene by killing its adult male citizens and enslaving the rest—a common practice with conquered peoples in Greece at the time. Better judgment prevailed, however, and at the eleventh hour Athens decided not to carry out this bloodthirsty sentence.

Meanwhile, the small town of Plataea was in trouble. This town had joined bravely in the defense of Greece against the Persians, and so was supposed to have earned the undying gratitude of all Greeks. But Plataea offended its powerful neighbor Thebes (now a Spartan ally) by deciding to join forces with Athens, in spite of its traditional ties to Thebes. A Theban army attacked Plataea in 431; then in 429 an army of the Peloponnesian League besieged it and destroyed the city in 427. The Athenian promise to defend it had meant little (**ii.73, iii.57**).

The greatest success of the Athenians was the capture in 425 of a band of 120 Spartan citizen soldiers on a small island called Sphacteria. So much did the Spartans value their citizens that they were willing to sue for peace on virtually any terms to get their men back. A leader named Cleon persuaded Athens not to make peace, however, and the first phase of the war continued until after Cleon's death, when it finally became clear that Athens had little to gain from further conflict. Peace was ratified in 421.

The Peace of Nicias (421–14) was an uneasy affair, as it did not resolve the fundamental problems between Athens and Sparta. Fighting began again soon after the peace was made, and a new generation of warlike leaders emerged. The most famous of these was Alcibiades, an aristocrat who was equally brilliant in politics and at war, and who is known to modern readers through his striking speech in Plato's fictional *Symposium*. In 416, Athens began the conquest of a neutral island, Melos. When the inhabitants refused to surrender, they were starved into submission; then the men were killed and the women and children enslaved. It was the worst blot on the history of Athens.

Introduction   xix

In 415 Alcibiades revived an old plan to expand Athenian influence by conquests in Sicily. Blocked by the Persian Empire from fully exploiting the commercial opportunities of the Black Sea, Athens could neither expand its influence nor secure its food supply without moving against Sicily. A glorious armada was whipped up out of the cream of the Athenian Empire for this expedition. Their main target was Syracuse, the largest and most powerful of the Greek cities on Sicily. Shortly after the force set sail, Alcibiades was recalled to face charges of crimes against religion—falsely brought, apparently, owing to the jealousy of his political rivals. Instead of returning to face his enemies at home, Alcibiades fled to Sparta with a mind full of plans by which the Spartans could (and did) achieve victory.

In 413, Syracuse defeated the Athenian expedition with the help of the Spartan general Gylippus, utterly destroying the Athenian and allied army and ships. Athens would never recover from this loss. In 412, many of the allies of Athens rebelled, and in 411 the desperate Athenians turned over the government to an oligarchy known as the Four Hundred, hoping that it would be more effective than the democracy had been. It was not; and the Athenian fleet, which was stationed on Samos, remained stubbornly democratic and brought about the restoration of democracy within the year. Thucydides' description of the chaotic maneuvering of various parties in Athens and on Samos brings his history to an unexpected close. He apparently did not live to carry out his intention of writing the full history of the war down to its end in 404.

The story was picked up by Xenophon in his *Hellenica* and is summarized at the end of this volume: in the end Athens was defeated, but not destroyed, by Sparta.

On Reading Thucydides

Like many literary texts, the *History* seems to do more to hide than to reveal its author's intentions, and yet most readers are left with the feeling that they know just what Thucydides thought: Pericles is good, human nature is bad, war and civil strife bring out the worst in us, and so forth. Conclusions about Thucydides' political judgments are drawn from three sources within the text: authorial statements, speeches, and narrative structures.

Authorial statements

Thucydides makes occasional remarks in his own persona. Few of these are substantial, however. Some solid material may be culled from the Archaeology of Book I (i.2–19) and some from descriptions of the plague and the Corcyrean civil war (iii.81–85). There are also two direct judgments about Athenian politics: a eulogy of Pericles (with corollary condemnation of the next generation of leaders), and a verdict on the government of the five thousand (ii.65 and viii.97). In addition, the narrative is peppered with judgments about people's motivations, of which the most famous (and apparently least justified) is the comment that Cleon was acting from fear when he tried to back out of commanding the final expedition to Pylos (iv.28). The most numerous authorial comments are asides of the form "as was to be expected"—*hōs eikos*, which is often well translated "as is natural." In this group falls a line from the passage cited above: when Cleon pulled back, the people reacted "as a mob usually does," and pressed Nicias to give Cleon the command.

There are also authorial judgments of character: to the eulogy of Pericles at **ii.65** should be added the positive comments on Brasidas at iv.81, Pisistratus at **vi.54**, and Nicias at **vii.86**, as well as the negative ones on Cleon (iv.21, 28, v.16) and Alcibiades (**vi.15**). Some of these judgments are conventional, others (like those for the tyrants) are radically revisionist. Each one calls for a study of its own. Whether or not Thucydides genuinely admires these characters, the language he uses seems to show what qualities he looks for.

What should we make of all these authorial statements? Nothing, I think, except what falls out from an interpretation of the entire text that includes them. Because these passages are normative, and because they are not attributed to any of the characters of the piece, they are taken to be "authorial." Really, however, Thucydides authored the entire book; and if some of these passages seem to ring in the authentic voice of Thucydides— the verdict on the five thousand is the best example—that is because of our sense for what is Thucydidean, a sense we have developed from our reading of the whole book. In the passage on the five thousand, Thucydides makes a brief and unprecedented break from his narrative mode to give a judgment that is entirely consonant with what we have already been led to expect from Thucydides—that he thinks the best government falls in between rule by the many and rule by the few. This expectation on our part makes us ready to believe that the passage expresses his own view. Such are the factors that convince us, and they are not internal to the passage in question. It would be foolish, therefore, to select authorial sentences from the *History* as if they were fragments uniquely recording the thought of their author.

We must also keep in mind that Thucydides had the gift of seeing all sides of complex issues, and we should be on our guard against irony everywhere in reading the *History*. Thucydides wrote in a literary tradition in which irony was the norm: every tragedy magnifies the glory of its hero before showing how his mistakes and character defects bring him down. This is not authorial praise for the hero, but rather a device for placing the hero in a moral context in which his fall is best explained: if a character knows more, or has more power, than is fitting for a human being, an Athenian audience knew his doom was near. In history as in tragedy Greek writers show the same mixture of pride, awe, and terror at the extent of human innovation and achievement. In tragedy, the mechanism for doom is driven by the gods; in Thucydides it is an all-too-human necessity that brings down those who overreach. The narrative structures are similar, however; so we should not be surprised if something like tragic irony shows up in the *History*.

Readers of Thucydides are lovers of Athens, and so tend to take the funeral oration as expressing Thucydides' own love of Athens; and then, loving Pericles because they love Athens, they tend to swallow Thucydides' eulogy of Pericles straight. Both passages are balanced by irony, however. This becomes clear, for example, to readers who set the Funeral Oration against the description of the plague. After the Funeral Oration praises the civilization of Athens; the account of the plague shows how easily the Athenians shed their veneer when times were hard. As for the eulogy of Pericles, it is hard to square with Thucydides' critical attitudes toward democracy and empire, which Thucydides knew to have been Pericles' legacy to Athens.

The speeches
Nearly one-fourth of the text of the *History* consists of speeches delivered elegantly in the first person by historical figures. As the speeches are teeming with insights, many scholars have held that they are our best source for Thucydides' own ideas; others scoff at this, saying that each speech represents only the point of view of a particular character at a particular time.[7] A third possibility is to try to identify Thucydidean elements within the speeches and separate them from what belongs to the speakers.

All three approaches are too simple. Understanding Thucydides is like understanding a playwright whose subject is history: he speaks few lines in his own person, but reveals much by the lines he thinks appropriate for

---

7. Werner Jaeger takes the generous view: the speeches are "above all else the medium through which [Thucydides] expresses his political ideas" (1945, I: 391). Hornblower takes the more austere line: "the sentiments contained in those speeches can never be used as evidence for his own opinions" (1987: 72).

others to speak. Study of the speeches must begin with a review of Thucydides' enigmatic introduction (i.22):

> What particular people said in their speeches, either just before or during the war, was hard to recall exactly, whether they were speeches I heard myself or those that were reported to me at second hand. I have made each speaker say what I thought his situation demanded, keeping as near as possible to the general sense of what was actually said.

The word translated "what... his situation demanded" (*ta deonta*) can also mean "what was appropriate," and may be a technical term for what was the right strategy in each case according to current rhetorical theory.[8]

The consensus of scholars is that Thucydides did not keep strictly to actual texts that were delivered. The speeches are too good, too artfully contrived, and too closely tied in with each other to be verbatim transcriptions of what was said. Still, many of them might well be paraphrases of their originals. On this point there is no general agreement: we do not know whether a given speech contains arguments that were actually used, and we have no sure way of telling paraphrase from historical fiction. Historians are left to speculate about what is likely to have been the case for each speech. The Melian Dialogue, for example, did not take place in public, so Thucydides was probably left to his own invention. Pericles' Funeral Oration, by contrast, seems to represent an occasion that would have been known to Thucydides' readers, and so he may have felt obliged to give an accurate report. Still, we do not have any reason to believe that Greek readers expected accuracy on such points.

In the end, although we cannot be sure where it crops up, we must conclude that there is fiction in the speeches; but even when they are fictional they are historical too, since they represent the imagination of a writer who wants to bring the truth to light by this means and is trying to be faithful to what the situation demanded—to *ta deonta*. But what sort of truth was Thucydides trying to serve in doing this? What did he mean by *ta deonta*? What a conventionally trained speaker of the period would have seen fit to say? What Thucydides thinks the speaker really should have said, all training aside? Or what would best reveal the speaker's thoughts and motivations and desires?

We simply do not know. Even if **i.22** were unambiguous we would still have to ask if it truly described Thucydides' practice. He was probably interested in all of the above. Certainly he was aware of the conventions of

---

8. See Hornblower, 1987: 46.

rhetoric, and he seems also to have cared about the ideals to which rhetoric should be put. But I think a frequent purpose of the speeches is to reveal the motives of the speakers. The speeches are part of Thucydides' larger project of bringing submerged realities to the surface, a project announced early on when he brings out what he believes is the real reason for the war:

> I believe that the truest reason for the quarrel, though least evident in what was said at the time, was the growth of Athenian power, which put fear into the Lacedaemonians and so compelled them into war (i.23, see p. 21 n. 64).

Generally, Thucydides wants to bring the darker side of human nature to light by revealing motives such as fear that speakers would want to conceal in real life.

Thucydides sees Cleon, for example, as a cowardly man who fears the people; yet in his speech against the Mytileneans he shows contempt for the people and their democratic processes (iii.37, ff.). No doubt a coward like Thucydides' Cleon would feel contempt for ordinary people, but why would he express that openly? Such cowardice commonly leads to flattery, not to open expressions of contempt. Similarly, the angry reproaches leveled at Sparta by the Corinthian spokesman (i.69) are more likely to represent what the Corinthians felt than what they said openly at the time.

A striking feature of the speeches is their virtual lack of dissimulation. Nicias, in the Sicilian debate, offers an interesting exception; in this case Thucydides bluntly explains Nicias' reasons for speaking as he does, contrary to his own opinion. (Nicias tries to stop the expedition indirectly, by raising its price tag, and fails.) By contrast, Cleon's deceptive speech over Pylos is described in the text but not reported. On the whole, I think, Thucydides' speakers are made to say what Thucydides thinks they actually believe, whether they would have said those things in public or not. When speakers rest their cases on justice, they appear to do so sincerely; when, as is more often the case, they prefer *realpolitik* to justice, they say so. A better rhetorical strategy would be to pretend to care about justice while pursuing the opposite, as Glaucon points out in the *Republic:* "the height of injustice is to seem just without being so" (361a). Thucydides is well equipped to see through such pretenses to virtue (ii.51), but he rarely shows people pretending. He shows us their speeches refracted through a lens of honesty. A measure of this is how little justice matters to speakers who have the power to disregard it. The plain outrage at injustice that is shown by the Spartan leader in Book I is as extraordinary as is the brevity of his speech (i.86).

Thucydides' speakers rarely persuade their audiences, but they seem often to have persuaded themselves. The Lacedaemonians, for example, are not moved by the arguments of either side in the debate at Sparta (i.88), while, in the same debate, the Athenians appear to be quite convinced by their own excuses for assuming an imperial role. Generally, the Athenians are shown to believe what they say again and again in their speeches: that their actions have been necessary and that their strategy will triumph over the chances of war. On both points they are self-deceived, as we shall see. Individual speakers too may be self-deceived, as when they exaggerate their own virtues or success (Alcibiades at vi.16 and Brasidas at iv.86).

So the speakers are often revealed, not for what they said, but for what they were, beneath their speaking. But what of Thucydides; what do we learn about him? He is revealed for what he thinks moves people to the things they do, and the view of human nature adumbrated in the descriptions of the plague and the Corcyrean civil war finds illustration in the speeches. But that is not all. The selection and arrangement of speeches is masterful. The concatenation of the Melian Dialogue with the Sicilian Debate, for example, is startling: the same Athenians who decried the hopes of the Melians plunge, a few pages later, into an unrealistic gamble. Or consider the curious interleaving of the stories of the sieges of Plataea and Mytilene, each ending in a brutal debate. After hearing how badly the Plataeans failed in their plea for justice, we can understand better why defenders of the Mytileneans argued on other grounds. In the end, the moral difference between Athens and Sparta at this point is reduced to this: that Sparta's interests required her to sacrifice Plataea, while Athens' interests permitted her to spare the majority of Mytileneans.

Narrative structures
Thucydides' selection and arrangement of narrative material similarly serves his purposes. The most salient example is his placement of the description of the plague immediately after the Funeral Oration of Pericles. The glories of Athens, as Pericles describes them, melt away under pressure of disease, and much of what has passed for virtue turns out to be sham. Again, it is not simply because he had eye-witnesses at hand that he tells us in vivid detail about the last days of Plataea or the Sicilian expedition. The Plataeans were led into their debacle by Athenian promises (ii.73—only a few pages after the eulogy of Pericles) and then abandoned, betrayed by the vagaries of Athenian democracy (iii.57). The Athenians should either have told Plataea they could not defend her or have given up Pericles' strategy. As it was, they evidently tried to have their strategy

Introduction

while promising a course of action—the defense of Plataea—that could only be achieved by abandoning that strategy. Athens later treated the expedition to Sicily in the same way, supporting the plan but taking its command away from the one man who could make it work. Both are sharp examples of the cost of incompetence in high places and the failure of democracy to provide clear, consistent leadership in time of war. The story is told in a way that is deceptively simple, but artfully arranged to leave its point in the reader's mind.

If I am right so far, there is nothing in the *History* that can be excluded, and nothing that has independent authorial force. The work must be read with care as a whole. All of it is animated by the enormous intelligence of its author.

Some scholars find this advice hard to follow: they cannot read Thucydides as a whole because, in their eyes, the book breaks down into sections that were written at different stages, and each of these must be taken on its own.[9] I shall not deal with the developmental hypothesis here, except to say that it must be a last resort. On the whole, the *History* is very tightly written, and its complex interlocking structures repay the most careful attention. It is a mosaic, of course, but a mosaic that appears to derive from a master plan, at least until it reaches the unfinished sections that comprise Book VIII.

Political Theory

The philosophical Thucydides lurks everywhere in the *History*. Can we, on the basis of many sightings, produce a composite picture of his political theory? Any attempt is speculative and controversial. Anyone who tries must blunder through the complex trail left by a man who could see all sides of the issues he treated. I will have space for only a general outline here.

Constitutions

Thucydides seems to hold that the main object of politics is stability and the avoidance of civil strife (*stasis*), which brings out the worst in people. Accordingly we would expect him to support the Lacedaemonian model of government, and reject the Athenian. This is borne out by the text, up to a point. The story it tells is built around the failure of Athens, a failure which was partly due to the vacillations of Athenian democracy and the

---

9. See Hornblower, 1987: Chapter 6.

instability of its constitution when subjected to great stress. These themes are illustrated in the failure to make peace after Sphacteria, in the mishandling of the Sicilian expedition, in the chaos of the year 411, and, of course, in the banishment of unsuccessful generals like Thucydides. Athenian democracy as Thucydides represents it needed to be controlled by a Pericles who could have the stabilizing effect of a monarch (ii.65); otherwise it tended to fall into the hands of demagogues, such as Cleon (iii.37, iv.21, 28, v.16), and could be seen as a tyranny of the many over the few. Democracy was felt to be oppressive by many die-hard conservatives, who longed for traditional upper-class privileges. Thucydides and most of our sources for the period belonged to this group. In addition, Thucydides has a dim view of human nature, and the same should go for democracy, since it seems to give human nature the largest, most untrammeled scope.

Was Thucydides, then, an admirer of the Spartan constitution? Certainly not, for he represents that system too as seriously flawed (viii.96). Sparta did not accept the good advice of Archidamus in Book I any more than Athens stuck by the strategy of Pericles; and Lacedaemonians too committed their share of atrocities. Nor is democracy entirely bad. Its strength is revealed in the Sicilian episode, for Syracuse was at the time a moderate democracy, and Thucydides sees this as making her a more powerful opponent for Athens (vii.55, cf. viii.96). Its people evidently felt they had a stake in the city and were for that reason willing to defend it. Thucydides also points out to us that democracy is more stable than a newly minted oligarchy (viii.89). In the end, he prefers a mixed constitution of the kind promised for the Five Thousand (viii.97); this, we must suppose, promised the stability and fairness that he looked for in government.

Justice

On the main points of ethics Thucydides' views do not depart from the standard views of his class and period.[10] Justice, piety, and other virtues are as they are thought to be, and are unchallenged goods, though fragile ones. Justice is the principal moral concept in the *History;* the word and its cognates ring through the book as if they mattered; and they would, too, if equals in power came to court or arbitration under established law. Justice consists in the following:

---

10. Ostwald, following a substantial tradition, 1988: 61, n. 31.

11. Thucydides admired the Pisistratids for preserving Athenian traditions and sympathized with the Peloponnesian war aim of supporting traditional autonomy in the cities (vi.54 and ii.8).

1. That traditional law be maintained.[11]
2. That disputes be settled without violence by a duly constituted authority.
3. That an agreement be kept, even when it is in the interests of one party to abrogate it.[12]
4. That punishment be meted out as retribution, proportional to the offense, and only to the guilty.[13]
5. That overreaching and avarice (*pleonexia*) be avoided.
6. That tyranny be avoided. (This follows directly from 1, as tyranny occurs when traditional law is abrogated.)

I have said that Thucydides is a traditionalist on justice, and so he is, but these six points alone do not make him so. In fact, he differs widely from the two main positions that had been advanced by sophists. The extreme position, represented by Callicles in Plato's *Gorgias*, is that conventional justice is bad for us because it runs against human nature. Instead of justice, which is the law of men, Callicles says we should follow the law of nature (*Gorgias* 483b–d).

Thucydides is no Callicles: though he shows how justice is often subverted by power, neither Thucydides nor any of his speakers ever suggests that justice is merely an empty convention, or that nature offers us a better law. All he shows is that nature, or necessity, or in one case both together,[14] are too powerful for justice. Thucydides clings to the traditional view of nature and justice: justice is good, but nature is dangerous and should therefore be kept under control.

The more moderate sophistic position is that of Protagoras, who holds that justice is a kind of second nature to us, something every Greek learns from society as he learns the language. This is a pleasantly optimistic

---

12. A violation of principles 2 and 3 (in the refusal of the Spartans to go to arbitration as agreed) was a principal cause of the war (**i.85, vii.18**).

13. The deterrent theory of punishment, which belonged to the new learning, is not offered by Diodotus as having anything to do with justice. It is Cleon's retributivism that is associated with justice (**iii.37, ff.**).

14. Even at **v.105**, where the Athenian spokesman comes closest to Callicles of anyone in the *History*, he stops short of saying that it is good or proper that the strong rule as many people as they can. He represents the rule of the strong neutrally, as a natural constraint. In representing it as a *constraint*, he implies that he feels a pull in the other direction. As often in Thucydides, an appeal to *anankê* to explain an injustice shows that the speaker is still loyal to justice as an ideal, but feels constrained from following it.

xxviii *Introduction*

model: if justice is like language, it is not easily forgotten; and though it is not as natural to us as claws to a lion, justice remains essential to normal human life.[15] Thucydides takes a harsher view. He has a sharp eye for pretenses of all sorts, and is not taken in by the posturings of his compatriots in the name of virtue. He sees not only how fragile the Greek moral system is, but how much of it is built upon deception. No one of Thucydides' contemporaries comes as close to him in this as do Plato's characters, Glaucon and Adeimantus, in Book II of the *Republic*. But while they state the thesis, Thucydides shows it, scene by scene, as he relentlessly exposes the motives of the Greeks to his scrutiny. Time and time again in the *History*, justice is honored more in speech than in action, and more by the weak than by the powerful. It is this that draws readers to the *History*: its frightening accuracy about the fragility of goodness in human dealings when power is involved.

Pericles' Funeral Oration praises Athens as a lesson for Greece. The irony of this in the larger context of Thucydides' story is shocking. Athens was a lesson for Greece, but not in an admirable way. Consider what lesson Athens almost taught at Mytilene and did teach at Melos, or what her army demonstrated outside Syracuse: don't follow the example of Athens. This point was conveyed with such force to posterity by Thucydides and others that democratic reformers in the nineteenth century, such as Grote, had to tell the story of Athenian democracy in a new way in order to restore its ideals to intellectual respectability.

Power

Thucydides has many words for power—*dunamis*, of course, but also *kratos* (control) and *archē* (empire) are prominent as are *anankē* (compulsion, necessity) and *bia* (force, violence). In international affairs, power is measured in the accumulation of wealth and the development of naval superiority.[16] Speeches at international gatherings have virtually no effect, and arbitration between states is irrelevant when interests truly conflict. Alliances are valuable to you just so long as you have the force to keep your allies at your side; consanguinity (as between Melos and Sparta, or Plataea and Thebes) carries no weight.

At the level of domestic politics, Thucydides' concern is mainly with

---

15. Plato, *Protagoras* 320d ff. Although not a direct quotation from Protagoras, the passage represents a view that was part of the new learning, and is probably Protagorean in general outline.

16. This is Thucydides' assumption throughout Book I, and yet Sparta, the greatest land power of Greece, was insignificant in both wealth and ships.

Introduction

Athenian democracy. Here, and here only, speeches make a difference—but not much. Pericles was able to manipulate the people to some extent, but his power rested more on his reputation for virtue than on his rhetoric, and even this power failed him when the war began to bite on the Athenians and they began to look for someone to bite in turn. Alcibiades was a successful speaker, on the whole, and his first great service to Athens, according to Thucydides, was a speech that prevented civil war (viii.86). Cleon, by contrast, maintained an uneasy hold on the people. When peace was possible after Pylos he was powerful enough to talk a weary people into continuing the war (iv.21); but in scenes Thucydides describes in greater detail, Cleon was first defeated in a rhetorical contest (over Mytilene) and then outmaneuvered by a more skillful politician (Nicias, when he called Cleon's bluff over Pylos). In fact, such success as Cleon had seems mainly due to luck. Even in democracy power rests more on understanding human nature than on knowing how to manipulate words. To avoid exile at the hands of the people, a leader must be able to predict the behavior of the democracy, vague and vacillating as it is (vii.48). Where Alcibiades and Thucydides failed, Nicias succeeded: his cautious and dilatory conduct of the Sicilian campaign kept him from losing his command, though it led in the end to total defeat. Such are the advantages of understanding how human nature serves democracy.

Human nature
Two features of the new learning were its positive view of human nature (*phusis*) and its critical attitude toward social conventions (*nomos*). Thucydides rejects both of these and harks back to the traditional view of nature as something wild and always in need of the trainer's strong hand. In this he is more like Plato than he is like other intellectuals of his period. War, civil strife, or natural disaster can easily strip away the good work of civilization. "War is a violent teacher," says Thucydides: it teaches people not only to be vicious, but to mask their vices with fine-sounding names. Loss of life saddens Thucydides, but he does not see it as a moral outrage in itself. After all, he was no pacifist, but a seasoned soldier and a member of a social class whose principal role in society involved bloodshed. He is appalled, however, by death in a civil brawl and shows a sense of outrage at the loss of virtue that accompanies it:

> Civil war brought many hardships to the cities, such as happen and will always happen as long as human nature is the same, although they may be more or less violent or take different forms, depending on the circumstances in each case. In peace and prosperity, cities and private individuals alike are

better minded because they are not plunged into the necessity of doing anything against their will; but war is a violent teacher: it gives most people impulses that are as bad as their situation when it takes away the easy supply of what they need for daily life.

Civil war ran through the cities; those it struck later heard what the first cities had done and far exceeded them in inventing artful means for attack and bizarre forms of revenge. And they reversed the usual way of using words to evaluate actions. (iii.82)

But war is not simply the cause of this. War and the loss of virtue are together consequences of something else: "the cause of all this was the desire to rule out of avarice and ambition, and the zeal for winning that proceeds from those two," he goes on to say. What causes the trouble, then, is the exercise of power in the interest of merely personal or civic gain—what the Greeks called *pleonexia*, avarice or overreaching. Now, is it inevitable that power will lead to injustice? Evidently not. Pericles, for all *his* faults, ruled like the Pisistratids before him without corruption, according to Thucydides. Bad as it is, human nature does not determine events. Chance, choice, and economic factors are all important to Thucydides' story. The observance of traditional laws and the cultivation of traditional virtues—including a moderate respect for the laws of one's neighbors—these would be enough to keep the wickedness in check, if only people could cling to them. There appears, however, to be a necessity in human events that brings on war.

Necessity

Ananke is usually translated "necessity," and this is right if taken as in the sentence "it was a military necessity to bomb Hiroshima." In Greek, as in English, such language often masks a choice. I have tried to render *ananke* with forms of "compulsion" and "compel," which suggest a human agency, because the basis of one person's *ananke* is usually the action—or expected action—of another.

Ananke arises in a wholly human context in Thucydides. It is not fate or the will of the gods, nor can it be reduced to mechanical laws of history or economics. It is not even the force behind human nature. Although he believes human behavior falls into patterns—that is why he thinks history is useful (i.22.4)—Thucydides does not appeal to the idea that psychological laws objectively determine individual choices. On the contrary, *ananke* is generally subjective in Thucydides: those who cite it in their speeches contend that it limits their range of choices and makes further discussion pointless. Plainly, their opponents do not agree. Thucydides makes only one appeal to *ananke* in his own voice, and that is in his explanation of the war: the growth of Athenian power "put fear into the Lacedaemonians and so compelled them into war" (**i.23**). As the story unfolds, we see that this *ananke* does indeed work through fear, and that it affects both sides: the Spartans feel they must curtail Athenian power while they still can; the Athenians feel that they cannot let any power slip from their grasp, lest the cities they have held down rise up and destroy them. Who is to blame? Not Sparta, if the war truly became inevitable with the growth of the Athenian empire, for then Athens would be to blame for starting the cycle of fear and felt necessity that was triggered by her overreaching. But Athens does not see the war in this light. In her defense before the Peloponnesians, her representatives appeal to *ananke* and the established principle that the weak be held down by the more powerful (**i.76**, cf. **v.105**): even Sparta, they say, would have been compelled by *ananke* to seize power forcibly, or else put itself at risk, if it had remained at the head of the anti-Persian league. In context we see that such *ananke* results from "ambition, fear, and advantage," with fear topping the list (**i.76**).

Fear, ambition, and self-interest are strong motives, but they do not actually make events in history inevitable, even in Thucydides. They merely make events feel inevitable to the principal actors. We the audience can see that the war was not inevitable from clues Thucydides leaves for us.[17] Sparta did not have to go to war; it could have followed the sage advice of Archidamus and gone to arbitration instead, as the Spartans realized later with regret (**vii.18**). Athens did not have to grow in the way it did—not, at least, for the reasons the Athenians gave. Had Sparta continued as head of the anti-Persian League, it would surely not have been compelled to set up an empire on the Athenian model. Neither Thucydides nor our other sources give us any reason to believe the Athenian counterfactual. The Peloponnesian League never did follow the Athenian model, even when it was victorious.[18]

This appears to be Thucydides' story, and it leaves no room for the alleged law of nature that the strong are always compelled to rule over the weak (**i.76, v.105**). This "law," which is peculiarly Athenian in

---

17. Kagan argues that the war was not inevitable, using evidence from Thucydides. He believes, however, as I do not, that Thucydides thought the war inevitable (1969: 366).

18. Athens and Sparta were ruled by different sorts of fears in any case: Athens feared for her supplies of grain and timber, but Sparta feared an uprising of the conquered people who worked her farms.

Thucydides, kicks in only when the strong have overreached, and are therefore in fear of the weak. The Spartans make nothing of *anankē* before attacking and subsequently destroying Plataea. All in all, hardly anyone but the Athenians makes such pleas, and these are steadfastly rejected by their weaker opponents, who are never persuaded that it was inevitable for Athens to destroy them.

Anankē is not the only illusion of the Athenians. They are also beguiled by *gnōmē*—planned strategy. This requires a chapter in itself: Athenian strategy led to one disaster after another, while their only great success, at Sphacteria, was due almost entirely to chance. A full study would show that Thucydides represents the Athenians as caught in elaborate self-deceptions, with their concept of *anankē* at the center of the web. *Anankē* is usually a bad excuse. It arises after avarice has led to injustice, which leads to fear of the downtrodden and that in turn produces the sense of *anankē* that drives the Athenians. The Athenians are partly right to feel that their actions are inevitable. Once begun, the cycle may be unstoppable; but the cycle did not have to begin, and moral decay is not inevitable in Thucydides' *History*, but has precise and (except for the plague) avoidable causes. Alliances can be maintained—witness the rise of the Peloponnesian League—and sound forms of government can be achieved—witness the rise of the Five Thousand and the reign of the Pisistratids. But when a special interest takes power (such as the common people in a city, or a dominant partner in an alliance), that starts the terrible cycle.

Plato and Thucydides

The philosopher and the historian have in common a fascination with Athens' loss of virtue during the Peloponnesian War, but they differ sharply on causes and cures. Both see the decline in terms of the rise of democracy, the growth of empire, and the new learning's critique of morality. Both emphasize the gap between the moral ideals of the Greeks and their experience of life, which was such that life could not possibly have taught them those ideals. Plato adds a metaphysical explanation for the gap between life and ideals (by postulating moral ideals that have a separate existence as Forms or Ideas) and supplies an ambitious scheme for closing the gap through radical reform in education (bringing the future philosopher-kings up from the cave of ignorance to see the Forms). In the *Republic* Plato attributes the moral decay of individuals to poor company and inadequate education. His solution is a society rebuilt around moral education, with strong controls over the appetites of ordinary people to prevent their succumbing to avarice and overreaching.

Thucydides gives no formal explanation, but what he implies is less optimistic than Plato's theory: education and tradition cannot be relied upon. They fail when subjected to stress, and once the cycle of moral decay begins, from avarice to a sense of *anankē*, there is no stopping it. Apparently the only hope is not to take this road at all, to maintain traditional governments and alliances, to cling to old values and virtues, to avoid the first small step towards overreaching. Antidemocratic and suspicious of change it may be, but this message comes from the depths of painful experience. It is what we would expect to hear from the tragic age of Greece.

BIBLIOGRAPHICAL NOTES

Translations.
The four best-known translations of Thucydides are Thomas Hobbes (1629), Richard Crawley (1876, revised ed. 1910), Benjamin Jowett (1881, revised ed. 1900), and Rex Warner (1954). I have consulted all of these in preparing my own.

Commentaries on the Greek text.
I have used all the available commentaries at every turn. Especially useful is the work in five volumes begun by Gomme and completed by Andrewes and Dover. The best philological commentary on a part of the text is a recent work on Book II by Rusten. There are also good school commentaries on Books VI and VII by Dover. The Molesworth edition of Hobbes's translation (1843) has useful notes.

Works about Thucydides.
A general discussion of Thucydides scholarship is in Dover (1973). A beginner to the study of Thucydides should read Hornblower (1987), W. R. Connor (1977 and 1984), and, especially, de Romilly (1951). On the philosophical side of Thucydides, Woodhead (1970) is helpful, and the careful studies of Ostwald on *autonomia* and *anankē* are invaluable for a scholar (1982, 1988). Farrar gives the most thorough recent treatment of Thucydides as a political philosopher (1988). Euben (1990) treats Thucydides' discussion of the civil war on Corcyra. The most famous concept study on Thucydides is Adam Parry's dissertation (1957).

Works about ancient Greece.
The J.A.C.T.[19] *World of Athens* (Cambridge, 1984) is a good place to begin. The new *Cambridge Ancient History*, vol. V (1992), edited by D. M. Lewis et al., gives the latest word on most topics of interest to readers of Thucydides. Ostwald (1986) covers Athenian politics and law.

Works about the Peloponnesian War.
Although controversial on some points, Kagan's series of volumes (1969–1987) is the most thorough. The study by de Ste. Croix (1970) is especially good on the background of the war. Peter Green's account of the Sicilian expedition is both good scholarship and good reading (1970).

Works Cited

Connor, W. R. *Thucydides.* Princeton, 1984.

———— "A Post-Modernist Thucydides?" *The Classical Journal* 72 (1977), pp. 289–98.

———— *The New Politicians of Fifth-Century Athens.* Princeton, 1971.

Cornford, Francis M. *Thucydides Mythistoricus.* London, 1907.

Dover, K. J. *Thucydides.* J.A.C.T. *Greece and Rome: New Surveys in the Classics #7*, Oxford, 1973.

Euben, Peter. *The Tragedy of Poltitical Theory.* Princeton, 1990.

Farrar, Cynthia. *The Origins of Democratic Thinking.* Cambridge, 1988.

Finley, John H. Jr. *Thucydides.* Oxford, 1942.

Gomme, A. W., A. Andrewes, and K. J. Dover, *A Historical Commentary on Thucydides.* 5 vols. Oxford, 1945–1981.

Green, Peter. *Armada from Athens.* London, 1970.

Grene, David. *Greek Political Theory: The Image of Man in Plato and Thucydides.* Chicago, 1965. (Originally published as *Man in his Pride: A Study in the Political Philosophy of Plato and Thucydides.* Chicago, 1950.)

Guthrie, W.K.C. *The Sophists.* Cambridge, 1971.

Hornblower, Simon. *Thucydides.* London, 1987.

———— *A Commentary on Thucydides.* vol. I (Books I–III). Oxford, 1991.

19. Joint Association of Classical Teachers.

Jaeger, Werner. *Paideia: The Ideals of Greek Culture.* 2d Ed. Trans. by Gilbert Highet. Oxford, 1945.

Kagan, Donald. *The Outbreak of the Peloponnesian War.* Ithaca and London, 1969.

―――― *The Fall of the Athenian Empire.* Ithaca and London, 1987.

Nussbaum, Martha C. *The Fragility of Goodness.* Cambridge, 1986.

Ostwald, Martin. *Autonomia: Its Genesis and Early History.* American Classical Studies II (1982).

―――― *From Popular Sovereignty to the Sovereignty of Law: Law, Society, and Politics in Fifth-Century Athens.* Berkeley, 1986.

―――― *Anankē in Thucydides.* American Classical Studies 18 (1988), Atlanta.

Parry, Adam Milman. *Logos and Ergon in Thucydides.* Harvard dissertation, 1957. Published in New York, 1981. Repr. Salem, N.H., 1988.

Romilly, J. de. *Thucydide et l'imperialisme athénienne.* 2d Ed. Paris, 1951. Translated as *Thucydides and Athenian Imperialism,* Oxford, 1963.

Rusten, J. S. *Thucydides, The Peloponnesian War, Book II.* Cambridge, 1989.

Ste. Croix, G.E.M. de. *The Origins of the Peloponnesian War.* London, 1972.

Schlatter, Richard. *Hobbes' Thucydides.* New Brunswick, 1975.

Strauss, Leo. *The City and Man.* Chicago, 1964.

Wills, Gary. *Lincoln at Gettysburg: The Words That Remade America.* New York, 1992.

Woodhead, A. Geoffrey. *Thucydides on the Nature of Power.* Cambridge, Mass., 1970.

Greece

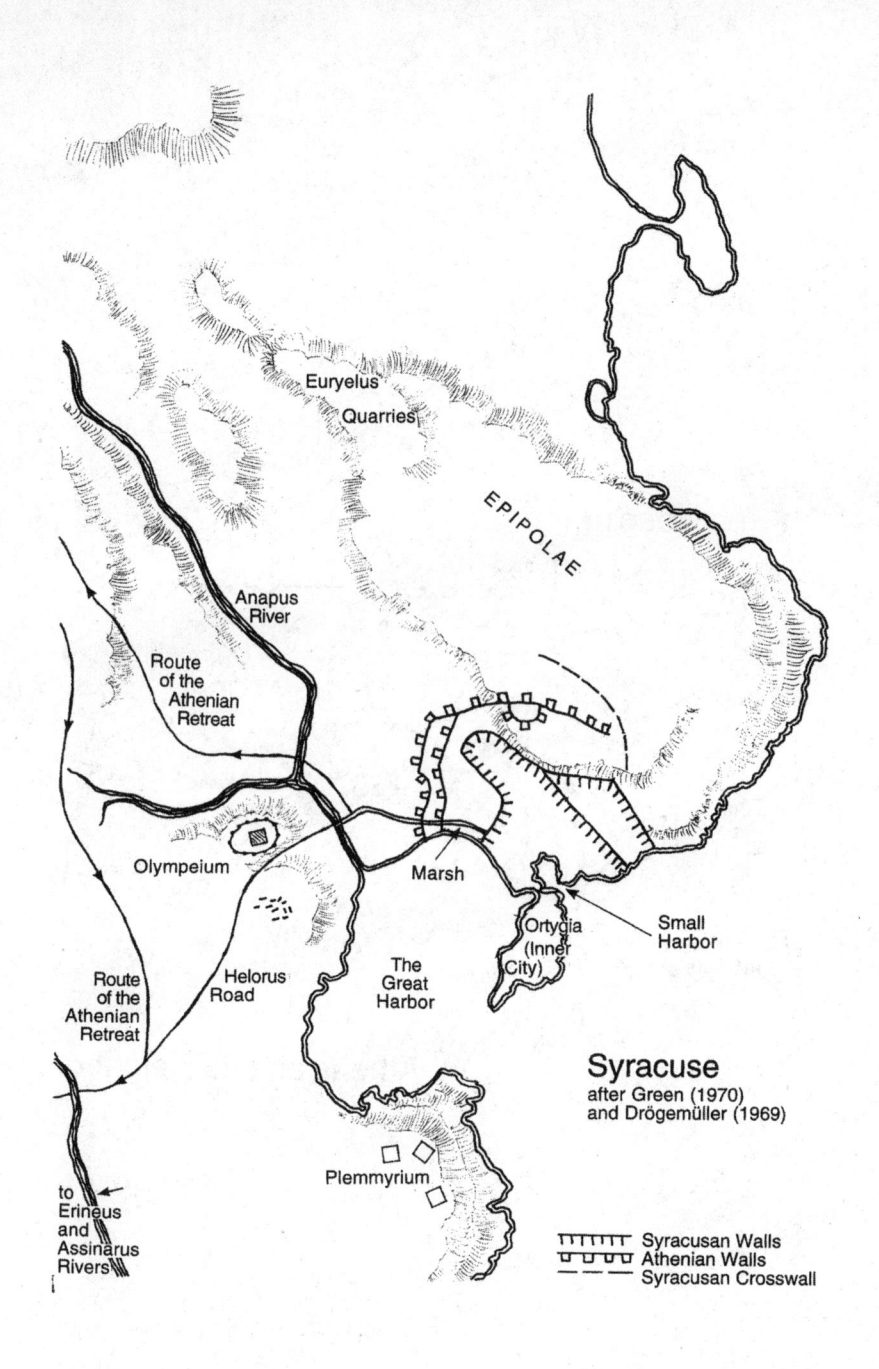

Syracuse
after Green (1970)
and Drögemüller (1969)

⊥⊥⊥⊥⊥ Syracusan Walls
⊔⊓⊔⊓ Athenian Walls
— — — Syracusan Crosswall

Athens and Its Neighbors

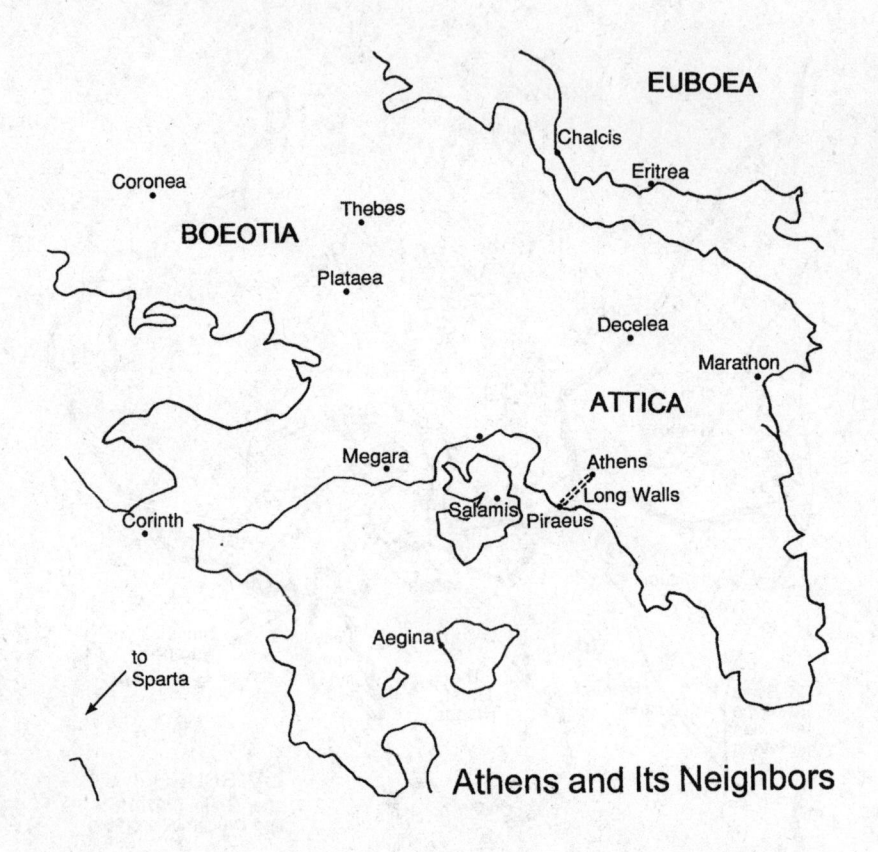

Thucydides

On Justice, Power, and Human Nature

1. Early History and Method

Thucydides begins with a brief preface followed by an investigation of the beginnings of Greek civilization. This section, known as the "Archaeology," is important mainly as an illustration of historical method. There Thucydides brings out, among other factors, the importance of economics in history and the value of sea-power.

a. Thucydides' preface [i.1]

Thucydides,[20] an Athenian, wrote up the war of the Peloponnesians and the Athenians as they fought against each other. He began to write as soon as the war was afoot, with the expectation that it would turn out to be a great one and that, more than all earlier wars, this one would deserve to be recorded. He made this prediction because both sides were at their peak in every sort of preparation for war, and also because he saw the rest of the Greek world taking one side or the other, some right away, others planning to do so.

This was certainly the greatest upheaval there had ever been among the Greeks. It also reached many foreigners—indeed, one might say that it affected most people everywhere. Because of the great passage of time it is impossible to discover clearly what happened long ago or even just before these events; still, I have looked into the evidence as far as can be done, and I am confident that nothing great happened in or out of war before this.

---

20. Thucydides usually refers to himself in the third person. He provides a second preface at v.26.

b. The archaeology [i.2–20]

Now Thucydides reconstructs the prehistory of Greece to support his thesis that no ancient display of power could compare with those of the Peloponnesian War. He makes astute use of all the evidence available to him—mythology, the Homeric poems, traditions of aristocratic families, king lists, archaeology, and even the current condition of other early peoples. He uses these resources critically and is guided at every stage by his conception of eikos—*what could reasonably be expected in the circumstances.*

[2] It is evident that what is now called "Hellas"[21] was not permanently settled in former times, but that there were many migrations, and people were ready to leave their land whenever they met the force of superior numbers. There was no trade, and they could not communicate with each other either by land or over the sea without danger. Each group used its ground merely to produce a bare living; they had no surplus of riches, and they planted nothing,[22] because they could not know when someone would invade and carry everything away, especially since they had no walls. They counted themselves masters of just enough to sustain them each day, wherever they were, and so made little difficulty about moving on. Because of this they had no strength, either in the size of their cities or in any other resources. The best land was always the most subject to these changes of inhabitants: what is now called Thessaly, also Boeotia, most of the Peloponnesus except for Arcadia, and whatever was most fertile in the rest of Greece. For the excellence of the land increased the power of certain men, and this led to civil wars, by which they were ruined; and all this made them more vulnerable to the designs of outsiders. Accordingly, Attica has been free from civil war for most of its history, owing to the lightness of its soil; and that is why it has always been inhabited by the same people.[23]

Here is strong support for this account: because of the migrations, the rest of Greece did not develop at the same rate as Athens, since the most able refugees from wars and civil strife all over Greece retired to the safety of Athens. There they became citizens, and they added so much to the citizen population that Attica could no longer support them, and colonies were sent out to Ionia.

21. 'Hellas' is the Greek name for Greece.
22. "Planted nothing": planted no vineyards or olive orchards, which take years to produce a crop.
23. Athenians believed they had always lived in Attica, and that their immigrants were refugees, rather than invaders. Thucydides accepts this myth, but it is not accepted by modern scholars (Hornblower).

1. Early History and Method

[3] I am further convinced of the weakness of Hellas in ancient times by this fact: before the Trojan War, Hellas evidently took no action in common. I do not believe, either, that the name "Hellas" was yet applied to the whole country. Before the time of Hellen, the son of Deucalion, there was no such name at all, but the various regions took the names of their own inhabitants, with "Pelasgian" naming the largest. When Hellen and his sons came to power in Phthiotis [a part of Thessaly], however, they were called in to the aid of other cities, which one by one came to be called Hellenes because of their association with them. That name cannot have prevailed over all of Greece until much later, however. The principal evidence for this is from Homer, who does not ever give them that name in general, though he was born long after the Trojan War. He does not use the name for anyone but those who came from Phthiotis with Achilles (who were the very first Hellenes); but he calls the others "Danaans," "Argives," or "Achaeans" in his poems. He does not use the term "foreigner" (*barbaros*) either, because, it seems to me, the Hellenes were not yet marked off by one name in opposition to them. City by city, then, they came to be called Hellenes if they understood each others' language, and later they all had this name; but before the Trojan War they did not enter into any action with their forces joined, owing to their lack of strength and communication; and they joined in that expedition only because they had learned to make more use of the sea.

[4] Minos, by all reports, was the first to build a navy;[24] he made himself master of most of what is now the Hellenic Sea, ruled the islands called the Cyclades, and sent colonies to most of them, expelling the Carians and setting up his own sons there as governors. Also, as one would expect, he freed the seas from piracy as much as he could, so that his revenue could reach him more easily.

[5] In ancient times, you see, the Greeks had turned to piracy as soon as they began to travel more in ships from one place to another, and so had the foreigners who lived on the mainland shore or on the islands. Their most powerful leaders aimed at their own profit, but also hoped to support the weak; and so they fell upon cities that had no walls or were made up of settlements. They raided these places and made most of their living from that. Such actions were nothing to be ashamed of then, but carried with them a certain glory, as we may learn from some of the mainlanders for whom this is still an honor, even today, if done nobly. The same point is proved by the ancient poets, who show that anyone who sails by, anywhere, is asked the same question—"Are you a pirate?"—and that those

---

24. By contrast, Herodotus consigns Minos to prehistory (iii.122).

who are asked are not insulted, while those who want to know are not reproachful.[25]

They also robbed each other on the mainland, and even now much of Greece follows this old custom—the Ozolean Locrians, for example, and the Aetolians and Acarnanians and mainlanders near them. The fashion of carrying iron weapons survives among those mainlanders as well, from their old trade of thieving. [6] All of Greece used to carry arms, you see, because houses were unfenced and travel was unsafe; and so they became accustomed to living every day with weapons, as foreigners do. The fact that some parts of Greece still do so testifies that the practice was once universal.

The Athenians were the first Greeks to put their weapons away and change to a more relaxed and luxurious style of life. It was due to this refinement that the older men among the rich there only recently gave up the fashion of wearing long linen robes and tying up the hair on their heads in knots fastened with golden cicadas.[26] (From them, because of their kinship with Athens, the same fashion spread to the older men of Ionia and lasted a long time.) The moderate sort of clothing that is now in style was first used by the Lacedaemonians, who had made the life-style of the rich equal to that of ordinary people, especially in regard to dress.[27] They were also the first to strip themselves naked for exercise and to oil themselves afterwards. In the old days athletes used to wear loincloths around their private parts when they competed, even at the Olympic Games, and it has not been many years since this custom ended. Even now there are foreigners, especially in Asia, whose athletes wear loincloths in boxing matches. And in many other ways one could show that the life-style of the ancient Greeks was similar to that of foreigners today.

[7] As for the cities, those that were settled more recently—since the advance of navigation—had a surplus of money and so were built with walls right on the coasts. They took over the isthmuses both for commercial reasons and to strengthen themselves individually against their neighbors. The older cities, however, were built further from the sea, owing to the greater danger of piracy on the islands as well as on the mainland. They

---

25. For example at *Odyssey* iii.71.

26. As cicadas seem to be born from the ground, they represented the Athenian belief that they had themselves sprung from the ground on which they lived.

27. The moderate sort of clothing was a short tunic. Spartan citizens tried to regard themselves as equals and to overlook the differences in wealth that actually occurred among them.

1. Early History and Method

robbed each other and any non-seamen who lived by the coast, with the result that even today those people are still settled inland.

[8] Most of the pirates were islanders, the Carians or Phoenicians who had settled most of the islands. The evidence for this is as follows: when the Athenians purified Delos during this war,[28] they dug up the graves of those who had died on the island and found that more than half were Carian. They knew this by the style of the weapons that were buried with them and by the burial customs, which are still in use.[29]

Once Minos' navy was afloat, navigation became easier, since he expelled the evil-doers from the islands and planted colonies of his own in many of them. And as those who lived along the coasts became more addicted to acquiring wealth, their settlements became more stable. Some, who had become richer than before, threw up walls around their towns. In their desire for gain, the weaker cities let themselves be subject to the stronger ones, while the more powerful cities used their surplus wealth to bring weaker ones under their rule. And that was the situation later, when they sent the expedition against Troy.

[9] In my view Agamemnon was able to get the fleet together because he had more power than anyone else at that time, and not so much because he was the leader of the suitors of Helen who were bound by oaths to Tyndareus.[30]

Those who received the clearest account of the Peloponnesians from their predecessors say that Pelops used the great wealth he brought from Asia and was the first to win power among the Peloponnesian people (who were very poor at the time). Because of this he gave his own name to the land, though he was an outsider. Afterwards, his descendants became still more powerful. After Eurystheus was killed in Attica by the Heraclids,[31] Atreus made himself king of Mycenae and the other lands Eurystheus had ruled. (Eurystheus had entrusted the rule of Mycenae to him when he set off on campaign, because of their family relationship. Atreus was his mother's brother and happened to be living at the time with Eurystheus, in

---

28. The Peloponnesian War. For the purification of Delos, see iii.104.

29. Although impressed by Thucydides' use of this evidence, most modern archaeologists think he mistook early Greek vases for Carian ones. (See the summary of literature in Hornblower.)

30. Helen's suitors were said to have sworn to her father Tyndareus that they would avenge any wrong done to the lucky suitor who married Helen.

31. Eurystheus was a member of the Perseids. The Heraclids, supposedly descendants of Heracles, had sought refuge in Athens from Eurystheus.

exile from his father for the death of Chrysippus.)[32] When Eurystheus did not come back, the Mycenaeans wanted Atreus to be king, partly out of fear of the Heraclids and partly because they thought Atreus was an able man and, at the same time, because he had served the interests of the majority. That is how the descendants of Pelops became greater than those of Perseus.[33]

Now Agamemnon was the son of Atreus and inherited this power; and besides this he had a stronger navy than anyone else. That is why I think he assembled his forces more on the basis of fear than good will. It is evident that most of the ships were his and that he had others to lend to the Arcadians, as Homer declares (whose evidence should be good enough for anyone).[34] Besides, in the "Giving of the Scepter" Homer says that Agamemnon was lord "of many islands and all Argos."[35] Now since he lived on the mainland, he could not have controlled islands (except for the neighboring ones, of which there were only a few) unless he had a navy. And we should infer the character of earlier enterprises on the basis of that expedition.

[10] Of course Mycenae was small, and the cities of that time may not seem to be worth very much; but such weak evidence should not count against believing that the expedition was as great as the poets have said it was, and as tradition holds. For if the Lacedaemonians' city were wiped out, and if only their temples and building foundations remained, I think people in much later times would seriously doubt that their power had matched their fame; and yet they own two fifths of the Peloponnesus and are leaders of the rest, along with many allies outside. Still, it would seem to have been rather weak, since it was not settled as one city around the use of costly temples or other buildings, but was made up of villages in the old Greek style.[36] If the same thing were to happen to Athens, however, one would infer from what was plain to see that its power had been double what it is.

We have no good reason, then, to doubt those reports about the size of

32. Atreus was one of the sons of Pelops; at the request of his mother, Atreus had helped to kill his half-brother Chrysippus—another son of Pelops.

33. Eurystheus' father was a descendant of Perseus.

34. *Iliad* ii.612.

35. *Iliad* ii.108.

36. Sparta was not enclosed by a wall until Roman times. The Athenians, by contrast, believed that Theseus had gathered their villages into one city at a very early date.

the army in the Trojan War, or to measure a city more by its appearance than its power. We should think of that army as indeed greater than those that went before it, but weaker than those we have now. This depends on our trusting Homer again on this point, where he would be expected as a poet to exaggerate; but on his account that army was still much weaker than modern ones: he makes the fleet consist of twelve hundred ships and reports that the Boeotian ships carried one hundred twenty men each, while those of Philoctetes carried fifty. I think he did this to show the maximum and minimum, but he makes no mention at all in his catalogue of the size of the other ships.[37] He does, however, show that all the rowers in Philoctetes' ships were also fighters, for he writes that all the oarsmen were archers. As for passengers on the ships, it is not likely that there were many, aside from the kings and other top people, especially since they had to cross the sea with military equipment on board, and in ships without the protection of upper decks, built in the old pirate fashion. So if we take the mean between the largest and smallest ships, we find that not many went to Troy, considered as a joint expedition from all of Greece.

[11] This is to be explained more by lack of wealth than by a shortage of men. Because of their lack of rations, they brought a smaller army—just the size they expected would be able to support itself while fighting. When they landed, they got the upper hand in fighting. (That is obvious; otherwise they could not have fortified their camp). After that, apparently, they did not use all their power, because they had to turn partly to farming in the Chersonese, and partly to piracy. Because they were dispersed in this way, the Trojans were better able to hold them off for those ten years and were an equal match for those Greeks who were left near Troy at any one time.

If they had gone out with plenty of rations, however, and concentrated their forces on continuous warfare without farming or piracy, they would easily have taken the city once they'd gotten the upper hand in fighting, since they were a match for the Trojans with the portion of the army that was present at any time. If they had settled down in a siege they would have taken Troy in less time with less trouble.[38]

---

37. Homer lists the participants in the Greek army at Troy in his Catalogue of Ships, *Iliad* ii.484 ff.

38. Thucydides writes from experience: siege warfare was very expensive for the Athenians, since it required keeping troops in the field for periods much longer than the brief campaigns to which they were accustomed. This no doubt explains the reluctance of Sparta to lay regular siege to Athens.

All enterprises were weak before the Trojan War for want of money, and this one was too, for all that it was the most famous expedition of ancient times. The facts show clearly that it was weaker than its fame would have it, and weaker than the verbal tradition that has come down to us from the poets.

[12] After the Trojan War the Greeks were still in motion, still resettling, and so could not make progress in one place. The Greeks came back from Troy after a long absence, and this brought about many changes: civil war broke out in most cities, and the people who were driven out founded new cities. The people now known as Boeotians were thrown out of Arnē by the Thessalians in the sixtieth year after Troy was taken; they settled in what is now Boeotia, but was then called Cadmeïs. (Only a portion of them were in that country before then, some of whom fought against Troy.) And in the eightieth year the Dorians seized the Peloponnesus along with the Heraclids.[39]

With much ado, then, and after a long time, peace came with security to Greece; and now that they were no longer being uprooted they began to send colonies abroad. The Athenians settled Ionia and most of the islands, while the Peloponnesians planted colonies in most of southern Italy and Sicily, as well as in some other parts of Greece. And all these were founded after the Trojan War.

[13] Now that Greece was becoming more powerful, and the Greeks were more interested in making money than before, tyrannies were set up in most of the cities; with their incomes growing larger (the hereditary kings before them had had only fixed revenues) the Greeks built navies and became more attached to the sea. The Corinthians are said to have been the first to change the design of ships almost to their present form, and to have built the first triremes in Greece at Corinth.[40] The Corinthian shipbuilder Ameinocles evidently built four ships at Samos, and he went to Samos about three hundred years before the current war ended [i.e, in 704]. The

---

39. The Dorian invasion is probably historical, though not as early as Thucydides puts it. According to legend, the Heraclids, who claimed descent from Heracles, were driven out of the Peloponnesus by the sons of Pelops and found asylum among the Dorians. Later they reclaimed their thrones with the aid of the Dorians, who took over the Peloponnesus and reduced the local population to a status like that of share-croppers.

40. Triremes were warships with three banks of oars (see Glossary). The fifty-oared ships Thucydides mentions elsewhere were an older type of warship that remained in use.

1. Early History and Method

earliest naval battle we know of was fought between Corinth and Corcyra, and that was only two hundred and sixty years before the same time [664].[41] Because it was settled on the Isthmus, Corinth had always been a center of commerce. (The old Greeks had traded by land more than by sea, so the Peloponnesians had no contact with outsiders except through Corinth.) So the Corinthians had the power of wealth, as the old poets show us when they named their land "the rich."[42] After the Greeks took more to the sea, the Corinthians scoured the sea of pirates with the ships they had; and their city had the power of a large income because they were a center for trade by sea and land alike.

Later, the Ionians got together a great navy in the time of Cyrus (the first Persian King) and his son Cambyses. The Ionians made war on Cyrus and for a time had control of the sea near them. Polycrates also had a strong navy; he was tyrant of Samos at the time of Cambyses, and used his navy to take over several islands, including Rheneia [near Delos] which he captured and dedicated to Apollo.[43] The Phocaeans, too, when they were settling Massalia [probably Marseilles] defeated the Carthaginians in a sea battle [about 600].

[14] These were the greatest naval powers, yet even they evidently used only a few triremes, though this was many generations after the Trojan War. Instead, they were made up of fifty-oared boats and long ships like those used at Troy. It was only shortly before the Persian War and the death of Darius (who was King of Persia after Cambyses) that the tyrants of Sicily and the Corcyreans had triremes in any number. These were the only navies worth mentioning in all of Greece before the Persian invasion. The people of Aegina had only a few ships, most of them of fifty oars, while the Athenians, and any others that had navies were no stronger. So it was only recently that Themistocles—during the war with Aegina, and when the Persian invasion was expected—persuaded the Athenians to build the ships in which they fought sea battles.[44] But even these ships were not completely decked over.

[15] Such, then, were the navies of the Greeks, both the ancient and

---

41. See Herodotus iii.49–53. The ancient quarrel between Corinth and Corcyra (modern Corfu) was one of the three chief causes of the Peloponnesian War. Scholars believe that Thucydides' date is too early by about seventy years.
42. Homer, *Iliad* ii.570.
43. On Polycrates, see Herodotus iii.122.
44. Such as the battle of Salamis in 480, which saved Greece from the Persian Navy.

the more recent ones. Those who used them nevertheless gained great power for themselves in increasing their wealth and ruling other peoples, for they sailed to the islands and conquered them (especially if they did not have enough land). But there was no warfare on land that would lead to any power; such wars as they had were all between neighbors, and the Greeks had not yet sent an army abroad to conquer any nation far from home. They never agreed to be subject to the greatest cities, you see, and they never put a common army together on an equal basis, but they fought each other only as citizens of individual states. The most they did was in the old war between Chalcis and Eretria, when the rest of Greece was divided into alliances with one side or the other.[45]

[16] While the rest were being held back from progress by other factors, the Ionians were conquered by the Persians. The Persian Kingdom was flourishing; and after Cyrus had conquered Croesus,[46] he marched against all the lands between the Halys River and the sea, subduing all the Ionian cities on the mainland. Later, Darius used his Phoenician navy to take control of the islands as well.[47]

[17] As for the tyrants that used to rule in the Greek cities, they looked only to their own interests—about their own persons and the glory of their own families, with as much safety as was possible. They resided for the most part in the cities and did no action worth remembering except against their neighbors—not even the tyrants of Sicily, who had arrived at the greatest power. Thus Greece was held back for a long time, because its cities could not do anything remarkable together, and no city dared try anything by itself.

[18] But after that, the last of the tyrants were most of them put down by the Lacedaemonians, both in Athens and in the rest of Greece where there were tyrannies, except for those of Sicily.[48] For although Lacedaemon was troubled with civil strife for longer than any other city we know after its foundation by the Dorians who live there now, it acquired good laws[49] even so at a very early time and has always been free from

---

45. The War of the Lelantine Plain (late 700s) was between the Euboean cities of Chalcis and Eretria and their respective allies.

46. Croesus was the king of Lydia whose wealth was legendary; Lydia was in Asia Minor (modern Turkey).

47. The tale of Cyrus's defeat of Croesus in 544 and subsequent conquest of Ionia is told in Book I of Herodotus' *Histories*.

48. In 510, the Lacedaemonians deposed Hippias in Athens.

tyrants. For up to the end of this war it has been over four hundred years that the Lacedaemonians have followed one and the same constitution; and this has made them strong in themselves, and also given them the ability to arrange matters in the other cities.

After the dissolution of tyrannies in Greece, it was not long before the battle was fought by the Persians against the Athenians in the fields of Marathon. And in the tenth year again after that, Xerxes, king of Persia, came with his great fleet into Greece to subjugate it. Since a great danger now threatened Greece, the leadership of the Greeks that formed an alliance in that war was given to the Lacedaemonians, because they were foremost in power. When the Persians invaded Athens, the Athenians, who had planned in advance to leave their city and were already packed, went aboard ships and became seamen. Soon after they had jointly beaten back the foreigners, all the Greeks—both those who had rebelled from the Persian king and those who had jointly made war against him—divided themselves and one part followed the Athenians while the other followed the Lacedaemonians. For these two cities appeared to be the mightiest; one had power by land, and the other by sea. But the alliance [of all Greece against the Persians] lasted only a while, for afterwards the Lacedaemonians and the Athenians began to disagree and made war on each other, along with their various allies. And any other Greek cities that quarreled went over to one side or the other. So Athens and Sparta spent the time between the war against the Persians and this present war partly in peace and partly in war (either one against the other or against allies in rebellion); and they both arrived at this war well furnished with military provisions and also very experienced in dealing with danger.

[19] The Lacedaemonians led their allies without requiring any payments from them, but took care that they were governed by oligarchy, which served their interests alone. Over time, however, the Athenians took into their hands the ships of all their allies except for Chios and Lesbos, and ordered each of them to make certain monetary payments. And so it came about that the military preparation of Athens alone was greater in the beginning of this war than that of the whole alliance between them and the rest of Greece had been when it was intact and flourishing at its greatest.

---

49. "Has had good laws": the expression is used for cities that are neither democracies nor tyrannies, and is often a code word for moderate oligarchy. See the use of this expression in connection with the establishment of oligarchy on Thasos (**viii.64**). On the constitution of Sparta, see Herodotus i.65 and p. xii.

[20] Such, then, was the state of Greece in the past as I found it, though particular pieces of evidence may be hard to believe.

c. On historical method [i.20.2–22]

People take in reports about the past from each other all alike, without testing them—even reports about their own country. Most of the Athenians, for example, think that Hipparchus was tyrant when he was killed by Harmodius and Aristogeiton, and don't know that it was Hippias who was in power, since he was the eldest son of Pisistratus, and Hipparchus and Thessalus were his brothers. In fact, on the very day, and at the very moment of the deed, Harmodius and Aristogeiton suspected that some of their accomplices had told Hippias about the plot. So they avoided him as having been forewarned, but they still wanted to do something daring before they were captured. When they met Hipparchus by chance at the Leocorium, where he was organizing the Panathenaic Procession, they killed him.[50]

Other Greeks have wrong opinions about many subjects that are current and not forgotten in the passage of time, for example, that the Lacedaemonian kings have two votes each, instead of one, and that they have a military unit there called "Pitanate," which never existed.[51] That shows how much the search for truth strains the patience of most people, who would rather believe the first things that come to hand. [21] But if the evidence cited leads a reader to think that things were mostly as I have described them, he would not go wrong, as he would if he believed what the poets have sung about them, which they have much embellished, or what the prose-writers have strung together, which aims more to delight the ear than to be true. Their accounts cannot be tested, you see, and many are not credible, as they have achieved the status of myth over time. But the reader should believe that I have investigated these matters adequately, considering their antiquity, using the best evidence available. People always think the greatest war is the one they are fighting at the moment, and when that is over they are more impressed with wars of antiquity; but, even so, this war will prove, to all who look at the facts, that it was greater than the others.

50. A longer version of this story is to be found in **vi.54–59**.
51. "Other Greeks have wrong opinions": This may simply refer to popular beliefs of the time; but it may also be implied criticism of Herodotus, who said the Spartan kings had two votes each at vi.57, and who referred to the Pitanate unit at ix.53.

1. Early History and Method

[22] What particular people said in their speeches, either just before or during the war, was hard to recall exactly, whether they were speeches I heard myself or those that were reported to me at second hand. I have made each speaker say what I thought the situation demanded, keeping as near as possible to the general sense of what was actually said.

And as for the real action of the war, I did not think it right to set down either what I heard from people I happened to meet or what I merely believed to be true. Even for events at which I was present myself, I tracked down detailed information from other sources as far as I could. It was hard work to find out what happened, because those who were present at each event gave different reports, depending on which side they favored and how well they remembered.[52]

This history may not be the most delightful to hear, since there is no mythology in it. But those who want to look into the truth of what was done in the past—which, given the human condition, will recur in the future, either in the same fashion or nearly so—those readers will find this *History* valuable enough, as this was composed to be a lasting possession and not to be heard for a prize at the moment of a contest.

---

52. See also v.26 and v.68 and vii.44 on Thucydides' methods and the difficulties he encountered in applying them.

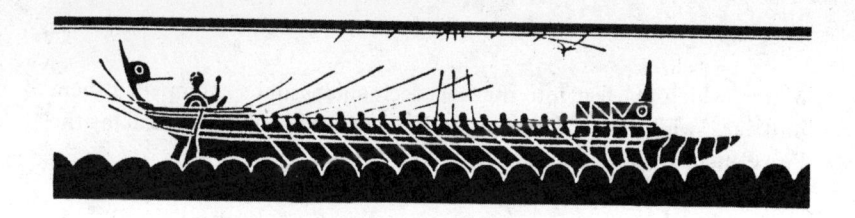

2. Origins of the War

a. Thucydides' explanation for the war [i.23]

The greatest action before this was the one against the Persians, and even that was decided quickly by two battles at sea and two on land.[53] But the Peloponnesian war went on for a very long time and brought more suffering to Greece than had ever been seen before: never had so many cities been captured and depopulated (some by foreigners, others by Greeks themselves at war with one another—some of which were resettled with new inhabitants); never had so many people been driven from their countries or killed, either in the war itself or as a result of civil strife.

Tales told about earlier times, but scantily confirmed in actuality, suddenly ceased to be incredible: tales of earthquakes, which occurred over most of the earth at this time, quite violent ones—eclipses of the sun, which were more frequent than is recorded in earlier times—great droughts in some places followed by famine—and, what caused enormous harm and loss of life, the plague.

All these hardships came upon them during this war, which began when the Athenians and Peloponnesians broke the Thirty Years' Peace that had been agreed between them after the conquest of Euboea. I will first write down an account of the disputes that explain their breaking the Peace, so that no one will ever wonder from what ground so great a war could arise among the Greeks. I believe that the truest reason for the quarrel, though least evident in what was said at the time, was the growth of Athenian

---

53. The sea battles of Salamis and Mycale (or possibly Artemisium), and the land battles of Thermopylae and Plataea.

power, which put fear into the Lacedaemonians and so compelled them into war,[54] while the explanations both sides gave in public for breaking the Peace and starting the war are as follows.

b. Debate at Sparta in 432 [i.68–88]

The immediate causes that were alleged were three Athenian actions: her siege of Potidaea, her decision to help defend the island of Corcyra against Corinth, and her decree restricting trade with Megara.

Potidaea was a Corinthian colony that had been part of the Athenian empire, but had rebelled against Athens (with Corinthian help) and been put under siege by Athens in 432.

The Island of Corcyra (modern Corfu) was also a colony of Corinth, but had no love for her mother city. Corinth had quarreled with her colony Corcyra over a place called Epidamnus, which was divided by civil war. Corinth supported the ruling democrats of Epidamnus, while Corcyra joined a group of exiled oligarchs in attacking them. Athens came in on the side of Corcyra, for fear that if Corinth defeated Corcyra, the Peloponnesians would have control of the Corcyrean fleet, the second largest in Greece.

Megara was Athens' immediate neighbor to the west; the Athenian decree prohibiting trade between Megara and Athens or any of the Athenian allies apparently caused hardship in the city, and this was much resented by the Peloponnesians.

Invited by Corinth, representatives of the cities in the Peloponnesian League gathered in Sparta in 432 to try to talk the Lacedaemonians into war with Athens. The Thirty Years' Peace Treaty had been in effect since 446, at least in theory, and the allies' goal was to show that Athens had broken it. The treaty had forced Athens to give up some of her conquests at the time. It listed the allies on both sides and barred each side from recruiting the other's allies. Apparently it also specified that future disagreements would be settled by arbitration.

Athens had a number of enemies at this point: Corinth was bitter about Athens' siege of Potidaea and support for Corcyra; the island of Aegina[55] com-

54. "Compelled them into war": scholars differ on how to take this. Comparison with parallel passages suggests that Thucydides does not mean that war was simply inevitable, but that people on both sides *felt* compelled to it by their mutual fear. Compulsion (*anankē*) is a subjective necessity. On the interpretation of *anankē* see above, p. xxx.

55. Aegina, an island close to Athens, had rebelled in 457 and been brought under firm Athenian control. We do not know precisely what sort of autonomy had been promised the Aegenitans earlier, or how they felt it had been infringed. On the concept of autonomy, see the Glossary.

2. Origins of the War

plained that Athens had violated her autonomy (which had been guaranteed in the treaty); and Megara was furious because Athenian markets were closed to her.

Sparta opened her assembly to a series of complaints from her allies against Athens, of which Corinth gave the last. Thucydides presents only the barest sketch of the preceding speeches, but he gives us his version of the Corinthian speech in full, followed by a reply from the Athenians. Afterwards the Spartans debated the issue among themselves: a king named Archidamus urged caution, but an official known as an ephor carried the day with a call for war.[56]

These four speeches constitute the famous Debate at Sparta.[57] All four are carefully composed in relation to one another, so that the structure of the debate rewards careful study. A remarkable feature of the debate is that the enemies of Athens have much to say against Athens, but they also comment at length about her military and cultural strength. We are led to see at the outset that Athens cannot lose this war unless she makes terrible mistakes or has extraordinarily bad luck. Thucydides is preparing us for the tragic downfall of Athens, which will in fact be due to a series of military errors compounded by bad luck.

SPEECH OF THE CORINTHIANS

[68] You have so much confidence in your own government and society, Lacedaemonians, that you are too suspicious of us outsiders when we have a complaint to make. This confidence gives you your self-control,[58] but it also makes you rather ignorant in foreign affairs. Many times we have warned you of the damage Athens was about to do to us, and each time you have ignored our guidance entirely. You suspect that we're speaking for our personal interests alone, and that is why you did not call the League together before we were hurt, but waited until it was actually happening to us.

And now we are in the best position to speak, since we have the worst complaints—we've been assaulted by Athens and neglected by you. Now, if the Athenians had done their injustices to Greece in secret, you would not know, and we would have to inform you. But as it is, who needs a long

---

56. On the Spartan constitution, see p. xii.
57. Scholars disagree about the historical status of such speeches in Thucydides. See i.22 and p. xxi.
58. "Self-control": *sōphrosunē*, a virtue associated with oligarchy and also with Lacedaemon. The Greek word cannot be contained by one English one; it is also translated in these pages as "prudence," "moderation," and "clear-headedness."

speech? You can see they have subjugated[59] some of us, while plotting against others, (especially our allies), and have long since mobilized for any war. Otherwise they would not have taken Corcyra from us by force or besieged Potidaea, when one of these is quite handy for attacks against our interests in Thrace, and the other could have provided us Peloponnesians with a very substantial navy.[60]

[69] And for all of this you are yourselves responsible, because you allowed them first to fortify their city after the Persian Wars and later to build the long walls.[61] From that day to this you have been taking freedom away, and not merely from the people they have subjugated, but from your allies as well. If you have the power to put a stop to subjugation, yet look the other way while it happens, then you have done it yourselves, more truly than if you had been the subjugators, yet all the more if you claim honor and virtue as the liberators of Greece![62]

Even now it has been hard to hold this meeting, and our agenda is unclear. We should no longer be asking whether we have suffered injustice, but how we may defend ourselves. The Athenians made up their minds and went into action against us without delay, while we were indecisive. But we know the path they follow, how the Athenians encroach upon their neighbors little by little. As long as they think you are blind to this and do not notice it, they will proceed with some caution; but once they realize that you are looking the other way, in full knowledge, then they will lay into us fiercely. You Lacedaemonians are the only Greeks who prefer procrastination to power as a defense, and you are the only ones who like to crush your enemies not at the start but when they've doubled their strength. You were supposed to be dependable, but your reputation has eclipsed the truth. We know ourselves that the Persians came from the ends of the earth to the Peloponnesus before you sent a significant force against them; and now you are looking the other way from the Athenians,

59. Subjugated: the Greek literally means "enslaved."
60. Corcyra (modern Corfu) had a navy of one hundred twenty triremes, the second largest in Greece. In fact, Corinth was the aggressor in her quarrel with Corcyra, and Athens had merely responded to calls for help against Corinth. Potidaea was of strategic importance for Athens' interests in the part of northern Greece known as Thrace, which was a source of gold as well as timber for ships. A former Corinthian colony, it had been a tributary member of the Athenian alliance until its rebellion against Athens in 432.
61. The long walls, guarding the road from Athens to its port, Piraeus, were built in 458.
62. See **i.18, ii.8,** and **viii.46** for the Spartan claim to be the liberators of Greece.

who are not far off as they were, but close by; and instead of attacking them for your own defense you are waiting for them to attack, when the odds against winning will be much worse for you. We also know that the Persian king was defeated mainly by his own mistakes, and that our survival so far against the Athenians has been due to their blunders more often than to any help from you. Really, hoping for help from you has destroyed some people who were unprepared because they relied on you.

Now please do not think we are speaking out of hostility; this is merely a complaint. Complaints are for friends who make mistakes, accusations for enemies who commit injustice. [70] Besides, we think we are in as good a position as anyone to find fault with our neighbors, especially in view of the great differences between the two sides, to which we think you are blind.

We don't think you have thought through what sort of people these Athenians are: your struggle will be with people totally different from yourselves. They love innovation, and are quick to invent a plan and then to carry it out in action, while you are good only for keeping things as they are, and you never invent anything or even go as far as necessary in action. Moreover, they are bold beyond their power, take thoughtless risks, and still hope for the best in danger; whereas your actions always fall short of your power, you distrust even what you know in your minds to be certain, and you never think you will be delivered from danger. Above all, they never hesitate; you are always delaying; they are never at home, and you are the worst homebodies, because they count on getting something by going abroad, while you fear you will lose what you have if you go out.

When they overcome their enemies, they advance the farthest; and when overcome by them, they fall back the least. And as for their bodies, they devote them utterly to the service of the city as if they were not their own, while they keep total possession of their minds when they do anything for its sake. Unless they accomplish what they have once set their minds on, they count themselves deprived of their own property. And if they do get what they went for, they think lightly of it compared to what their next action will bring, but if they happen to fail in any attempt, they turn to other hopes and make up the loss that way. You see, they alone get what they hope for as soon as they think of it, through the speed with which they execute their plans.

At this they toil, filling all the days of their lives with hard work and danger. What they have, they have no leisure to enjoy, because they are continually getting more. They do not consider any day a holiday unless they have done something that needed to be done; and they think that an idle rest is as much trouble as hard work. So that, in a word, it is true to say that they are born never to allow themselves or anyone else a rest.

[71] That is the character of their city, Lacedaemonians, and yet you still procrastinate! You don't realize that you will enjoy the longest peace if you make your intention clear never to put up with injustice, while using your own military with justice. You think fairness lies in a defense that does no harm to others and brings no damage on yourselves. This would hardly work even with neighbors similar to you. As we have just now shown you, however, your customs are quite old-fashioned compared to theirs. New ways necessarily prevail over old, in politics as in technology; unchanging traditions may be best for a city at peace, but a city faced with the many necessities of war must have many innovations as well. That is why there have been more changes in Athens than here, because of their wide experience.[63]

So now is the time to put an end to your torpor! Help Potidaea and the others, as you promised, by immediately attacking Attica, so you will not betray your friends and kindred to their worst enemies and drive us in despair to seek out some other alliance. There would be no injustice in that, either to the gods who received our oaths or to the people who heard them. Treaties are broken not by those who go elsewhere because they were abandoned, but by those who fail to help the ones they swore to help. But if you decide to become engaged, we will stay with you, since to change allies then would be a sacrilege, and we would not find more compatible allies in any case. Think carefully about all this, and try not to let the Peloponnesus sink under your leadership below the level at which it was given you by your ancestors.

[72] So spoke the Corinthians. Athenian ambassadors happened to be at Sparta already on other business, and when they heard the speeches against them they decided they should present themselves to the Lacedaemonians, not to defend themselves on the charges brought by the cities, but to persuade the Lacedaemonians to consider the whole issue at greater length rather than make a quick decision. Besides, they wished to point out how powerful their city was, refreshing the memories of the old while instructing the young on what they had missed. They believed their speech would turn them more to peace than to war. So they went to the Lacedaemonians and asked for permission to speak to the assembly. On being invited to do so, they came forward and spoke as follows:

63. The changes in Athens are the democratic reforms. For Thucydides' mixed views on the effectiveness of democracy at war, see Introduction, p. xxv.

SPEECH OF THE ATHENIANS[64]

[73] Our mission here was not to argue with your allies, but to represent our city on another matter. Still, when we heard the great outcry against us we came forward, not to respond to the charges made by the cities, (for you are no law court set over our speeches and theirs), but so that you will not be too easily persuaded by your allies into making a bad decision on important matters. Besides, we want to review the whole case against us and show that we are not being unreasonable in holding on to our possessions, and also that we are a city to be reckoned with.

There is no need to speak of the distant past, for which hearsay is a better witness than what you listeners have seen. The Persian Wars, however, and events you know from your own experience, must come into this speech, although it is a nuisance for us to keep bringing them up. In our actions at that time we took risks to achieve benefits that partly went to you in actual fact; at this point we should not be deprived of all our glory, for what it's worth. This story will be told, not by way of asking favors, but as evidence to show you what sort of city will be your opponent if you make the wrong decision.

We say that at Marathon we faced the Persians first and alone.[65] And when they came a second time, when we were too weak to resist by land, we took to our ships with all our people and joined in the battle at Salamis [in 480], which kept them from sailing down to the Peloponnesus and destroying one city after another with a fleet so large that you would have been unable to combine forces against it. The best evidence for this comes from the Persian king himself: as soon as he was beaten at sea he quickly took the greater part of his army and went back home, seeing that his power was no longer what it had been.

[74] That is how it was, and it is clear that, when the Greek cause depended on her ships, we Athenians provided the three things that contributed most to the victory: the largest number of ships, the most intelligent commander, and the most unhesitating zeal. (1) We supplied just under

---

64. The Athenian speech does not respond to specific charges of the Corinthians such as the matter of Potidaea. Instead it responds to what Thucydides earlier called "the truest reason for the quarrel" (i.23): the growth of the Athenian empire, which was also a general theme of the Corinthian speech (i.69). Thus, in shaping this debate, Thucydides relegates "the explanations both sides gave in public" to the sidelines: this is a debate about the empire.

65. Plataean troops were also engaged in the Battle of Marathon in 490.

two thirds of the four hundred ships.⁶⁶ (2) Themistocles, the Athenian leader, gets the most credit for positioning the battle in the narrow strait, which clearly saved our cause; and you honored him for this more highly than any other outsider who came to your city. (3) We showed the most daring zeal when no one came to help us from further south and all of Greece to the north of us had been subjugated by the Persians. Then we decided it was right for us to leave our city and sacrifice our property. We did not want to abandon the common cause of our remaining allies or split off and so become useless to them, so we took to our ships without any anger at you for not coming to our defense any sooner.

We insist, therefore, that our action did you at least as much good as it did us. You did come to help—when we had nothing left to save—and you did so more out of fear for yourselves than for us, since you left behind cities that were still full of your homes, which you hoped to enjoy in the future. We, however, set out from a city that was no more, we risked our lives for homes that survived only in a slender hope, and we did our share of fighting to save you while saving ourselves as well.⁶⁷ If we had surrendered to the Persians earlier, as the others had done, out of fear for our land, or if we had not had the courage to take to our ships—if we had thought ourselves defeated—then there would have been no point in your fighting the Persians at sea: you did not have enough ships, and the Persians would have taken everything they wanted without a blow.

[75] Really, Lacedaemonians, in view of our zeal and intelligent strategy during the Persian Wars, do we deserve to be treated with such extreme hostility by the Greeks, even though we do have an empire? After all, we did not take the empire by violence; it was the allies themselves who came and begged us to take command when you were unwilling to stay with us and finish off the war against the Persians.⁶⁸ After that action we were compelled to develop our empire to its present strength by fear first of all, but also by ambition, and lastly for our own advantage.⁶⁹ Once we

---

66. An exaggeration: there were two hundred Athenian ships in an allied fleet of a little under four hundred.
67. In 480, when the second Persian invasion under Xerxes reached Athens, the Athenians sent their wives and children to safety on the islands and put every available man on board their fighting ships.
68. Soon after 479, the Spartans withdrew from the war against the Persians, and the Athenians took over the cause.
69. The three motives are *deos, timē, and ōphelia*. Fear is Thucydides' favorite explanation for violence and injustice, and he sees it operating even when it is well below the surface. The word translated "ambition" literally means "honor."

2. Origins of the War

had come to be hated by most people,[70] when some had already rebelled and been put down and you had turned away from our former friendship to suspicion and hostility, then we thought it would not be safe to risk letting anyone go free, especially since the rebels went over to your side.[71] No one should be blamed for looking after his own interests to fend off such great dangers.

[76] You Lacedaemonians, for example, use your position of leadership in the Peloponnesus to arrange affairs in the cities there to your own advantage. If you had stayed on as leaders of the alliance against the Persians, you would have been as much hated by all as we are now, and we are sure that your leadership would have been no less painful to the allies than ours has been. You too would have been compelled to rule with a strong hand or else put yourselves in danger. We have not done anything in this that should cause surprise, and we have not deviated from normal human behavior: we simply accepted an empire that was offered us and then refused to surrender it. If we have been overcome by three of the strongest motives—ambition, fear, and our own advantage—we have not been the first to do this. It has always been established that the weaker are held down by the stronger.[72] Besides, we took this upon ourselves because we thought we were worthy of it, and you thought so too, until now that you are reckoning up your own advantage and appealing to justice—which no one has ever preferred to force, if he had a chance to achieve something by that and gain an advantage.

When people follow their natural human inclination to rule over others,

---

70. "Hated by most people": see **ii.8**, **i.99**, and **iii.47**. This is probably an exaggeration, as much of the empire appears to have been loyal to Athens even in adversity. The issue is debated by scholars. Is Thucydides to be trusted on this point? Or is he taking a narrowly oligarchical perspective? Did ordinary Athenians see their empire this way? Was Athens seen as a supporter of democracy in the subject cities? Did the empire in fact become more harsh around 432 and ease up afterwards under pressure of war? In i.99 Thucydides explains the decline of Athenian popularity in these terms: The allies began by making payments so as to avoid contributing troops or ships in the war against Persia. Then, when they failed to meet their financial obligations, Athenian forces would come against them. Since they had cut back on their own military forces, they would have no adequate means of defense against Athens, and so they continued in the empire, full of resentment.

71. Athens had been badly scared by the rebellion of the nearby island of Euboea in 446; that was why she had agreed to the Thirty Years' Peace.

72. See the Melian Dialogue, **v.105**, and Democritus fr 267: "By nature it is fitting for the stronger to rule."

they deserve to be praised if they use more justice than they have to, in view of their power. And we think that if anyone else had our position, you would really see how moderate we have been; yet our very fairness has brought contempt on us instead of the praise we deserve.

[77] Although we have been at a disadvantage in lawsuits arising from treaties with our allies and have allowed them trial in our own city by impartial laws, we have nevertheless been given a reputation for litigiousness.[73] No one notices that others, who have empires in other places, and are less moderate toward their subject states than we, are never upbraided for it. Those who have the power to use force, you see, have no need at all to go to law. And yet because these men have been used to dealing with us on equal terms, if they lose anything at all which they think they should not have lost, either by sentence of our courts or by the power of our government, they are not thankful for the large amount that they retain. Instead, they complain more about their slight loss than they would if we had put law to one side and openly seized their goods at the start. For in that event, not even they could deny that the weaker must give way to the stronger. People are apparently more passionate over injustice than violence, because then they feel that someone who is their equal has taken an unfair advantage, while they accept violence from someone stronger as a matter of necessity. At least, when they suffered worse things under the rule of the Persians, they accepted them; but now they find our empire hard to bear. And that was to be expected: the present is always the worst to those who are subject to the rule of others.

As for you, if you should defeat us and reign yourselves, you would soon find a change from the love they bear you now out of fear of us, at least if you are planning the sort of behavior you showed when you were their leaders for that short time against the Persians.[74] The customs in your country are not compatible with those of others; and to make matters worse, when any one of you travels abroad, he neither follows your cus-

---

73. The interpretation of this passage is in question. According to the alternative reading, preferred by Hornblower, the Athenians were losing cases tried abroad and therefore shifted trials to Athens so that they could get a fairer hearing *for themselves*. This can be defended from the Greek, but would not fit a context in which the Athenians are pleading their fairness to their allies.

74. "The sort of behavior you showed": The Spartan general Pausanias had alienated a number of allies soon after his victory at Plataea (i.94–95); but another Spartan general, Brasidas, was to be highly successful in winning friends for Sparta in northern Greece (p. 97). Events showed, however, that Sparta could be a harsh master (see iii.93).

toms nor those of the rest of Greece.

[78] Make your decision with the slow deliberate care due to important matters, and don't bring trouble on yourselves by giving in to other people's opinions and complaints. Before you go to war, you must realize how unpredictable war is. The longer it lasts the more it is likely to turn on chance. The odds of disaster are the same for both sides, and no one can see where the dangers lie. People tend to go into war the wrong way around, starting with action and turning to discussion only after they have come to harm. We are not making that mistake, and neither are you, so far as we can see. So, while it is still possible for both sides to use good judgment, we ask you not to dissolve the treaty or break your oaths, but to submit our differences to arbitration according to the agreement. If not, the gods who heard the oaths are our witnesses, and once you have started the war we will do our best to resist wherever you show the way.

So spoke the Athenians. After the Lacedaemonians had heard the complaints of their allies against Athens, as well as the Athenian speech, they put everyone else out of their assembly and discussed the situation among themselves. The opinions of the majority came down to this: that the Athenians were guilty of injustice, and they should go to war right away. But their king, Archidamus, who had a reputation for intelligence and prudence, came forward and spoke as follows:

SPEECH OF ARCHIDAMUS

[80] I have seen too many wars, Lacedaemonians, (and so have you, if you're my age) to have any desire for the business out of that ignorant belief, to which ordinary people succumb, that war is safe and good. If you think about it with a clear mind, you will see that this war we are discussing would be no small one. Our strength would be comparable if we were to fight Peloponnesians who are our neighbors, where we could reach any place quickly. But these men live in a distant land, and besides they are superbly trained at sea and have all sorts of excellent resources—private and public wealth, ships, horses, infantry, the largest population of any city in Greece, and many tax-paying allies as well. How could we lightly undertake a war with men like these? Unprepared as we are, where could we get the confidence to rush into war? From our ships? We are weaker there, and it would take time to build and train a navy to match theirs. From our money? There we are even weaker, since we have no public treasury and cannot easily raise money from our citizens.

[81] Perhaps one of you takes heart from our heavy infantry, which is superior to theirs in quality and numbers, because this would allow us to invade them frequently and waste their lands. But they have plenty of land in their empire, and will bring in whatever they need by sea. If, on the other hand, we try to get their allies to rebel, we will have to provide them with naval support, as they are mostly islanders. So what kind of war will this be? Unless we take control of the sea, or cut off the income that supports their navy, we will be defeated on almost every front. And then we will have gone too far to make an honorable peace, especially if everyone thinks we started the quarrel. We must not indulge in the false hope that we will end the war quickly if we destroy their crops. No, I am afraid that we shall leave this war as a legacy to our children. We cannot expect the Athenians to give up their ambitions slavishly to save their land, or, with their experience, to be easily shattered by war.

[82] Now I am not asking you to be so blind to the damage Athens is doing to your allies that you let them get away with it and do nothing to arrest them in their schemes.[75] But do not take up arms just yet. Send to them instead, and make demands, without implying too clearly whether you plan to make war or give way, and use the time to prepare our forces. We should acquire allies, either Greek or foreign, who can add a naval force or money to our power. (No one should be blamed for saving themselves by taking help from foreigners as well as Greeks—not if Athens is plotting against them, as she is against us.[76]) We should also stockpile our own resources. If Athens accepts our demands, so much the better; if not, we'll let two or three years go by and then attack them, if we choose, from a stronger position. And perhaps once they've seen our preparations, and realized that we really do mean to back up our demands, they'll give in more easily, before their farmland is ruined and while they can still decide to save the goods they have now, which are not yet destroyed. Remember,

---

75. "To be so blind": this is one of the accusations of Corinth, above, **i.69**.

76. "No one should be blamed": see **i.75**, where the Athenians introduce this line of thought, that a city cannot be blamed for actions taken in its own defence. Seeking help from foreigners (which in this case probably meant using Persian money or ships against Athens) was a terrible thing to do so soon after the long hard war to keep Persians out of Greek affairs. An early Spartan attempt to deal with Persia was derailed by the Athenians (**ii.67**). Towards the end of the war, however, almost twenty years after this debate, Sparta did use Persian help to defeat Athens. As elsewhere in the debate, Thucydides is probably foreshadowing the outcome of the war.

their land is nothing but a hostage to us, and as such it is more useful to us the better cultivated it is. You ought to spare Athenian farmland as long as possible, and not make them so desperate that they are harder to control. If we are hurried by the complaints of our allies into wasting their land before we are prepared, then be careful we don't bring down shame and trouble on the Peloponnesus. Complaints can be resolved, whether they are from cities or individuals, but a war engages everyone for the sake of a few personal interests, a war's progress cannot be foreseen, and there is no decent way to end it easily.

[83] Now, although there are many of us, no one should think it is cowardice that prevents us from quickly attacking that one city. They have just as many allies as we do, and theirs give them money. After all, war depends more on finance than on weapons, since money lets you put weapons to use; and this is especially true when a land-power takes on a sea-power. We should collect money first, therefore, before we are carried away by our allies' speeches. We are the ones who will bear most of the responsibility for the outcome, either way, so we should take the time to look ahead.

[84] Yes, we are slow and make delays; that is their biggest complaint about us. But don't be ashamed of that. If we begin the war in haste, we'll have many delays before we end it, owing to our lack of preparation. Besides, our city has always been famous, always free; and this slowness of ours is really nothing but clear-headed self-control. It is this that gives us our unique ability to restrain our arrogance in success, and to yield less than other people to misfortune. When people try to excite us with praise into doing something dangerous, we do not let the pleasure of it overcome our better judgment; and if someone tries to spur us on with harsh criticism, we do not let ourselves be swayed by our anger. Our discipline makes us good soldiers and gives us good judgment. We are good soldiers because our self-control is the chief cause of a sense of shame, and shame of courage;[77] while we have good judgment because our education leaves us too

---

77. "Our self-control ... courage": literally, "A sense of shame takes the biggest part in self control, and courage takes the biggest part in shame." When x takes part in y, it is y that explains x. For the interpretation of this difficult passage, see Nussbaum (1986: 508, n. 24), and my note on iii.83. Self-control (*sōphrosunē*), the chief virtue associated with Sparta, is essentially linked to a sense of shame (*aidōs*), which is closely akin to shame (*aischunē*). Shame leads to courage because men who have a sense of shame will not want to be seen doing anything cowardly.

ignorant to look down on our laws,[78] and our self-control is too strict for disobeying them. We have none of that useless intelligence that condemns the enemy's forces in a fine speech but fails to deliver as good an attack in the field. Instead, we think the plans of our neighbors are as good as our own, and we can't work out whose chances at war are better in a speech. So we always make our preparations in action, on the assumption that our enemies know what they are doing. We should not build our hopes on the belief that they will make mistakes, but on our own careful foresight. And we should not think there is much difference between one man and another, except that the winner will be the one whose education was the most severe.

[85] These practices were passed down to us by our ancestors and they have always helped us. Do not let them go; and do not let yourselves be rushed into a decision in a brief part of a day, when it concerns many lives and cities, a great deal of money, and our honor. Instead, decide at leisure. We can do that, more easily than most people, because of our strength. Send to the Athenians about Potidaea, and send to them about the injustices of which our allies complain. I urge this because they are ready to go to arbitration, and in such a case it is not lawful to attack them first, as if they were in the wrong. But do prepare for war in any case. This decision will be the strongest, and it will put the most fear into our enemies.

That was what Archidamus said. Then Sthenelaïdas, who was one of the ephors that year, stood up last and spoke thus:

SPEECH OF STHENELAÏDAS[79]

[86] I don't understand all these words the Athenians use. They praised themselves a lot, but nowhere did they deny the injustice they've shown to our allies and the Peloponnesus. Yes, they were good men against the Persians at one time, but they are bad men to us now, and they deserve double punishment for changing from good to bad. We've stayed the same, then and now: we will not disregard any injustice to our allies, if we are clearheaded, and we will punish Athens without delay, since there is no delay in our allies' suffering.

Others may have plenty of money and ships and horses, but we have

---

78. Sophists were forbidden to bring the new learning to the Lacedaemonians. See Plato, *Hippias Major* 283–84.

79. A truly Laconic speech. Spartans were famous for brevity in speaking and our word "laconic" is derived from the name of their homeland. Sthenelaïdas plays no other part in the *History*.

2. Origins of the War

good allies and they should not be betrayed to the Athenians. This issue is not to be settled in arbitration or speeches, since the damage is not being done in a speech; no, this calls for swift punishment with all our strength. Don't let anyone teach us it's proper to stop and discuss injustice while it's being done to us; what's really proper is for those who are planning *injustice* to spend a lot of time in discussions.

Vote for war, then, Lacedaemonians! Be worthy of Sparta and don't let Athens grow any stronger! Don't betray your allies either, but with the gods' help let us attack the aggressors!

[87] With these words, since he was an ephor,[80] he put the vote to the assembly of the Lacedaemonians. They decide matters there by shouting rather than counting votes, and he said he could not tell which shout was louder. In fact, he wanted them to show their opinion openly, so as to whip up enthusiasm for making war. So he said, "Any of you Lacedaemonians who thinks the treaty is broken and the Athenians are in the wrong, go over there," pointing out a place to them, and, "Anyone who does not think so, get on the other side." They stood up and divided, and by far the greater number thought the treaty had been broken. Then they called the allies back in and told them that they had decided the Athenians were guilty of injustice, but that they wanted to call a formal meeting of all the Peloponnesian League and put it to the vote, so that if they made war it would be on the basis of a common decision.

This done, the allies went home, while the Athenians stayed on to finish the business that had brought them. This decision of the assembly (that the treaty had been broken) was made in the fourteenth year of the Thirty Years' Peace, which began after the rebellion in Euboea.[81]

[88] The main reason the Lacedaemonians voted that the treaty had been broken and that the war should begin was not that the allies' speeches had persuaded them. They made this decision because they were afraid Athenian power would continue to grow, seeing that most of Greece was already subject to them.[82]

---

80. Sparta had five elected officials known as Ephors (overseers).

81. The debate took place in 432; the treaty was negotiated in 446, after Athens had put down a rebellion on Euboea, the island just north of Attica (i.114–15). Much later, the Lacedaemonians came to regret their decision to start the war (vii. 18).

82. Speeches in Thucydides rarely affect action, although they frequently bring to light the motives for action. As we have observed before, fear, not reason, is the principal cause of war and other human evils, according to Thucydides (p. xxxi, see i.23).

Thucydides now flashes back to the fifty years that followed the Persian War and led to the current crisis. In a rapid summary (known as the "Pentecontaetia," or "Fifty Years' Tale") he tells of the rise of Athens and the increasing friction between it and the Peloponnesians (i. 89-118). We omit this digression and turn directly to the events that opened the war.

c. Meeting of the Peloponnesian League in 431
[Summary of i.118-24]

After their decision against Athens, the Spartans sent to the oracle at Delphi to ask if they should go to war. They received an encouraging reply. Then they held a meeting of the Peloponnesian League as promised. Once again, the Corinthians gave the last speech, and Thucydides supplies us with a version of it. The Corinthians argued that the Peloponnesians would have the advantage in the war, mainly on these grounds:

1. *The Peloponnesians had more and better disciplined ground troops.*
2. *Although Athens currently had the larger navy, the Peloponnesians had access to funds from the treasuries of Olympia and Delphi, and could use these to hire sailors away from Athens, which depended heavily on mercenaries.*
3. *The Peloponnesian League would volunteer contributions to their war effort, while the Athenian Empire was forced to pay tribute.*
4. *Athens was vulnerable to rebellions within her empire, and to the establishment of a fort in Attica.*[83]

The Corinthians then urged the members of the League to bring Athens to her knees. If they failed, they would let Athens establish herself as a tyrant state in Greece. They urged the Peloponnesians to move quickly to save Potidaea ("a Dorian city besieged by Ionians") before it would be too late. The best hope for lasting peace, they said, would be to win the war against Athens.

Their last words were a stirring call to war:

> Allies, you must see that we have arrived at the moment of necessity and that our advice is best: you should vote for war. Have no fear of immediate danger; but keep your hearts set on the wider peace that flows from danger. War gives us a more secure peace, you see, while staying out of war allows us no

---

83. This foreshadows the fortification of Decelea in 413 (p. 127) and will be answered by Pericles (**i.142**).

comparable security. Keep in mind that a tyrant city has been set up in Greece, and it has been set up against all of us alike; some of us it rules already, the rest it plans to add to its empire. Let us attack it and bring it down, so that we may live on without danger and may liberate the others from subjugation. (i.124. 2–3)

d. *Pericles' war speech [i.140–46]*

After the League had decided on war, the Lacedaemonians sent a delegation to Athens. They demanded that the Athenians raise their siege of Potidaea, set Aegina free, and rescind the decree blocking commerce with Megara. Only on these conditions, they said, would peace be possible. The Athenians refused, giving their reasons for continuing as they were. Then came the final delegation from Sparta with this message: "The Lacedaemonians would like there to be peace—and there will be peace, but only if you let the Greeks have their autonomy."[84]

Then the Athenians called an assembly to consider their options, and decided to make up their minds and answer once and for all. Many people came forward to speak on each side; some thought they should go to war, others that they should rescind the Megarian Decree so that it would not stand in the way of peace. Then Pericles—who was at that time the foremost Athenian and the most able in speech or action—gave the following advice:[85]

PERICLES' WAR SPEECH

[140] My opinion has always been the same, Athenians: don't give in to the Peloponnesians. Of course I know the passion that leads people into war does not last when they're actually engaged in it; people change their minds with the circumstances. But I see I must still give nearly the same advice now as I gave before; and I insist that if you agree to this as common policy you support it even if things go badly for us—otherwise you've no

---

84. "Autonomy" (*autonomia*): independence, really "having your own laws." See Glossary.

85. "Most able in speech or action": the sophist Protagoras promised to make his students "most able in speech or action" (Plato, *Protagoras* 318e). Pericles was deeply involved in the new learning and had spent much time with Protagoras.

right to boast of your intelligence if all goes well, since events can turn out as stupidly as people's intentions, and that is why we usually blame chance when things don't turn out as expected.

It is obvious that the Lacedaemonians have been plotting against us, now more than ever. We agreed in the Thirty Years' Peace to refer our differences to mutual arbitration, while each party kept what it had in the meanwhile.[86] But they have not yet asked for arbitration, and they have not accepted our offers either; they prefer war to speeches as a means of clearing away the charges against them, and they're already giving orders when they come, instead of complaining as they did before. They are commanding us to leave Potidaea, restore autonomy to Aegina, and rescind our decree against Megara; now these latest arrivals are warning us to let the Greeks have their autonomy. No one should think that the war will be over a trifle if we do not rescind the Megarian decree (which is what they emphasize the most—that if we rescind the decree there won't be a war). There mustn't be any suspicion remaining among you that the war was over a small matter: this "little matter" holds all the firmness of your resolve, and the proof of our judgment. If you give way on these points you will immediately be ordered to give up something greater, since they will expect you to be afraid and give way over that as well. A stiff refusal from you, however, will teach them clearly to treat you more as equals.

[141] Make up your minds right now either to give in before we get hurt, or, if we do go to war—as *I* think best—not to yield to any demand whatever, great or small, and to hold on to our possessions without fear. The effect is the same—subjugation—whether the claim is large or small, so long as it comes as a command from equals to their neighbors, before arbitration.

Now as for the war and the resources on both sides, once you hear a detailed account you must see that we'll be just as strong as they will. First, the Peloponnesians work their own land and have no wealth either in private or public hands.[87] Second, they have no experience of extended or overseas warfare, since their attacks on each other are kept brief by their

---

86. "In the meanwhile": almost all editors supply such a phrase, although it is not in the text. The point is that in agreeing to the Thirty Years' Peace the Peloponnesians cannot have agreed to let Athens keep her gains permanently, and they did not ratify the Athenian Empire.

87. Since the Lacedaemonians were not dependent on imported grain, as Athens was, they had not developed the sort of commercial system which, along with its mines, had made Athens rich.

2. Origins of the War

poverty. Such people are unable to man ships or send out armies of foot soldiers with any frequency, for they'd be far from their own property while still depending on their own food supplies. Besides, they would be blockaded by sea. Wars must be supported by wealth that is available, not by forced contributions.[88] And those who work their own land are more willing to risk their lives in war than their money, since they have some confidence of surviving but are not sure their money won't be spent, especially if their war should be prolonged (as is likely) beyond what they expected. The Peloponnesians and their allies are able to hold out against all the other Greeks in a single battle, but they are unable to make war against those whose preparations are different from their own. Their League does not have a common council to take quick decisive action as needed; instead, they all have equal votes, and because they are not akin[89] each group pursues its own interest, which means that nothing gets decided. Some, you see, want more than anything to exact revenge, while others want to keep damage to their own property at a minimum. They take a long time before a meeting, and then devote only a fraction of it to any common business, while spending the greater part on their individual concerns. Meanwhile, no one thinks that his neglect of common interests will do any harm—let someone else look after his share of the common interest. The result is that no one notices how everyone's individual judgments are ruining the common good for them all.

[142] The main point however is that they will be hindered by lack of money, since they will have to delay action while they wait to raise funds. But in war, the critical moment will not wait. And we should not have a moment's fear of their fort-building or their navy.[90] As for a fort in Attica,

---

88. The Athenians had to resort to forcing money from their allies as early as 428/7, to support the siege of Mytilene (iii. 19). There must be some irony in Thucydides' comment about Pericles at ii.65: "he also foresaw what the city could do." Pericles' critical remarks about forced contributions seem more true of Athens than of Sparta.

89. "Because they are not akin": the Peloponnesian League included Dorians and Aeoloians, and there were substantial cultural differences within these groups as well. See vi.17 for a similar prediction—not borne out in the event—about the mixed population of Sicily.

90. The Corinthians had observed that Athens would be vulnerable to having a Peloponnesian fort set up in her territory, an idea the Spartans did not take up until it was proposed to them by the Athenian Alcibiades many years later. In fact, Sparta's navy and fort-building did eventually defeat Athens; Thucydides may be ironically foreshadowing events that are far in the future.

it would be hard enough in peace-time to build a citadel that would be our match, let alone in war, when we are fortified against it. If they build only an observation post, on the other hand, they may damage some of our land by raiding it, and they may take in runaway slaves; but this would not be enough to keep us from sailing to their land and building forts there or retaliating with our navy, which is our great strength.

Our naval experience has actually done us more good on land than their infantry experience has done for their navy. And they won't easily learn to be experts at sea. You yourselves have not yet mastered it completely, though you've been studying it since right after the Persians came; how then could men who are farmers rather than sailors do anything worthwhile? Besides, they'll have no chance to practice, because we will blockade them constantly with a large fleet. They might take courage from superior numbers, set their ignorance aside, and venture out against a light blockade; but if they are shut in by a large navy then they will not stir that way at all, their lack of practice will make them even less skillful than before, and they will be even more cautious because of that. Naval warfare requires professional knowledge as much as anything else does: it is not possible to learn by practicing it occasionally on the side; on the contrary, if you're studying naval warfare you can't do anything else on the side.

[143] What if they would carry off the money at Olympia or Delphi and try to hire away our foreign sailors at a larger salary?[91] That would be dangerous to us only if we could not match them by manning a fleet with our own citizens and resident aliens. As it is, however, we *can* do this. Besides—and this is really decisive—we have more captains and junior officers among our citizens than all the rest of Greece, and they are better qualified, too. Furthermore, to say nothing of the risks involved, no sailor would agree to be outlawed by his own country, accept a weaker chance of winning, and join forces with the other side for only a few days of bonus payments.[92]

That is more or less how I think things stand for the Peloponnesians. As for us, our position is free of all the faults I found in theirs, and we have great advantages in other areas as well. If they invade our territory on foot, we shall go to theirs by sea. And the advantage will be ours even if we waste only part of the Peloponnesus while they waste all of Attica. They cannot replace their land without a battle, while we have plenty of land in the

---

91. See above, p. 30. This is another of the Corinthian proposals.
92. Although all Athenian sailors were paid, it did not follow that they included large numbers of mere mercenaries, as the Corinthians had assumed. Pericles is right to imply here that allied sailors felt some loyalty to Athens.

islands and on the mainland. That's how great a thing it is to have control of the sea!⁹³

Consider this: would we be any safer from attack if we were islanders? Now we should really think like islanders and give up our land and our farmhouses, but keep watch over the sea and our city. We must not get so angry over losing our farms that we engage the Peloponnesians in battle when they outnumber us. If we won, we would have to fight against just as many men again; and if we were defeated we would lose our allies, which are the source of our strength, as they'll not keep quiet unless we're strong enough to fight them. We mustn't cry over our land and farms, but save our mourning for the lives of men: farmland won't give us men, but men can win farmland. If I thought I could persuade you, I'd tell you to go out and destroy the farms yourselves, and prove to the Peloponnesians that you will never surrender in order to save your land.

[144] Many other things give me hope that we shall win through, unless you intend to enlarge your empire while still engaged in the war, or choose to take on new risks.⁹⁴ I am more afraid of our own mistakes, you see, than I am of our opponents' schemes. But all this should come clear in another speech, at the time of action.

For the present, let us send the ambassadors back with this answer: (1) We will give the Megarians the use of our market and ports if the Lacedaemonians will cancel their policy of expelling us and our allies as aliens (since nothing in the treaty blocks either our current policy or theirs). Also, (2) we will give the Greek cities their autonomy (if they were autonomous when we signed the treaty), as soon as the Lacedaemonians grant autonomy to their own cities to enjoy as they see fit, and not merely to serve Lacedaemonian interests. And (3) we would like to go to arbitration in accordance with the treaty. We will not begin a war, but we will punish those who do.

This is an answer that follows justice and suits the dignity of our city as well. Nevertheless, you must realize that although we are being forced into this war, if we embrace it willingly we will have less pressure from the enemy. Remember too that the greatest danger gives rise to the greatest honor for a city or a private man. Our ancestors, after all, stood up to the Persians; they started with less than we have now, and even gave up what they had. It was more good planning than good luck, and more daring than power, that enabled them to repel the Persian king and raise our city to its

---

93. On the importance of sea power, see above i.7, i.13 ff., and i.82.

94. Here Thucydides foreshadows the ill-fated expedition to take over Syracuse on Sicily (p. 111, ff.).

present heights. We must measure up to our ancestors: resist our enemies in every possible way and try to deliver the city undiminished to those who come after.

[145] That was Pericles' speech. The Athenians thought his advice was best, and voted to do as he had told them. They answered the Lacedaemonians as he had proposed, in every particular and on the main point too: "They would do nothing on command, but were ready to resolve the accusations on a fair and equal basis by arbitration as specified in the treaty." Then the Lacedaemonians went home, and after that there came no more ambassadors.

[146] These, then, were the complaints and the issues on which the two sides differed before the war—complaints which arose from events at Epidamnus and Corcyra.[95] The two sides were still in communication, however, and went to each other without heralds, though not without suspicion, for what was happening amounted to a breach of the treaty and a reason for war.

e. The war begins with an attack on Plataea [ii.1–8]

The war between the Athenians and Peloponnesians, involving allies on both sides, began when all communication ceased between them, except through heralds, and they made war without intermission from then on. The events have been written up in the order in which they occurred, by summer and winter seasons.[96]

Summary of ii.2–7

The Thirty Years' Peace had lasted just fourteen years. In the early spring of 431, some three hundred Theban soldiers stole by night into the city of Plataea with the connivance of Theban sympathizers inside. (Although Thebes considered it part of Boeotia, Plataea had been a longstanding ally of Athens, and Plataean troops had fought with Athenians in the glorious victory of Marathon over the Persian invaders.)

When the Theban soldiers woke the town, there was no fighting at first, and the Plataean leaders agreed to join Thebes in an alliance. But when they saw how few attackers there were, the ordinary people of Plataea—who did not wish

---

95. See above, p. 16.
96. War at the time was seasonal. Thucydides has chosen the device of organizing his story around the two traditional campaigning periods of each year.

to break from Athens—prepared to attack the Thebans before dawn. Fighting in the dark and in a city unknown to them, the Thebans were soon beaten. Many were killed, and the survivors fled into a large building, mistaking its door for the gate to the city wall, and so became prisoners. A larger force of Thebans arrived late, owing to heavy rains, and was not able to support them, but the force decided to take prisoners from Plataean farms outside the city, in hopes of exchanging them for those who had been captured inside. Then the Plataeans threatened to kill the Theban prisoners unless the Theban army left their territory. When the main Theban army left, however, Plataea did not return the prisoners as promised, but killed all 180 of them.

On hearing the news, Athens sent Plataea a garrison and supplies for withstanding a siege, while women, children, and nonmilitary personnel were removed to Athens for safety. Then both Athens and Sparta sent to their allies for support, and the war began in earnest.

Why most Greeks supported the Lacedaemonians [ii.8]

Neither side made small plans, and both put their whole strength into the war. This was only to be expected, for in the beginning of an enterprise everyone is most eager. Besides, there were many young men in the Peloponnesus at that time, and many in Athens, who for want of experience undertook the war quite willingly. And the rest of Greece watched in suspense as its two principal cities came into conflict. Many prophecies were told, and many sung by the priests of the oracles, both in the cities about to make war and in others. There was also an earthquake in Delos a little before this, where the earth had never been shaken before in the memory of the Greeks. This was said to be a sign of what was going to happen afterwards, and people believed that. And if anything else of this sort happened by chance, people started looking for an explanation.

Men's sympathies for the most part went with the Lacedaemonians, especially because they gave out that they would recover the Greeks' liberty. Everyone, private citizens and cities alike, endeavored in word and deed to assist them as much as they could; and everyone thought that the affair would be held back if they were not part of it. That is how angry most people were against the Athenians, some out of the desire to be set free from their empire, and others for fear of falling under it.

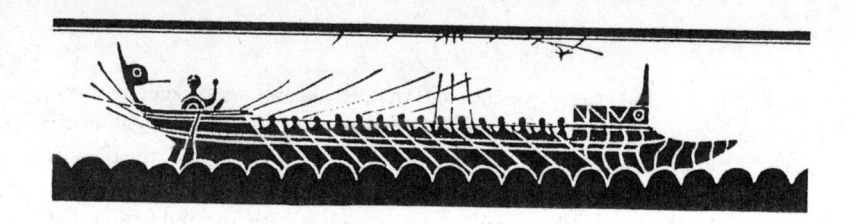

3. Pericles and the Plague

a. *The Funeral Oration of Pericles [ii.35–46]*

During the first winter of the war Athens held a public funeral for the soldiers and sailors who had lost their lives in various minor actions of the war. Pericles delivered a speech which Thucydides reconstructed as follows. It is the most famous speech that has come down to us from antiquity.[97] Pericles praises Athens in terms that do great credit to the city and to himself.

PERICLES' FUNERAL ORATION

[35] Most of those who have spoken before me on this occasion have praised the man who added this oration to our customs because it gives honor to those who have died in the wars; yet I would have thought it sufficient that those who have shown their mettle in action should also receive their honor in an action, as now you see they have, in this burial performed for them at public expense, so that the virtue of many does not depend on whether one person is believed to have spoken well or poorly.

It is a hard matter to speak in due measure when there is no firm consensus about the truth. A hearer who is favorable and knows what was done will perhaps think that a eulogy falls short of what he wants to hear and knows to be true; while an ignorant one will find some of the praise to be exaggerated, especially if he hears of anything beyond his own talent—because that would make him envious. Hearing another man praised is bearable only so long as the hearer thinks he could himself have done what

---

97. On its influence see Gary Wills (1992).

he hears. But if a speaker goes beyond that, the hearer soon becomes envious and ceases to believe. Since our ancestors have thought it good, however, I too should follow the custom and endeavor to answer to the desires and opinions of every one of you, as far as I can.

[36] I will begin with our ancestors, since it is both just and fitting that they be given the honor of remembrance at such a time. Because they have always lived in this land,[98] they have so far always handed it down in liberty through their valor to successive generations up to now. They deserve praise; but our fathers deserve even more, for with great toil they acquired our present empire in addition to what they had received, and they delivered it in turn to the present generation. We ourselves who are here now in the prime of life have expanded most parts of the empire; and we have furnished the city with everything it needs to be self-sufficient both in peace and in war. The acts of war by which all this was attained, the valiant deeds of arms that we and our fathers performed against foreign or Greek invaders—these I will pass over, to avoid making a long speech on a subject with which you are well acquainted. But the customs that brought us to this point, the form of government and the way of life that have made our city great—these I shall disclose before I turn to praise the dead. I think these subjects are quite suitable for the occasion, and the whole gathering of citizens and guests will profit by hearing them discussed.

[37] We have a form of government that does not try to imitate the laws of our neighboring states.[99] We are more an example to others, than they to us. In name, it is called a democracy, because it is managed not for a few people, but for the majority. Still, although we have equality at law for everyone here in private disputes, we do not let our system of rotating public offices undermine our judgment of a candidate's virtue; and no one is held back by poverty or because his reputation is not well-known, as long as he can do good service to the city.[100] We are free and generous not only in our public activities as citizens, but also in our daily lives: there is no

---

98. Athenians believed they had sprung from the very soil of Attica (see **i.2**).

99. The contrast is with Sparta, which was said to have borrowed its form of government from cities in Crete. Observe also the wider contrast between **ii.37–40** and Archidamus' discussion of Spartan customs at **i.84**.

100. "We do not let our system of rotating public offices undermine our judgment of a candidate's virtue": The exact meaning of this sentence is in doubt. Pericles is evidently defending Athens against the charge that the best men are not given the most power in democracies. He is probably referring to the use of the lottery and the related system of the rotation of offices, which ensured the participation of a wide variety of citizens in democracy (p. xiii).

suspicion in our dealings with one another, and we are not offended by our neighbor for following his own pleasure. We do not cast on anyone the censorious looks that—though they are no punishment—are nevertheless painful. We live together without taking offense on private matters; and as for public affairs, we respect the law greatly and fear to violate it, since we are obedient to those in office at any time, and also to the laws—especially to those laws that were made to help people who have suffered an injustice, and to the unwritten laws[101] that bring shame on their transgressors by the agreement of all.

[38] Moreover, we have provided many ways to give our minds recreation from labor: we have instituted regular contests and sacrifices throughout the year, while the attractive furnishings of our private homes give us daily delight and expel sadness. The greatness of our city has caused all things from all parts of the earth to be imported here, so that we enjoy the products of other nations with no less familiarity than we do our own.

[39] Then, too, we differ from our enemies in preparing for war:[102] we leave our city open to all; and we have never expelled strangers in order to prevent them from learning or seeing things that, if they were not hidden, might give an advantage to the enemy. We do not rely on secret preparation and deceit so much as on our own courage in action. And as for education, our enemies train to be men from early youth by rigorous exercise, while we live a more relaxed life and still take on dangers as great as they do.

The evidence for this is that the Lacedaemonians do not invade our country by themselves, but with the aid of all their allies; when we invade our neighbors, however, we usually overcome them by ourselves without difficulty, even though we are fighting on hostile ground against people who are defending their own homes. Besides, no enemy has yet faced our whole force at once, because at the same time we are busy with our navy and sending men by land to many different places. But when our enemies run into part of our forces and get the better of them, they boast that they have beaten our whole force; and when they are defeated, they claim they

---

Individual merit was a factor in the advance screening of candidates for selection by such means. Thucydides may also be referring to the relevance of individual merit to the election of generals. On the issues, see Hornblower and Rusten.

101. Unwritten law is associated by other authors with matters of religious importance. See *Antigone* 454, Xenophon's *Memorabilia* iv.4.19, and Pseudo-Lysias 6.10. See Hornblower for further references.

102. Here the implicit contrast with Sparta is especially striking. Pericles attributes to Athens everything contrary to what was well known about Sparta.

were beaten by all of us. We are willing to go into danger with easy minds and natural courage rather than through rigorous training and laws, and that gives us an advantage: we'll never weaken ourselves in advance by preparing for future troubles, but we'll turn out to be no less daring in action than those who are always training hard. In this, as in other things, our city is worthy of admiration.

[40] We are lovers of nobility with restraint, and lovers of wisdom without any softening of character.[103] We use wealth as an opportunity for action, rather than for boastful speeches. And as for poverty, we think there is no shame in confessing it; what is shameful is doing nothing to escape it. Moreover, the very men who take care of public affairs look after their own at the same time; and even those who are devoted to their own businesses know enough about the city's affairs. For we alone think that a man who does not take part in public affairs is good for nothing, while others only say he is "minding his own business."[104] We are the ones who develop policy, or at least decide what is to be done;[105] for we believe that what spoils action is not speeches, but going into action without first being instructed through speeches. In this too we excel over others: ours is the bravery of people who think through what they will take in hand, and discuss it thoroughly; with other men, ignorance makes them brave and thinking makes them cowards. But the people who most deserve to be judged tough-minded are those who know exactly what terrors or pleasures lie ahead, and are not turned away

---

103. "We are lovers of nobility with restraint, and lovers of wisdom without any softening of character" (*philokaloumen te gar met' euteleias kai philosophoumen aneu malakias*): the most famous sentence in Thucydides. Like many of Thucydides' memorable sentences it admits of a variety of interpretations.

I have translated *kalon* here as "nobility," meaning nobility of character, but the reader should be warned that it can mean beauty as well. *Met' euteleia* could also mean "without excessive expenditure," but this seems inappropriate. If Pericles means that Athens is not extravagant, his claim is preposterous in view of his magnificent building program. "Lovers of wisdom" translates *philosophoumen*, which is cognate to our "philosophize" but has a much wider meaning. For the charge that such studies make people soft, see especially Aristophanes' *Clouds* and Plato's *Gorgias* 485–86 with *Republic* 410e.

104. "Minding his own business" [being *apragmōn*] is the opposite of "being a busybody" [*polupragmosunē*], which the Greeks considered unseemly.

105. Although not all Athenians were involved in developing policy, all were involved in the making of decisions in the assembly. This elegant point hangs on a single particle, *ge*. For this interpretation, see Rusten's and Hornblower's notes on the passage. Pericles holds that it is up to the leaders of Athens to develop policy and then to instruct the people to carry it out.

3. Pericles and the Plague

from danger by that knowledge. Again we are opposite to most men in matters of virtue:[106] we win our friends by doing them favors, rather than by accepting favors from them. A person who does a good turn is a more faithful friend: his goodwill towards the recipient preserves his feeling that he should do more;[107] but the friendship of a person who has to return a good deed is dull and flat, because he knows he will be merely paying a debt—rather than doing a favor—when he shows his virtue in return. So that we alone do good to others not after calculating the profit, but fearlessly and in the confidence of our freedom.

[41] In sum, I say that our city as a whole is a lesson for Greece, and that each of us presents himself as a self-sufficient individual, disposed to the widest possible diversity of actions, with every grace and great versatility. This is not merely a boast in words for the occasion, but the truth in fact, as the power of this city, which we have obtained by having this character, makes evident.

For Athens is the only power now that is greater than her fame when it comes to the test. Only in the case of Athens can enemies never be upset over the quality of those who defeat them when they invade; only in our empire can subject states never complain that their rulers are unworthy. We are proving our power with strong evidence, and we are not without witnesses: we shall be the admiration of people now and in the future. We do not need Homer, or anyone else, to praise our power with words that bring delight for a moment,[108] when the truth will refute his assumptions about what was done.[109] For we have compelled all seas and all lands to be open to us by our daring; and we have set up eternal monuments on all sides, of our setbacks as well as of our accomplishments.[110]

Such is the city for which these men fought valiantly and died, in the firm belief that it should never be destroyed, and for which every man of you who is left should be willing to endure distress.

[42] That is why I have spoken at such length concerning the city in general, to show you that the stakes are not the same, between us and the

---

106. "virtue": *aretē*. This traditionally involved doing good to one's friends and harm to one's enemies; that is why Pericles uses the concept here to introduce the topic of friendship among cities.

107. This is what the context seems to require. The Greek allows a number of interpretations.

108. See i.21.

109. This recalls Thucydides' criticisms of earlier historians (i.20).

110. This last phrase could also mean: "Of the evil we have done to our enemies, and of the good we have done to our friends."

enemy—for their city is not like ours in any way—and, at the same time, to bring evidence to back up the eulogy of these men for whom I speak. The greatest part of their praise has already been delivered, for it was their virtues, and the virtues of men like them, that made what I praised in the city so beautiful. Not many Greeks have done deeds that are obviously equal to their own reputations, but these men have. The present end these men have met is, I think, either the first indication, or the final confirmation, of a life of virtue. And even those who were inferior in other ways deserve to have their faults overshadowed by their courageous deaths in war for the sake of their country. Their good actions have wiped out the memory of any wrong they have done, and they have produced more public good than private harm. None of them became a coward because he set a higher value on enjoying the wealth that he had; none of them put off the terrible day of his death in hopes that he might overcome his poverty and attain riches. Their longing to punish their enemies was stronger than this; and because they believed this to be the most honorable sort of danger, they chose to punish their enemies at this risk, and to let everything else go. The uncertainty of success they entrusted to hope; but for that which was before their eyes they decided to rely on themselves in action. They believed that this choice entailed resistance and suffering, rather than surrender and safety; they ran away from the word of shame,[111] and stood up in action at risk of their lives. And so, in the one brief moment allotted them, at the peak of their fame and not in fear, they departed.

[43] Such were these men, worthy of their country. And you who remain may pray for a safer fortune, but you must resolve to be no less daring in your intentions against the enemy. Do not weigh the good they have done on the basis of one speech. Any long-winded orator could tell you how much good lies in resisting our enemies; but you already know this. Look instead at the power our city shows in action every day, and so become lovers of Athens. When the power of the city seems great to you, consider then that this was purchased by valiant men who knew their duty and kept their honor in battle, by men who were resolved to contribute the most noble gift to their city: even if they should fail in their attempt, at least they would leave their fine character [*aretē*] to the city. For in giving their lives for the common good, each man won praise for himself that will never grow old; and the monument that awaits them is the most splendid—not where they are buried, but where their glory is laid up to be remembered

---

111. I.e., the one thing they have feared is the reputation for cowardice. Note the frequent use of the contrast between word and action in Thucydides.

forever, whenever the time comes for speech or action. For to famous men, all the earth is a monument, and their virtues are attested not only by inscriptions on stone at home; but an unwritten record of the mind lives on for each of them, even in foreign lands, better than any gravestone.

Try to be like these men, therefore: realize that happiness lies in liberty, and liberty in valor, and do not hold back from the dangers of war. Miserable men, who have no hope of prosperity, do not have a just reason to be generous with their lives; no, it is rather those who face the danger of a complete reversal of fortune for whom defeat would make the biggest difference: they are the ones who should risk their lives. Any man of intelligence will hold that death, when it comes unperceived to a man at full strength and with hope for his country, is not so bitter as miserable defeat for a man grown soft.

[44] That is why I offer you, who are here as parents of these men, consolation rather than a lament. You know your lives teem with all sorts of calamities, and that it is good fortune for anyone to draw a glorious end for his lot, as these men have done. While your lot was grief, theirs was a life that was happy as long as it lasted. I know it is a hard matter to dissuade you from sorrow, when you will often be reminded by the good fortune of others of the joys you once had; for sorrow is not for the want of a good never tasted, but for the loss of a good we have been used to having. Yet those of you who are of an age to have children may bear this loss in the hope of having more. On a personal level new children will help some of you forget those who are no more; while the city will gain doubly by this, in population and in security. It is not possible for people to give fair and just advice to the state, if they are not exposing their own children to the same danger when they advance a risky policy. As for you who are past having children, you are to think of the greater part of your life as pure profit, while the part that remains is short and its burden lightened by the glory of these men. For the love of honor is the one thing that never grows old, and useless old age takes delight not in gathering wealth (as some say), but in being honored.[112]

[45] As for you who are the children or the brothers of these men, I see that you will have considerable competition. Everyone is used to praising the dead, so that even extreme virtue will scarcely win you a reputation equal to theirs, but it will fall a little short. That is because people envy the living as competing with them, but they honor those who are not in their way, and their good will towards the dead is free of rivalry.

112. "As some say": Simonides, for example (Plutarch *Moralia* 786B).

And now, since I must say something about feminine virtue, I shall express it in this brief admonition to you who are now widows: your glory is great if you do not fall beneath the natural condition of your sex, and if you have as little fame among men as is possible, whether for virtue or by way of reproach.

[46] Thus I have delivered, according to custom, what was appropriate in a speech, while those men who are buried here have already been honored by their own actions. It remains to maintain their children at the expense of the city until they grow up. This benefit is the city's victory garland for them and for those they leave behind after such contests as these, because the city that gives the greatest rewards for virtue has the finest citizens.

So now, when everyone has mourned for his own, you may go.

b. The plague: human nature laid bare by a natural disaster [ii.47–54]

During the second year of the war, in 430, when refugees from the countryside were crowded into Athens for safety from Lacedaemonian raiding parties, a terrible plague struck Athens. Thucydides plunges into a vivid account of the plague right after reporting Pericles' Funeral Oration. The juxtaposition of these two passages is a striking instance of Thucydides' style: the funeral oration gives us a bright picture of a wonderfully civilized city; the story of the plague shows how easily civilization slips away when times are hard.

[47] Such was the funeral they held that winter, and with the end of that season the first year of the war came to a close.

In the very beginning of summer the Peloponnesians and their allies, with two-thirds of their forces as before, invaded Attica under the command of Archidamus, King of Lacedaemon. After they had settled in, they started wasting the country around them.[113]

They had not been in Attica for many days when the plague first began among the Athenians. Although it was said to have broken out in many other places, particularly in Lemnos, no one could remember a disease that was so great or so destructive of human life breaking out anywhere before. Doctors, not knowing what to do, were unable to cope with it at first, and

---

113. During the war, the Spartans regularly invaded Attica at harvest time and destroyed the crops. In 430, however, their occupation of Attica was apparently the longest of this phase of the war, about forty days (**ii.57**).

3. Pericles and the Plague

no other human knowledge was any use either. The doctors themselves died fastest, as they came to the sick most often. Prayers in temples, questions to oracles—all practices of that kind turned out to be useless also, and in the end people gave them up, defeated by the evil of the disease.

[48] They say it first began in the part of Ethiopia that is above Egypt, and from there moved down to Egypt and Libya and into most of the Persian Empire. It hit Athens suddenly, first infecting people in Piraeus [the port of Athens], with the result that they said the Peloponnesians must have poisoned the water tanks (they had no wells there at the time). Afterwards the plague moved inland to the city, where people died of it a good deal faster. Now anyone, doctor or layman, may say as much as he knows about where this probably came from, or what causes he thinks are powerful enough to bring about so great a change. For my part, I will only say what it was like: I will show what to look for, so that if the plague breaks out again, people may know in advance and not be ignorant. I will do this because I had the plague myself, and I myself saw others who suffered from it.[114]

[49] This year of all years was the most free of other diseases, as everyone agrees. If anyone was sick before, his disease turned into this one. If not, they were taken suddenly, without any apparent cause, and while they were in perfect health. First they had a high fever in the head, along with redness and inflammation of the eyes; inside, the throat and tongue were bleeding from the start, and the breath was weird and unsavory. After this came sneezing and hoarseness, and soon after came a pain in the chest, along with violent coughing. And once it was settled in the stomach, it caused vomiting, and brought up, with great torment, all the kinds of bile that the doctors have named.[115] Most of the sick then had dry heaves, which brought on violent spasms which were over quickly for some people, but not till long after for others. Outwardly their bodies were not very hot to the touch, and they were not pale but reddish, livid, and flowered with little pimples and ulcers; inwardly they were burning so much with fever that they could not bear to have the lightest clothes or linen garments on them—nothing but mere nakedness, and they would have loved to throw

---

114. What was the plague? On Thucydides' description it does not exactly match any disease that is known to us now. Either the disease is extinct or we must read Thucydides' account of it with considerable charity. See Rusten and Hornblower.

115. See *Republic* 405d on the interest of doctors in naming things, where Plato shows a similar contempt for medical science.

themselves into cold water. Many of them who were not looked after did throw themselves into water tanks, driven mad by a thirst that was insatiable, although it was all the same whether they drank much or little. Sleeplessness and total inability to rest persisted through everything.

As long as the disease was at its height, the body did not waste away, but resisted the torment beyond all expectation, so that they either died after six or eight days from the burning inside them, or else, if they escaped that, then the disease dropped down into the belly, bringing severe ulceration and uncontrollable diarrhea; and many died later from the weakness this caused, since the disease passed through the whole body, starting with the head and moving down. And if anyone survived the worst of it, then the disease seized his extremities instead and left its mark there: it attacked the private parts, fingers, and toes. Many people escaped with the loss of these, while some lost their eyes as well. Some were struck by total amnesia as soon as they recovered, and did not know themselves or their friends.

[50] This was a kind of disease that defied explanation, and the cruelty with which it attacked everyone was too severe for human nature.[116] What showed more clearly than anything else that it was different from the diseases that are bred among us was this: all the birds and beasts that feed on human flesh either avoided the many bodies that lay unburied, or tasted them and perished. Evidence for this was the obvious absence of such birds: they were not to be seen anywhere, and certainly not doing that. But this effect was more clearly observed in the case of dogs, because they are more familiar with human beings.

[51] Now this disease was generally as I have described it, if I may set aside the many variations that occurred as particular people had different experiences. During that time no one was troubled by any of the usual sicknesses, but whatever sickness came ended in this. People died, some unattended, and some who had every sort of care. There was no medical treatment that could be prescribed as beneficial, for what helped one patient did harm to another. Physical strength turned out to be of no avail, for the plague carried the strong away with the weak, no matter what regimen they had followed.

But the greatest misery of all was the dejection of mind in those who found themselves beginning to be sick, for as soon as they made up their minds it was hopeless, they gave up and made much less resistance to the disease. Another misery was their dying like sheep, as they became in-

---

116. "Too severe for human nature": the disease was more severe than a normal human disease. Some Athenians must have seen the plague as sent by the gods, perhaps as retribution for Athenian imperial policy.

3. Pericles and the Plague

fected by caring for one another; and this brought about the greatest mortality. For if people held back from visiting each other through fear, then they died in neglect, and many houses were emptied because there was no one to provide care. If they did visit each other, they died, and these were mainly the ones who made some pretense to virtue. For these people would have been ashamed to spare themselves, and so they went into their friends' houses, especially in the end, when even family members, worn out by the lamentations of the dying, were overwhelmed by the greatness of the calamity. But those who had recovered had still more compassion,[117] both on those who were dying and on those who were sick, because they knew the disease first-hand and were now out of danger, for this disease never attacked anyone a second time with fatal effect. And these people were thought to be blessedly happy, and through an excess of present joy they conceived a kind of light hope never to die of any other disease afterwards.

[52] The present affliction was aggravated by the crowding of country folk into the city, which was especially unpleasant for those who came in. They had no houses, and because they were living in shelters that were stifling in the summer, their mortality was out of control. Dead and dying lay tumbling on top of one another in the streets, and at every water fountain lay men half-dead with thirst. The temples also, where they pitched their tents, were all full of the bodies of those who died in them, for people grew careless of holy and profane things alike, since they were oppressed by the violence of the calamity, and did not know what to do. And the laws they had followed before concerning funerals were all disrupted now, everyone burying their dead wherever they could. Many were forced, by a shortage of necessary materials after so many deaths, to take disgraceful measures for the funerals of their relatives: when one person had made a funeral pyre, another would get before him, throw on his dead, and give it fire; others would come to a pyre that was already burning, throw on the bodies they carried, and go their way again.

[53] The great lawlessness that grew everywhere in the city began with this disease, for, as the rich suddenly died and men previously worth nothing took over their estates, people saw before their eyes such quick reversals that they dared to do freely things they would have hidden before— things they never would have admitted they did for pleasure. And so, because they thought their lives and their property were equally ephemeral, they justified seeking quick satisfaction in easy pleasures. As for doing what had been considered noble, no one was eager to take any further pains

---

117. More compassion, that is, than those who pretended to virtue. Thucydides is consistent in his scornful view of claims to virtue.

for this, because they thought it uncertain whether they should die or not before they achieved it. But the pleasure of the moment, and whatever contributed to that, were set up as standards of nobility and usefulness. No one was held back in awe, either by fear of the gods or by the laws of men: not by the gods, because men concluded it was all the same whether they worshipped or not, seeing that they all perished alike; and not by the laws, because no one expected to live till he was tried and punished for his crimes. But they thought that a far greater sentence hung over their heads now, and that before this fell they had a reason to get some pleasure in life.[118]

[54] Such was the misery that weighed on the Athenians. It was very oppressive, with men dying inside the city and the land outside being wasted. At such a terrible time it was natural for them to recall this verse, which the older people said had been sung long ago:

> A Dorian war will come,
> and with it a plague.

People had disagreed about the wording of the verse: some said it was not *plague (loimos)* but *famine (limos)* that was foretold by the ancients; but on this occasion, naturally, the victory went to those who said 'plague,' for people made their memory suit their current experience. Surely, I think if there is another Dorian war after this one, and if a famine comes with it, it will be natural for them to recite the verse in that version.

Those who knew of it also recalled an oracle that was given to the Lacedaemonians when they asked the god [Apollo] whether they should start this war or not. The oracle had said: *they would win if they fought with all their might, and that he himself would take their part* [i.118]. Then they thought that their present misery was a fulfillment of the prophecy; the plague did begin immediately when the Peloponnesians invaded, and it had no appreciable effect in the Peloponnesus, but preyed mostly on Athens and after that in densely populated areas. So much for the plague.

---

118. Although we have no hard figures for this, we believe that over a quarter of the Athenian population was killed by the plague. This reduction in manpower further restricted the military options available to Athens. In iii.87–88, Thucydides reports how the plague struck Athens again in the winter of 427 and lasted over a year. He gives the casualty figure as forty four hundred hoplites, 300 horsemen, and innumerable ordinary people. With very little change, this account of the plague was put into Latin epic verse by the philosopher Lucretius (*De Rerum Natura*, Book VI).

c. Military operations of 430 [ii.55–58]

[55] After the Peloponnesians had wasted the plain, they fell upon the territory called Paralia as far as Mt. Laurion [the western coast of Attica], where Athens had silver mines. First they wasted the part of it that looks towards the Peloponnesus, and then they turned to the part that faces Andros and Euboea. Pericles was general then, and he kept to his strategy in the previous invasion—that the Athenians not go out against them.[119]

[56] But he started to equip one hundred ships to sail against the Peloponnesus while they were still on the plain and had not yet gone into Paralia; and as soon as they were ready, he put to sea. In these ships he had four thousand hoplites, as well as three hundred horsemen in older ships that were then for the first time made into horse transports. Chios and Lesbos joined him with fifty ships.

When the Athenian expedition sailed, they left the Peloponnesians still in Paralia. They first came to Epidaurus in the Peloponnesus and wasted much of the land there; they also attacked the city with some hope of taking it, but were disappointed. Putting out from Epidaurus they wasted the lands of Troezen, Halieis, and Hermione (all places along the coast of the Argolid in the Peloponnesus). From there they sailed to Prasiae, a small maritime town of Laconia. There they wasted the land, took the town, and sacked it. After doing this they went home and found that the Peloponnesians were no longer in Attica, but had also gone home.

[57] All this time, while the Peloponnesians were in Attica and the Athenians campaigning by sea, the plague went on killing the Athenians, both in the army and in the city. A result of this, we are told, is that the Peloponnesians left the country sooner out of fear of the plague, when they learned it was in the city from deserters and by seeing the funerals. Still, this invasion was the longest they ever made in Attica—almost forty days—and they wasted all of the land.

[58] The same summer, Hagnon and Cleopompus, who were generals along with Pericles, took the army he had used and immediately campaigned against the Chalcideans near Thrace and against Potidaea, which was still besieged. On their arrival they brought battering rams against Potidaea, and tried in every way to take it. But they had no success either in taking the city or in doing anything else worthy of so large a force, for the plague struck them there too and pressed them hard, nearly destroying the army. The Athenian soldiers who had been there before, and who had been

---

119. See **i.143** and **ii.22**.

in good health before that, caught the disease from Hagnon's army.[120] (As for Phormio and his sixteen hundred, they were not now in the Chalcidice.)

So Hagnon came home with his ships to Athens, after losing 1050 men out of 4000 to the plague in less than forty days.

The soldiers who were there before stayed on in that place and continued the siege of Potidaea.

d. Pericles' last speech [ii. 59–64]

After the second Spartan invasion of Attica, the spirits of the citizens began to flag and they turned in anger against Pericles, who was responsible for the decision to let the Lacedaemonians lay waste to Attica.

[59] After their second invasion by the Peloponnesians, now that their land had been wasted a second time, and the plague was lying over them along with the war, the Athenians changed their minds[121] and blamed Pericles for persuading them to make war—as if the troubles that had come their way were due to him—and were in a hurry to come to terms with the Lacedaemonians. They sent ambassadors to them, without effect. They were altogether at their wit's end, and so they attacked Pericles.

When he saw that they were angry over their present circumstances, and were doing exactly what he had expected, he called an assembly—he was still general at the time—intending to put heart into them, to turn aside their anger, and so to make their minds calmer and more confident.

He stood before them and spoke as follows:

PERICLES' LAST SPEECH

[60] I expected you to get angry with me, and I can see why it has happened. I have called this assembly to remind you of certain points and to rebuke you for your misplaced anger at me and for your giving in too easily to misfortune.

I believe that if the city is sound as a whole, it does more good to its private citizens than if it benefits them as individuals while faltering as a collective unit. It does not matter whether a man prospers as an individual: if his country is destroyed, he is lost along with it; but if he meets with misfortune, he is far safer in a fortunate city than he would be otherwise.

---

120. The original expedition had numbered three thousand hoplites (ii.31).
121. See **viii.1** and the Old Oligarch ii.17.

3. Pericles and the Plague

Since, therefore, a city is able to sustain its private citizens in whatever befalls them, while no one individual is strong enough to carry his city, are we not all obliged to defend it and not, as you are doing now, sacrifice our common safety? In your dismay at our misfortunes at home you are condemning yourselves along with me—me for advising you to go to war and yourselves for agreeing to it. And it is I at whom you are angry, a man who is second to none (in my opinion) for recognizing and explaining what must be done—I, a patriot, beyond corruption. A man who knows something but cannot make it clear might as well have had nothing in mind at all; while a man who can do both will not give such loyal advice if he has no love for his city; and a man who has all this and loyalty too, but can be overcome by money, will sell everything for this alone. It follows that if you were persuaded to go to war because you thought I had all those qualities, even in a moderately higher degree than other people, there is no reason for me to bear a charge of injustice now.

[61] Of course, for people who have the choice and are doing well in other ways, it is very foolish to go to war. But if (as is the case with us) they are compelled either to submit directly to the rule of their neighbors, or else to take on great dangers in order to survive, a man who runs away from danger is more to be blamed than one who stands up to it.

For my part, I am the man I was. I have not shifted ground. It is you who are changing: you were persuaded to fight when you were still unharmed, but now that times are bad, you are changing your minds; and to your weak judgment my position does not seem sound. That is because you already feel the pain that afflicts you as individuals, while the benefit to us all has not yet become obvious; and now that this great reversal has come upon you in so short a time you are too low in your minds to stand by your decisions, for it makes your thoughts slavish when something unexpected happens suddenly and defies your best-laid plans. That is what has happened to you on top of everything else, mainly because of the plague.

Still, you live in a great city and have been brought up with a way of life that matches its greatness; so you should be willing to stand up to the greatest disasters rather than eclipse your reputation. (People think it equally right, you see, to blame someone who is so weak that he loses the glorious reputation that was really his, as it is to despise someone who has the audacity to reach for a reputation he should not have.)

So set aside the grief you feel for your individual losses, and take up instead the cause of our common safety.

[62] As for your fear that we will have a great deal of trouble in this war, and still be no closer to success, I have already said something that should

be enough for you: I proved many times that you were wrong to be suspicious of the outcome. I will tell you this, however, about your greatness in empire—something you never seem to think about, which I have not mentioned in my speeches. It is a rather boastful claim, and I would not bring it up now if I had not seen that you are more discouraged than you have reason to be. You think your empire extends only to your allies, but I am telling you that you are entirely the masters of one of the two usable parts of the world—the land and the sea. Of the sea, you rule as much as you use now, and more if you want. When you sail with your fleet as it is now equipped, there is no one who can stop you—not the King of Persia or any nation in existence. This power cannot be measured against the use of your land and homes, though you think it a great loss to be deprived of them. It makes no sense to take these so seriously; you should think of your land as a little kitchen garden, and your house as a rich man's trinket, of little value compared to this power. Keep in mind too that if we hold fast to our liberty and preserve it we will easily recover our land and houses; but people who submit to foreign domination will start to lose what they already had. Don't show yourselves to be doubly inferior[122] to your ancestors, who took the empire—they did not inherit it from others—and, in addition, kept it safe and passed it on to you. No, what you should do is remember that it is more shameful to lose what you have than to fail in an attempt to get more. You should take on the enemy at close quarters, and go not only with pride, but with contempt.[123] Even a coward can swell with pride, if he is lucky and ignorant; but you cannot have contempt for the enemy unless your confidence is based on a strategy to overcome them—which is your situation exactly. Even if you have only an even chance of winning, if you are conscious of your superiority it is safer for you to be daring, for in that case you do not depend on hope[124] (which is a bulwark only to those who have no resources at all), but on a strategy based on reality, which affords a more accurate prediction of the result.

[63] You have reason besides to support the dignity our city derives from her empire, in which you all take pride; you should not decline the trouble, unless you cease to pursue the honor, of empire. And do not think that the only thing we are fighting for is our freedom from being subju-

---

122. "Doubly inferior": in neither winning an empire nor passing it on to your sons.

123. Not only with *phronēma* but with *kataphronēma*. A word play of the kind taught by sophists.

124. See the Melian Dialogue, v.103.

gated: you are in danger of losing the empire, and if you do, the anger of the people you have ruled will raise other dangers. You are in no position to walk away from your empire, though some people might propose to do so from fear of the current situation, and act the part of virtue because they do not want to be involved in public affairs. You see, your empire is really like a tyranny—though it may have been thought unjust to seize, it is now unsafe to surrender.[125] People who would persuade the city to do such a thing would quickly destroy it, and if they set up their own government they would destroy that too. For those who stay out of public affairs survive only with the help of other people who take action; and they are no use to a city that rules an empire, though in a subject state they may serve safely enough.

[64] Don't be seduced by this sort of men. After all, it was you who decided in favor of this war along with me; so don't be angry at me. What the enemy did when they invaded was just what was to be expected when we refused to submit to them; and this plague has struck contrary to all expectations—it is the only thing, of all that has happened, that has defied our hopes. I know that I have become hated largely because of this; but that is an injustice, unless you will also give me credit whenever you do better than you'd planned to do. What heaven sends we must bear with a sense of necessity, what the enemy does to us we must bear with courage—for that is the custom in our city; that is how it used to be, and that custom should not end with you.

Keep this in mind: our city is famous everywhere for its greatness in not yielding to adversity and in accepting so many casualties and so much trouble in war; besides, she has possessed great power till now, which will be remembered forever by those who come after us, even if we do give way a little now (for everything naturally goes into decline): Greeks that we are, we have ruled most of the Greeks, and held out in great wars against them, all together or one city at a time, and our city has the most wealth of every sort, and is the greatest. And yet a man of inaction would complain about this! No matter, anyone who is active will want to be like us, and those who do not succeed will envy us. To be hated and to cause pain is, at present, the reality for anyone who takes on the rule of others, and anyone who

---

125. For the thought that the empire was founded on injustice, and was therefore like a tyranny, see **i.122, ii.8, iii.37**. This was, of course, the basic Lacedaemonian charge against Athens. For the idea that justice cannot be served safely, see **v.107**. For Alcibiades' view that an empire must grow in order to survive, see **vi.18**.

makes himself hated for matters of great consequence has made the right decision; for hatred does not last long, but the momentary brilliance of great actions lives on as a glory that will be remembered forever after.

As for you, keep your minds on the fine future you know will be yours, and on the shame you must avoid at this moment. Be full of zeal on both counts. Send no more heralds to the Lacedaemonians, and do not let them know how heavy your troubles are at present. The most powerful cities and individuals are the ones that are the least sensitive in their minds to calamity and the firmest in their actions to resist it.

e. *Thucydides' judgment of Pericles [ii.65]*

Thucydides tells us that this speech did restore public confidence in the war, but not in Pericles. Other sources tell us Pericles was removed from public office, his accounts were examined, and he was tried for the misappropriation of public funds. He was found guilty and made to pay a fine.[126] In the following year, however, Pericles was reelected to high office, and Thucydides gives us the following assessment of the man, his manner of politics, and his strategy for the war:

[65] With this speech Pericles tried to appease the anger of the Athenians and to divert their attention from their present afflictions. They were persuaded on the public matter, and no longer sent embassies to the Lacedaemonians, but applied themselves more to the war. As individuals, however, they were upset by what had happened to them—the people were upset because they had been deprived of the little they had, and the powerful because they had lost their fine possessions in the country, along with their houses and costly furnishings. Most of all, however, it was because they had war instead of peace. As a group, they did not give up their anger against him until they had punished him with a fine. Not long after, however, as is common with a mob, they made him general again and turned all public affairs over to him, for their pain over their private domestic losses was dulled now, and they thought he was the best man to serve the needs of the city as a whole.

As long as he was at the head of the city in time of peace, he governed it with moderation and guarded it securely; and it was greatest under him.

126. Pericles' fine was said to have been fifty talents, a substantial sum (see Glossary). Sources differ as to how much Pericles was fined and for what alleged crime. Compare Plutarch (32,35) and Diodorus (12.45.4). Plato's tale that the charge was theft is open to doubt (*Gorgias* 515e).

3. Pericles and the Plague

After the war was afoot, it was obvious that he also foresaw what the city could do in this. He lived two years and six months after the war began. And after his death his foresight about the war was even better recognized, for he told them that if they would be quiet and take care of their navy, and not seek to expand the empire during this war or endanger the city itself, they should then have the upper hand. But they did the opposite on all points, and in other things that seemed not to concern the war they managed the state for their private ambition and private gain, to the detriment of themselves and their allies. Whatever succeeded brought honor and profit mostly to private individuals, while whatever went wrong damaged the city in the war.

The reason for Pericles' success was this: he was powerful because of his prestige and his intelligence, and also because he was known to be highly incorruptible. He therefore controlled the people without inhibition, and was not so much led by them, as he led them. He would not humor the people in his speeches so as to get power by improper means, but because of their esteem for him he could risk their anger by opposing them. Therefore, whenever he saw them insolently bold out of season, he would put them into fear with his speeches; and again, when they were afraid without reason, he would raise up their spirits and give them courage. Athens was in name a democracy [ii.37], but in fact was a government by its first man. But because those who came after were more equal among themselves, with everyone aiming to be the chief, they gave up taking care of the commonwealth in order to please the people.[127]

Since Athens was a great imperial city, these mistakes led to many others, such as the voyage against Sicily, which was due not so much to mistaking the power of those they attacked, as it was to bad decisions on the part of the senders, which were no use to the people they sent.[128] They weakened the strength of the army through private quarrels about popular leadership, and they troubled the state at home with discord for the first time. After their debacle in Sicily, when they lost most of their navy along

---

127. "They gave up taking care of the commonwealth": Thucydides is highly critical of the next generation of Athenian leaders, such as Cleon. See Connor, 1971.

128. "Bad decisions on the part of the senders" refers primarily to the recall of Alcibiades from the expedition (p. 125). In fact, as Thucydides well knew, Athens had badly underestimated the power of her enemies in Sicily. (For the meaning of this sentence, see Hornblower. Some translators take the sentence to mean that Athens did not adequately supply or reenforce the expedition, but this is plainly false.)

with the rest of the expedition, and the city was divided by civil strife, they still held out eight years[129] against their original enemies, who were now allied with the Sicilians, against most of their own rebellious allies besides, and also eventually against Cyrus, the son of the King of Persia, who took part with, and sent money to, the Peloponnesians to maintain their fleet. And they never gave in until they had brought about their own downfall through private quarrels.

So Pericles had more than enough reasons to predict that the city might easily outlast the Peloponnesians in this war.

With these words Thucydides takes Pericles offstage, although he lived and led Athens for another year before succumbing to effects of the plague.

---

129. The mss read "three years." But as the war continued eight, most editors emend the text at this point.

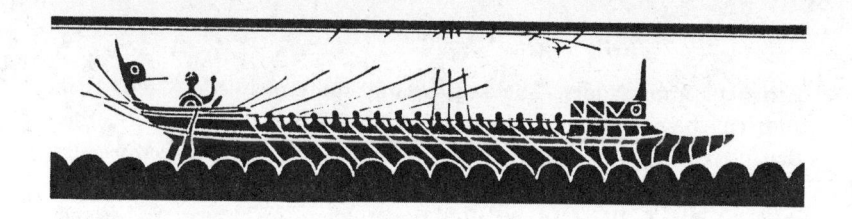

4. Justice and power: Plataea and Mytilene

a. Further events of 430 [ii.66–70]

[66] That same summer, the Lacedaemonians and their allies sent an expedition of one hundred ships against Zacynthus, an island lying opposite Elis. The inhabitants were a colony of Achaeans from the Peloponnesus, but were allied with the Athenians. A thousand Lacedaemonian hoplites sailed with this fleet under the command of the Spartan Cnemus. They landed and wasted the greater part of the territory; but since the islanders did not yield, they put off again and went home.

[67] At the end of the same summer, Aristeus of Corinth and the Lacedaemonian ambassadors Aneristus, Nicolaus, and Pratodamus, along with Timagoras of Tegea and Pollis of Argos (who was in his private capacity) were travelling to Asia to the King of Persia, to persuade him to give them money, and to draw him into their alliance. On the way they came first to Sitalces in Thrace, with the desire to persuade him also, if they could, to forsake their alliance with Athens and to send forces to Potidaea, which the Athenian army now besieged. Besides, they wanted to cross the Hellespont with his help to meet Pharnaces, who was going to send them on to the King. But the Athenian ambassadors Learchus and Ameiniades happened to be with Sitalces, and they persuaded Sitalces' son, Sadocus, who had become a citizen of Athens, to put them into their hands, so that they would not cross to the King and do harm to the city that was now, in part, his own. He was persuaded; and as they journeyed through Thrace to take ship to cross the Hellespont, he had them captured before they embarked by men he had sent along, with orders to turn them over to the

Athenian ambassadors. They—Learchus and Ameiniades—took them and sent them to Athens. When they arrived, the Athenians were afraid that if Aristeus were to escape he would do them much more mischief, because even before then he had been found to be responsible for some of their troubles in Potidaea and all of the problems in Thrace. And so they put them all to death that same day, without trial and without letting them say what they wanted, and threw them into a ravine. They thought it was only justice to use the same means of punishment the Spartans had used first, when they killed and threw into ravines the Athenian and allied merchants they captured sailing in freighters around the Peloponnesus. At the beginning of the war the Lacedaemonians had killed everyone they captured by sea as an enemy, whether they were allies of the Athenians or neutral.

[68] About the same time, at the end of the summer, the Ambraciots raised a large force of foreigners and campaigned with them against Amphilochian Argos and the rest of that territory. The quarrel between them and the Argives had arisen from this:

This Argos and the rest of Amphilochia was founded by Amphilochus, the son of Amphiaraus, after the Trojan War. When he came home he was not happy with the situation in Argos [in the Peloponnesus], and so he built this city in the Gulf of Ambracia and called it Argos after the name of his own country. It became the greatest city, with the most powerful inhabitants, of all Amphilochia. Many generations later, however, they fell on hard times and pressed the Ambraciots (who shared their border with Amphilochia) to join them as fellow colonists. They learned the Greek language they now speak from the Ambraciots who had joined them, for the rest of the Amphilochians were foreigners. After some time, the Ambraciots drove out the Argives, and held the city by themselves. At this, the Amphilochians gave their allegiance to the Acarnanians,[130] and both together called in the Athenians, who sent them thirty ships under the command of Phormio. When Phormio arrived, he took control of Argos and enslaved the Ambraciots, while the Amphilochians and Acarnanians jointly settled the city. This was the beginning of the alliance between the Athenians and Acarnanians.

The Ambraciots therefore derived their hatred of the Argives from this period of enslavement. Later, after the war began, they made the campaign I mentioned, with an army consisting of themselves, the Chaonians, and

---

130. The date of this alliance is uncertain, but it is most likely to have been formed in the early 430's and to have been one of the provocations of the war.

4. Justice and power: Plataea and Mytilene

other neighboring foreigners. When they came to Argos, they took control of the countryside; but when they could not take the city by assault they returned home and disbanded, each to his own people. This was what was done that summer.

[69] In the following winter, the Athenians sent twenty ships around the Peloponnesus under the command of Phormio. Taking Naupactus as his base, he guarded the passage there so that no one could sail in or out of Corinth or the Gulf of Crisa. They sent another six ships to Caria and Lycia under the command of Melesander, both to collect money and to keep Peloponnesian pirates from darting out from there to molest merchant shipping from Phaselis, Phoenikē, and that part of the mainland. But when he landed in Lycia with the force of Athenians and their allies he had on board, Melesander was overcome in battle and killed, with the loss of part of his army.

[70] That same winter (in 430/29) the Potidaeans could no longer withstand the siege,[131] for they saw that the Peloponnesians' invasions of Attica would not make the Athenians lift the siege. Their food supply had failed, and they did what they had to do in order to eat, some of them even tasting each other's flesh. And so they began negotiations for an agreement with the commanders of the Athenian army surrounding them—with Xenophon, Hestiadorus, and Phanomachus. The Athenian commanders accepted the agreement because they saw how miserable their army was in that cold place and knew that Athens had already spent two thousand talents on the siege.[132]

These were the conditions of the treaty: the Potidaeans would leave with their wives and children and the force that had come to help them; each man would take one cloak, and each woman two, and they would take a certain sum of money for travelling expenses. And so they departed under a truce, some to the Chalcidice, others where they were able to go.

But the people in Athens called the commanders in question for making this agreement without asking them (for they thought they could have taken the city on any terms).[133] Afterwards, they settled Potidaea with a colony of their own citizens.

That was what happened that winter (430/29), and so ended the second year of this war, as written up by Thucydides.

131. The siege had begun in 432. See p. 16.

132. See Plato's *Symposium* 220a–c for an account of the conditions under which the besieging army lived.

133. Had they captured the city in battle, the Athenians could have sold its people as slaves.

b. The siege of Plataea [ii.71–78]

[71] The next summer (in 429), the Peloponnesians and their allies did not invade Attica, but sent their army against Plataea under the command of Archidamus, king of the Lacedaemonians. He had pitched camp, and was about to waste the land, when the Plataeans sent ambassadors to him with these words:

"Archidamus, and you Lacedaemonians, your attack on the land of Plataea is neither just nor worthy of yourselves and your ancestors. Remember when Pausanias of Lacedaemon liberated Greece from the Persians with the help of those Greeks who were willing to risk joining him: after the terrible battle that was fought on our land, Pausanias made a sacrifice to Zeus Liberator in the *agora* of Plataea, and calling together all of the allies, he granted this right to the Plataeans: that their land and their city should be theirs to hold with autonomy; that no one should make war against them unjustly or try to make them a subject people; and that if anyone did, the allies then present would do their best to defend Plataea. These rights your ancestors granted us for our valor and zeal in that emergency. Now, however, you are doing the opposite: you've come with the Thebans, our worst enemies, to make us subject to them. We call the gods to witness, therefore—your ancestral gods and the gods of this land, by whom those oaths were made—and we tell you this: do no injustice to the land of Plataea, and do not violate your oaths. Let us live under our own laws as Pausanias declared we should."

[72] As the Plataeans were speaking, Archidamus interrupted them and said:

"There is justice in what you say, Plataeans, if your actions will match your words. Use the right Pausanias granted you: keep your own laws and help us liberate the others who took the same risks [at the battle of Plataea], who were party to the same oaths, and who are now subject to the Athenians. It is for the liberation of these people and others that all this military preparation has been made, and this war started. You should really join us and keep the oaths yourselves; if not, then do as we asked earlier and keep quiet, mind your own business, and don't join either side. Accept both sides as your friends and do not make war on either one. That would satisfy us."

So said Archidamus.

After hearing him, the Plataean ambassadors went back into the city and communicated what he had said to the people. Then they told him that they could not do as he asked unless the Athenians agreed, since their wives and children were in Athens and they were afraid for the entire city

4. Justice and power: Plataea and Mytilene

as well: once the Spartans had gone, the Athenians might come and disregard their neutrality, or the Thebans might take advantage of their promise to admit both sides as friends and try to take the city back for themselves.

Then Archidamus said this to encourage them:

"Give your city and houses over to us Lacedaemonians, show us the boundaries of your land, tell us how many olive trees you have, and anything else you can count. Then move wherever you want, for as long as the war lasts. When it is over, we will give you back what we have received. Until then we will keep it in trust, working the land and paying you whatever rent will be enough for you."

[73] On hearing this they went back into the city and, after meeting with the people, said that they would first communicate Archidamus' request to the Athenians; if the Athenians agreed, they would do as he asked. Till then they requested a truce in which their land would not be wasted. Archidamus made a truce for as many days as the journey was expected to take and did not cut down the trees or vines. The Plataean ambassadors arrived in Athens, discussed the matter with the Athenians, and returned with this message to those who were in Plataea:

"In the past, say the Athenians, since we became their allies, they have never abandoned us to those who would do us injustice; and now they will not neglect us either. They will send us as much help as they can, and they are pressing us, by the oaths of our ancestors, not to make any changes in our alliance."

[74] When the ambassadors made this report, the Plataeans decided not to betray the Athenians, but to see their land wasted if necessary and to put up with whatever misery should befall them. They decided not to go out again, but to give their answer from the walls: that they could not do as the Lacedaemonians asked.

When they had given this answer, King Archidamus first called on the gods and heroes of the land as his witnesses:

"All you gods and heroes who protect Plataea, be my witnesses that, because they first broke the oath we swore together, there has been no injustice at all in our entering their land, where our ancestors defeated the Persians after praying to you, and where you made the ground favorable for the Greeks in the contest. And there will be no injustice in what we are about to do now,[134] because, although we have made many reasonable offers, we have had no luck with them. Consent, then, to our punishing those

---

134. The Spartans later came to believe that this action put them in the wrong, since the Thebans had invaded Plataea in peacetime (vii.18, cf. iii.56).

who started the injustice, and agree to their paying the price to those who exact it in accordance with law."

[75] After making this plea to the gods, he prepared his army for war.

First they built a palisade around the city from trees they had felled, so that no one could get out; and then they heaped up earth in a ramp against the city wall, hoping to take the city quickly, since they had so large an army at work. They cut wood on Mt. Cithaeron and built structures on either side of it, laying the wood criss-cross to serve as walls, so that the ramp would not spread out too far. As filler for it they brought stones and earth and anything else they could throw in to finish the ramp. They worked on this for seventy days and nights continuously,[135] dividing into shifts so that some could carry while others had time for sleep or food. They were compelled to keep at their task by the Lacedaemonian officers who were in charge of supervising the work of the allied contingents.

When the Plataeans saw the ramp rising, they built a framework of wood and put it on top of their own wall where the ramp was being piled up, and they laid bricks inside it which they had taken from nearby houses they had demolished. The timber served to bind the bricks together, so that the structure would not be weakened as it grew taller. They covered this with hides and leather so that the workers would be safe, and to protect the timbers against fire-bearing arrows. So the height of the wall rose greatly on one side, and the ramp went up as fast on the other.

Another device the Plataeans used was this: they broke a hole in their own wall where the ramp touched it[136] and pulled earth from it into the city. [76] But the Peloponnesians found this out, and packed mud into mats of reeds and threw these bricks into the gap. Because these bricks had been reinforced by reeds, they did not spread out and could not be carried away, as the earth was.

Foiled on that plan, the Plataeans gave it up; but then they dug a tunnel from the city under the ramp, working out the precise location, and again hauled off the filling of the ramp. For a long time they were not detected by those outside, so that although the Lacedaemonians kept adding material, the ramp was less finished, because it was being taken away from underneath and always settling into the place that was hollowed out.

Still, the Plataeans were afraid they could not hold out even by this method, since there were only a few of them against many, so they in-

---

135. As campaigns rarely lasted over forty days (see ii.57), this figure is probably an error in the manuscript. Seven or seventeen days is more likely.

136. The bottom of the ramp touched the wall, though its upper portion left a gap (ii.77).

4. Justice and power: Plataea and Mytilene

vented this device as well: they gave up working on the high wall opposite the ramp, and, beginning on this side and that, from where the city wall was lower, they built another wall in the form of a crescent bending in towards the city. If the great wall were taken, they could hold this one and make the enemy build yet another ramp—and this ramp, being further in, would be twice as much work, and the enemy would be more exposed to shots from both sides.

At the same time as they were building the ramp, the Peloponnesians brought their battering rams against the city. They used one of these against the high wall opposite the ramp and shook down a large part of it, frightening the Plataeans. They used others against other parts of the wall. The Plataeans deflected some of these rams by snagging them with loops of rope; others they broke with huge logs that they hung by both ends on long iron chains from two poles that jutted out over the wall like a pair of antennae. They would pull the log up crosswise to the poles and then, when the battering ram was about to strike, they would take their hands off the chains and let the log drop and break off the beak of the ram by the force of its fall.

[77] After this, the Peloponnesians realized that they could not take the city under these difficult conditions, with their battering rams useless and their ramp faced by a wall. They prepared, therefore, to put a wall around the city. But first they decided to try the effect of fire, to see if they could burn the city down when a wind came up, since Plataea was a rather small city, and they were trying every sort of scheme to take it without the expense of a long siege. So they brought bundles of sticks and threw them from the ramp into the space between it and the wall, which, since they had many hands, they quickly filled. Then they heaped up other bundles in the rest of the city, wherever they could reach from the height of the ramp; and they lighted bundles with pitch and brimstone and threw them in, raising such a flame as had never been seen (not at least in a man-made fire; in mountain forests, of course, trees have caught fire owing to friction caused by the wind and have flamed up of their own accord). This fire was a very large one, however, and the Plataeans, who had survived everything else, came close to being destroyed by it. Large parts of the city were inaccessible, and if there had been a wind to whip it up (as the enemy hoped) they would not have come through. But, as it happened, we are told that a heavy rain fell along with thunder, quenched the flames, and brought this danger to an end.

[78] When the Peloponnesians failed in this as well, they dismissed the majority of their army, retaining only a part. Then they built a wall around the city, assigning a section of the perimeter to each of their allies. There

was a ditch inside the wall and another outside it, from which they made the bricks. When it was all finished, around the rising of Arcturus [in mid-September], they left guards for half the wall (the other half being guarded by Boeotians), and went home, dismissing the army to the cities from which they came.

Before this, the Plataeans had already sent their wives and children, along with everyone else who was no use in war, to Athens. There were four hundred of them who remained under siege, with eighty Athenians and a hundred and ten women to make bread. These were all who were there when they were laid under siege; no one else was inside the wall, free or slave.

Such was the beginning of the siege of Plataea.

c. The Mytilenean debate [iii. 37–51]

Thucydides breaks off the story of Plataea to tell us of other events, and soon turns to the rebellion of Mytilene. Mytilene is the principal town on the island of Lesbos, which lies off the coast of Asia Minor. Although they had enjoyed special privileges in the Athenian Empire, the Mytileneans rebelled against Athens in the summer of 428. Most of the rest of the island of Lesbos joined the rebellion.

The Mytileneans endured a lengthy siege by the Athenians in the hope that a Peloponnesian force would come to their aid. Meanwhile, their ambassadors made a plea for help to the Peloponnesians who were meeting at Olympia right after the Games (iii.9–14). They complained that their alliance with Athens, though beneficial in the beginning to both sides, had degenerated to the point at which it was held together only by the fear each side had of the other (iii.12). The Mytileneans expected the Athenians to take away their remaining rights at any moment, and so they decided to strike first. Unfortunately, circumstances forced them to go into rebellion earlier than they had planned, before they were prepared. Now, therefore, they really needed the help of the League. The Peloponnesians welcomed them into the League, but without control of the sea they were unable to offer significant help.

When Mytilene began to run out of food and realized that the Peloponnesians would not be able to save them, the democrats threatened to come to terms with the Athenians on their own. The oligarchic leaders of Mytilene were thus forced to surrender to the Athenian general, whose name was Paches. The only condition was that nothing be done to harm the Mytileneans until their representatives could be sent to Athens to plead their case before the Athenian people.

4. Justice and power: Plataea and Mytilene

The Athenians were enraged by the rebellion of what they considered a privileged ally. They therefore decreed that all the Mytilenean men of military age be put to death and the rest enslaved. The day after this decree, many Athenians had second thoughts and an assembly was convened to reconsider the issue. Here is the debate as Thucydides reconstructs it:

SPEECH OF CLEON[137]

[37] For my part, I have often seen that a democracy is not capable of ruling an empire, and I see it most clearly now, in your change of heart concerning the Mytileneans. Because you are not afraid of conspiracies among yourselves in your daily life, you imagine you can be the same with your allies, and so it does not occur to you that when you let them persuade you to make a mistake, or you relent out of compassion, your softness puts you in danger and does not win you the affection of your allies; and you do not see that your empire is a tyranny,[138] and that you have unwilling subjects who are continually plotting against you. They obey you not because of any good turns you might do them to your own detriment, and not because of any good will they might have, but only because you exceed them in strength. But it will be the worst mischief of all if none of our decisions stand firm, and if we never realize that a city with inferior laws is better if they are never relaxed than a city with good laws that have no force, that people are more use if they are sensible without education than if they are clever without self-control, and that the more common sort of people generally govern a city better than those who are more intelligent. For those intellectuals love to appear wiser than the laws and to win a victory in every public debate—as if there were no more important ways for them to show their wisdom! And that sort of thing usually leads to disaster for their city. But the other sort of people, who mistrust their own

---

137. It was Cleon who had persuaded the assembly to pass the original motion for killing the Mytileneans. At this time, Cleon was the most powerful leader in Athens, typical of those who were called demagogues by the Greeks. He exercised this power without holding any elected high office, but exerted tremendous influence on Athens through his speaking ability. This meant that he could formulate policies and push them through the Assembly without being held accountable, as were all Athenian officials at the end of their terms. Cleon and his like were bitterly resented by upper-class writers such as Thucydides, who takes him to be typical of the new generation of politicians that in his view corrupted Athens after the death of Pericles.

138. See Pericles' last speech, **ii.63**.

wits, are content to admit they know less than the laws and that they cannot criticize a speech as powerfully as a fine orator can; and so, as impartial judges rather than contestants, they govern a city for the most part very well. We should do the same, therefore, and not be carried away by cleverness and contests of wit, or give to you, the people, advice that runs against our own judgment.

[38] As for me, I have the same opinion I had before, and I am amazed at these men who have brought this matter of the Mytileneans into question again, thus causing a delay that works more to the advantage of those who have committed injustice. After a delay, you see, the victim comes at the wrongdoer with his anger dulled; but the punishment he gives right after an injury is the biggest and most appropriate. I am also amazed that there is anyone to oppose me, anyone who will try to prove that the injustice the Mytileneans have committed is good for us and that what goes wrong for us is really damaging to our allies. Clearly, he must have great trust in his eloquence if he is trying to make you believe that you did not decree what you decreed. Either that, or he has been bribed to try to lead you astray with a fine-sounding and elaborate speech.

Now the city gives prizes to others in contests of eloquence like this one, but the risks she must carry herself. You are to blame for staging these rhetorical contests so badly. The habits you've formed: why you merely look on at discussions, and real action is only a story to you! You consider proposals for the future on the basis of fine speeches, as if what they proposed were actually possible; and as for action in the past, you think that what has been done in front of your own eyes is less certain than what you have heard in the speeches of clever fault-finders. You are excellent men— at least for being deceived by novelties of rhetoric and for never wanting to follow advice that is tried and proved. You bow down like slaves to anything unusual, but look with suspicion on anything ordinary. Each of you wishes chiefly to be an effective speaker, but, if not, then you enter into competition with those who are. You don't want to be thought slow in following their meaning, so you applaud a sharp point before it is even made; and you are as eager to anticipate what will be said, as you are slow to foresee its consequences. You seek to hear about almost anything outside the experience of our daily lives, and yet you do not adequately understand what is right before your eyes. To speak plainly, you are so overcome with the delight of the ear that you are more like an audience for the sophists than an assembly deliberating for the good of the city.

[39] To put you out of these habits, I tell you that the Mytileneans have done us a far greater injustice than any other single city. For my part, I can

4. Justice and power: Plataea and Mytilene

forgive those cities that rebelled because they could not bear being ruled by us, or because they were compelled to do so by the enemy. But *these* people were islanders, their city was walled, and they had no fear of our enemies except by sea, where they were adequately protected by their fleet of triremes. Besides, they were governed by their own laws, and were held by us in the highest honor. That they should have done this! What is it but a conspiracy or a betrayal? It is not a rebellion, for a rebellion can only come from people who have been violently oppressed, whereas these people have joined our bitterest enemies to destroy us! This is far worse than if they had made war on us to increase their own power.

They'd learned nothing from the example of their neighbors' calamities—everyone who has rebelled against us so far has been put down—and their prosperity did not make them at all cautious before rushing into danger. They were bold in the face of the future and they had hopes above their power to achieve, though below what they desired. And so they started this war, resolved to put strength before justice, for as soon as they thought they could win, they attacked us, who had done them no injustice.

It is usual for cities to turn insolent when they have suddenly come to great and unexpected prosperity. In general, good fortune is more secure in human hands when it comes in reasonable measure, than when it arrives unexpectedly; and, generally, it is easier to keep misfortune away than to preserve great happiness. Long ago we should have given the Mytileneans no more privileges than our other allies, and then they would not have come to this degree of insolence, for generally it is human nature to look with contempt on those who serve your interests, and to admire those who never give in to you.

They should be punished right now, therefore, as they deserve for their injustice. And do not put all the blame on the oligarchs and absolve the common people, for they all alike took up arms against you. The democrats could have come over to our side and would long since have recovered their city, but they thought it safer to join in the oligarchs' rebellion.

Now consider your allies. If you inflict the same punishment on those who rebel under compulsion by the enemy, as on those who rebel of their own accord, don't you think anyone would seize the slightest pretext to rebel, when if they succeed they will win their liberty, but if they fail they will suffer nothing that can't be mended? And then we would have to risk our lives and our money against one city after another. If we succeed we recover only a ruined city, and so lose its future revenue, on which our strength is based. But if we fail, we add these as new enemies to those we had before, and the time we need to spend fighting our old enemies we must use up fighting our own allies.

[40] We must not, therefore, give our allies any hope that pardon may be secured by bribery or by persuading us that "it is only human to err." For these people conspired against us in full knowledge and did us an injury of their own will, while only involuntary wrongs may be pardoned. Therefore I contend then and now that you ought not to alter your former decision, and you ought not to make the mistake of giving in to the three things that are most damaging to an empire: pity, delight in speeches, and a sense of fairness. It may be right to show pity to those who are like-minded, but not to those who will never have pity on us and who must necessarily be our enemies for ever after. As for the rhetoricians who delight you with their speeches—let them play for their prizes on matters of less weight, and not on a subject that will make the city pay a heavy price for a light pleasure, while the speakers themselves will be well rewarded for speaking well. And as for fairness, we should show that only towards people who will be our friends in the future, and not towards those who will still be as they are now if we let them live: our enemies.

In sum I say only this: if you follow my advice, you will do justice to the Mytileneans and promote your own interests at the same time. But if you see the matter differently, you will not win their favor; instead, you will be condemning yourselves: if they were right to rebel, you ought not to have been their rulers. But then suppose your empire is not justified: if you resolve to hold it anyway, then you must give these people an unreasonable punishment for the benefit of the empire, or else stop having an empire so that you can give charity without taking any risks.

If you keep in mind what it would have been reasonable for them to do to you if they had prevailed, then you—the intended victims—cannot turn out to be less responisve to perceived wrong than those who hatched the plot, and you *must* think they deserve the same punishment they'd have given you—especially since they were the first to commit an injustice. Those who wrong someone without any excuse are the ones who press him the hardest, even to the death, when they see how dangerous an enemy he will be if he survives; for (they will think) if one side is wronged without cause, and escapes, he will be more harsh than if the two sides had hated each other equally in the beginning.

Therefore, do not be traitors to yourselves. Recall as vividly as you can what they did to you, and how it was more important than anything else for you to defeat them then. Pay them back now, and do not be softened at the sight of their present condition, or forget how terrible a danger hung over us at that time. Give these people the punishment they deserve, and set up a clear example for our other allies, to show that the penalty for rebellion is death. Once they know this, you will less often have occasion to neglect your enemies and fight against your own allies.

[41] So spoke Cleon. After him, Diodotus, the son of Eucrates, who in the earlier assembly had strongly opposed putting the Mytileneans to death, came forward this time also, and spoke as follows:

SPEECH OF DIODOTUS[139]

[42] I find no fault with those who have brought the Mytilenean business forward for another debate, and I have no praise for those who object to our having frequent discussions on matters of great importance. In my opinion, nothing is more contrary to good judgment than these two—haste and anger. Of these, the one is usually thoughtless, while the other is ill-informed and narrow-minded. And anyone who contends that discussion is not instructive for action is either stupid or defending some private interest of his own. He is stupid if he thinks there is anything other than words that we can use to consider what lies hidden from sight in the future. And he has a private interest if he wants to persuade you to do something awful, but knows that a good speech will not carry a bad cause, and so tries to browbeat his opponents and audience with some good slander instead: the most difficult opponents are those who also accuse one of putting on a rhetorical show for a bribe. If the accusation were merely of ignorance, a speaker could lose his case and still go home with a reputation more for stupidity than injustice; but once corruption is imputed to him, then he will be under suspicion even if he wins, and if he loses he will be thought both stupid and unjust. Such accusations do not do the city any good, since it loses good advisers from fear of them. The city would do best if this kind of citizen[140] had the least ability as speakers, for they would then persuade the city to fewer errors. A good citizen should not go about terrifying those who speak against him, but should try to look better in a fair debate. A sensible city should neither add to, nor reduce, the honor in which it holds its best advisers, nor should it punish or even dishonor those whose advice it does not take. This would make it less attractive for a successful speaker to seek greater popularity by speaking against his better judgment, or for

---

139. Of Diodotus we know only what we learn from Thucydides' representation of him in this debate.

140. "This kind of citizen": people like Cleon.

an unsuccessful one to strive in this way to gratify the people and gain a majority.

[43] But we do the opposite of that here; and besides, if anyone is suspected of corruption, but gives the best advice anyway, we are so resentful of the profit we think he is making (though this is uncertain), that we give up benefits the city would certainly have received. It has become the rule also to treat good advice honestly given as being no less under suspicion than bad, so that a man who has something rather good to say must tell lies in order to be believed, just as a man who gives terrible advice must win over the people by deception. Because of these suspicions, ours is the only city that no one can possibly benefit openly, without deception, since if anyone does good openly to the city, his reward will be the suspicion that he had something secretly to gain from this.

But on the most important matters, such as these, we orators must decide to show more foresight than is found in you short-sighted citizens, especially since we stand accountable for the advice we give, but you listeners are not accountable to anyone, because if you were subject to the same penalties as the advisers you follow, you would make more sensible decisions. As it is, whenever you fail, you give in to your momentary anger and punish the man who persuaded you for his one error of judgment, instead of yourselves for the many mistakes in which you had a part [cf. viii.1].

[44] For my part, I did not come forward to speak about Mytilene with any purpose to contradict or to accuse. Our dispute, if we are sensible, will concern not their injustice to us, but our judgment as to what is best for us. Even if I proved them guilty of terrible injustice, I still would not advise the death penalty for this, unless that was to our advantage. Even if they deserved to be pardoned, I would not have you pardon them if it did not turn out to be good for the city. In my opinion, what we are discussing concerns the future more than the present. And as for this point that Cleon insists on—that the death penalty will be to our advantage in the future, by keeping the others from rebelling—I maintain exactly the opposite view, and I too am looking at our future well-being. I urge you not to reject the usefulness of my advice in favor of the apparent attractions of his. In view of your present anger against the Mytileneans, you may agree that his argument is more in accord with justice. But we are not at law with them, and so have no need to speak of justice. We are in council instead, and must decide how the Mytileneans can be put to the best use for us.

[45] The death penalty has been ordained for many offenses in various cities, and these are minor offenses compared to this one; yet people still risk their lives when they are buoyed up by hope, and no one has ever gone

4. Justice and power: Plataea and Mytilene

into a dangerous conspiracy convinced that he would not succeed. What city would ever attempt a rebellion on the supposition that her resources, whether from home or from her alliance with other states, are too weak for this? They all have it by nature to do wrong, both men and cities, and there is no law that will prevent it. People have gone through all possible penalties, adding to them in the hope that fewer crimes will then be done to them by evildoers. It stands to reason that there were milder punishments in the old days, even for the most heinous crimes; but as the laws continued to be violated, in time most cities arrived at the death penalty. And still the laws are violated.

Either some greater terror than death must be found, therefore, or else punishment will not deter crime. Poverty compels the poor to be daring, while the powerful are led by pride and arrogance into taking more than their share. Each human condition is dominated by some great and incurable passion that impels people to danger. Hope and passionate desire,[141] however, dominate every situation: with desire as the leader and hope as the companion, desire thinking out a plan, and hope promising a wealth of good fortune, these two cause the greatest mischief, and because they are invisible they are more dangerous than the evils we see. Besides these, fortune [*tuchē*] plays no less a part in leading men on, since she can present herself unexpectedly and excite you to take a risk, even with inadequate resources. This happens especially to cities, because of the serious issues at stake—their own freedom and their empire over others—and because an individual who is acting with everyone else has an unreasonably high estimate of his own ability. In a word, it is an impossible thing—you would have to be simple-minded to believe that people can be deterred, by force of law or by anything else that is frightening, from doing what human nature is earnestly bent on doing.

[46] We should not, therefore, make a bad decision, relying on capital punishment to protect us, or set such hopeless conditions that our rebels have no opportunity to repent and atone for their crime as quickly as possible. Consider this: if a city in rebellion knew it could not hold out, as things are it would come to terms while it could still pay our expenses and make its remaining contributions; but if we take Cleon's way, wouldn't any city prepare better for a rebellion than they do now, and hold out in a siege to the very last, since it would mean the same whether they gave in late or early? And what is this if not harmful to us—to have the expense of a siege because they will not come to terms, and then, when we have taken a city,

---

141. "Passionate desire": *eros*. On hope, see v.103.

to find it ruined and to lose its revenue for the future?[142] You see, our strength against our enemies depends on that revenue.

We should not, then, be strict judges in punishing offenders, and so harm ourselves; instead, we should look for a way to impose moderate penalties to ensure that we will in the future be able to make use of cities that can make us substantial payments. We should not plan to keep them in check by the rigor of laws, but by watching their actions closely. We are doing the opposite now, if we think we should punish cruelly a city that used to be free, was held in our empire by force, rebelled from us for a good reason—to restore its autonomy—and now has been defeated. What we ought to do in the case of a city of free men is not to impose extreme penalties after they rebel, but to be extremely watchful before they rebel, and to take care that the idea of rebellion never crosses their minds. And once we have overcome them, we should lay the fault upon as few of them as we can.

[47] Consider also how great a mistake you will be making on this score if you follow Cleon's advice: as things are, the democrats in all the cities are your friends, and either they do not join the oligarchs in rebellion or, if they are forced to, they remain hostile to the rebels, so that when you go to war with them, you have their common people on your side; but if you destroy the democrats of Mytilene, who had no part in the rebellion, and who delivered the city into your hands of their own will as soon as they were armed, then you will, first, commit an injustice by killing those who have done you good service, and, second, accomplish exactly what oligarchs everywhere want the most: when they have made a city rebel, they will immediately have the democrats on their side, because you will have shown them in advance that those who are not guilty of injustice suffer the same penalty as those who are. And even if they were guilty, however, we should pretend that they were not, so that the only party still allied with us will not become our enemy. And in order to keep our empire intact, I think it much more advantageous for us to put up with an injustice willingly, than for us justly to destroy people we ought not to destroy. And as for Cleon's idea that justice and our own advantage come to the same in the case of punishment—these two cannot be found to coincide in the present case.

[48] Now I want you to accept my proposal because you see that it is the best course, and not because you are swayed more by pity or a sense of fairness. I would not have you influenced by those factors any more than

---

142. See iii.39 where Cleon makes the point to which this responds.

4. Justice and power: Plataea and Mytilene

Cleon would. But take my advice and judge the leaders of the rebellion at your leisure, while you let the rest enjoy their city. That will be good for the future, and it will strike fear into your enemies today. Those who plan well against their enemies, you see, are more formidable than those who attack with active force and foolishness combined.

[49] So spoke Diodotus. After these two quite opposite opinions were delivered, the Athenians were at odds with each other, and the show of hands was almost equal on both sides. But the opinion of Diodotus prevailed.

On this they immediately sent out another ship in haste, so they would not find the city already destroyed by coming in after the first ship (which had left a day and a night earlier). The Mytilenean ambassadors provided wine and barley cakes for the second ship and promised them great rewards if they overtook the first. And so they rowed in such haste that they ate their barley cakes steeped in wine and oil while they rowed, and took turns rowing while others slept.[143] They were lucky in that there was no wind against them. And since the first ship was not sailing in any haste on its perverse mission, while the second one hurried on in the manner described, the first ship did arrive first, but only by the time it took Paches to read the decree. He was about to execute the sentence when the second ship came in and prevented the destruction of the city. That was how close Mytilene came to destruction.

[50] As for the other men Paches had sent away as being most to blame for the rebellion, the Athenians did kill them as Cleon had advised, just over a thousand of them. They also razed the walls of Mytilene and confiscated their ships. Afterwards, they stopped collecting payments directly from Lesbos. Instead, they divided the land (all but that of Methymna[144]) into three thousand allotments, of which they consecrated three hundred to the gods, the rest going to Athenians who were chosen by lot and sent out as allotment holders. The people of Lesbos were required to pay them two silver *minas*[145] annually for each lot, and worked the land themselves. The Athenians also took over the communities that Mytilene had controlled on the mainland and made them subject to Athens. So ended the business on Lesbos.

[51] The same summer, after the recovery of Lesbos, the Athenians

---

143. The normal practice was for sailors to eat and sleep on land.
144. Methymna had not joined the rebellion.
145. As two *minas* was roughly a hoplite's annual pay, this may have been intended to support a hoplite garrison. See Hornblower.

made war against the island of Minoa[146] (which lies near Megara), under the command of Nicias. The Megarians had built a tower there for use as a garrison, and Nicias wanted it as an Athenian look-out post that would be nearer to Megara than Budorum or Salamis, so he could use it to prevent the Peloponnesians from sailing their triremes out of Megara unobserved (as had happened before with raiding expeditions) as well as from sending anything into Megara by sea. First he captured two towers on the side of the island facing Nisaea [the port of Megara], thus securing a passage for his ships between the mainland and the island; then he walled off the section that faced the mainland, (for it might have received aid by a bridge over the shallows where the island was near the mainland). He finished this in a few days and, after establishing a garrison in a fort there, went home with his army.

d. The Plataean debate [iii.52–68]

Thucydides had interrupted his account of Mytilene to record an incident at Plataea, which was undergoing siege through the same winter of 428/7. When the Plataeans ran low on food, they planned to break through the Peloponnesian lines and escape on a dark and stormy night (iii.20-24). About half of them decided to stay, but 220 troops made the daring attempt. Thucydides' tale of the breakout is so vivid it could only have come from an eyewitness. Of the 220 who made the attempt, an incredible 212 reached Athens in safety. The remaining Plataeans lasted until summer, when they too had to capitulate.

[52] About the same time that summer the Plataeans ran out of food and were no longer able to withstand the siege; so they surrendered to the Peloponnesians. This is what happened:

The Peloponnesians assaulted the walls, but the people inside could not defend themselves. When the Lacedaemonian commander saw how weak they were, he did not want to take the place by force. He had orders for this from Lacedaemon, so that if they made a treaty with Athens that would restore all land taken in war, then they would not have to give up Plataea if it had come over of its own accord. So the Lacedaemonian commander sent a herald to the Plataeans to ask if they would give up the city of their own accord and accept them as judges to punish those who had done any injustice, and to punish no one without judicial procedure. The herald told

---

146. No such island is known to us; a process of silting must have made Minoa part of the mainland. Apparently it was close to the port used by Megara.

them this, and they—for they were then at their weakest—gave up the city. Then the Peloponnesians fed the Plataeans for as many days as it took the judges (of whom there were five) to come from Lacedaemon. When they arrived, no formal charge was announced. Instead, they called the Plataeans forward and asked them this one question: "Had they done any good service for the Lacedaemonians or their allies in the present war?" The Plataeans, however, begged to speak at greater length, and appointed as their speakers Astymachus and Lacon, who had represented Lacedaemon in Plataea. They came forward and spoke as follows:

SPEECH OF THE PLATAEANS

[53] We gave up our city to you, Lacedaemonians, because we trusted you and did not expect to undergo this sort of trial, but some more lawful proceeding instead; and we agreed to submit to your judges (as we are doing), rather than others, because we thought we would be treated quite fairly that way. But now we are afraid we have been wrong on both points: we have reason to suspect that we are facing the most terrible penalties in this trial, and that you are not impartial. We gather this from the fact that there has been no formal charge that we could answer (as it was we asked permission to give this speech), and also from the fact that your question was short and worded so that a true answer would convict us while a false one would be refuted. Since, however, we have nowhere else to turn in our present straits, we are compelled to do what seems safest—to make a speech before we take our chances. A word unspoken that might have saved us could be a reproach to people in our situation later on.

Besides, it will be hard for us to persuade you. If we had not known each other, we might have helped ourselves by producing testimony of which you were unaware. As things stand, however, you already know everything we have to tell you. Our fear is not that you have already found our virtue to be less than yours and will make that your accusation, but that you have already judged our case in order to please another city. [54] Nevertheless, we will make the case we have that justice is on our side in the quarrel with Thebes; we will remind you of our good services to you and the rest of Greece, and in this way we will try to persuade you.

As for that short question, whether we have done anything to help the Lacedaemonians and their allies in this war, we answer as follows: if you ask us as enemies, we say we have done you no injustice by not helping you; but if you consider us friends, then you are the ones who have done the greater wrong, by making war on us. When there was peace, however, and during the Persian War, we behaved ourselves well: we were not the first to break the peace this time, and in that earlier war we were the only Boeotians[147] who joined you to fight for the freedom of Greece. Though we are not sailors we fought in the sea-battle of Artemesium, and in the battle on our own land we were with you and Pausanias.[148] We took part beyond our means against every other threat to the Greeks at that time. We also helped you Lacedaemonians in particular after the earthquake when the revolt of the Helots who seized Ithome struck terror into Sparta.[149] At that time we sent you a third of our forces, which you have no reason to forget.

[55] That is the sort of people we decided to be, during those important events of the past. Since then we have been enemies, but that is your fault. We asked for an alliance when Thebes attacked us, but you rejected us and told us to turn to the Athenians, since they were nearby and you lived far away.[150] Nevertheless, you have had no more trouble than you should from us in this war, and you would have had none in the future. We did not rebel against the Athenians when you asked us to do so, but that is not an injustice. For they were the ones who helped us against Thebes when you held back, and it would have been ignoble to betray them, especially since they treated us well. It was at our urging that we became allies and were given a share in their citizenship;[151] so we had reason to follow all their commands with alacrity. When you or the Athenians are leaders of the allies, then it is the leaders, rather than the followers, who are to blame for whatever goes wrong when evil is done.

[56] The Thebans have done us many injustices; you know yourselves about the latest of these, which is the cause of our present troubles. They seized our city when a treaty was in effect, and at a sacred time of the month

---

147. The Plataeans exaggerate; Thespiae, also in Boeotia, resisted the Persians at great cost to themselves (Herodotus vii.132, viii.50).

148. The Greeks fought two indecisive naval battles with the Persians at Artemesium (not far from Thermopylae) in 480. At Plataea, however, they won an overwhelming victory on land in 479 under the Lacedaemonian general Pausanias.

149. The Helots were a subject people to the Lacedaemonians, who kept them in a form of serfdom. They were frequently in rebellion, and on more than one occasion seized and fortified the mountain of Ithome, most recently in 464.

150. Probably in 519. See Herodotus vi.108.1–3.

151. The Plataeans were never full citizens; their survivors apparently enjoyed honorary citizenship after these events, and this may have given them some rights. See Hornblower.

too; we were right to punish them then, in accordance with the law that holds everywhere: piety allows one to repel an aggressor.[152] So there is no reason why we should be made to suffer on their account. If you measure justice by your immediate benefit and their hostility, you will make it obvious that you are not true judges of what is right, but merely serving your own interests. And yet though the Thebans seem useful to you now, we and the other Greeks were far more useful to you then, when you were in greater danger. As things are now you terrify other people when you attack them, but in former times it was the Persians who threatened us all with servitude, and the Thebans were on their side. Justice demands that you compare the zeal we showed then with any offense we may have committed now. You will find that one far outweighs the other, especially since it came at the right time, when hardly any of the Greeks dared oppose Xerxes' power with their valor. At that time the greater praise went to those who did not selfishly find safety in the face of the attack but to those who dared do what was best voluntarily and at great risk. We were in the former group and given the highest honors; now we are afraid that the same sort of choice will lead to our destruction, since we sided with the Athenians as justice required, rather than with you, as would have been to our advantage. You should always exercise the same judgment in similar cases and realize that your advantage lies in what is good for your allies, when they can be certain of your gratitude for their virtue and when your immediate interests are, in a sense, served.

[57] Keep in mind also that you are now thought to be an example of heroism to most of the Greeks. Your judgment in this trial will not go unnoticed, because you are widely praised and we are without blame. If your decision about us is unreasonable, watch out: people may not accept an improper sentence against good men, even if it is given by better ones; and they may resent it if you decide to dedicate spoils taken from us in the common temples, since we have done good service to Greece. It will be thought horrible that Plataea should be destroyed by Lacedaemonians, and that you—whose fathers honored our valor by inscribing the name of our city on the tripod at Delphi[153]—should now blot us out entirely from all of Greece to gratify the Thebans. Look how far our troubles have gone: we were ruined when we were conquered by the Persians, and now we have been defeated by the Thebans through you, who used to be our greatest

---

152. Piety is a principal theme of the Plataeans. Here it is tantamount to justice, elsewhere it has more religious overtones (as in the honor they have done to the Spartan dead, iii.58).

153. The tripod with this inscription can be seen in the Hippodrome in Istanbul.

friends; and we have been put through two great ordeals—first to die of hunger if we did not give up the city to you, and now to be on trial for our lives.

Although our zeal in defense of Greece exceeded our power, we Plataeans are now abandoned by everyone, alone and unprotected. None of our former allies is helping us. You Lacedaemonians were our only hope, but now we fear you are not reliable.

[58] We beseech you, then, for the sake of the gods who sanctified our alliance and for the sake of our excellent service to Greece, be moved by us and change your minds about whatever the Thebans have persuaded you to do. Ask them instead to return you this courtesy: be content not to kill those you ought to spare. Then you will earn sincere gratitude rather than thanks for a shameful act, and you will not be giving others pleasure at the cost of evil to yourselves.[154] You can take our lives quickly enough, but it will be hard work for you to live down the infamy of this deed. We are not your enemies but well-wishers who were compelled to make war; and therefore you cannot have a good reason for punishing us. The pious judgment, then, would be for you to put our lives in safety, if you remember that you received us by our voluntary submission with our arms held out as suppliants (for the law in Greece forbids killing people who do that). Keep in mind also that we have been your benefactors through everything. Look at the tombs of your fathers who were buried here after they were killed by the Persians; we have honored them yearly at public expense with clothing and other customary offerings that our land produces in season. We have offered them the first fruits of every crop as companions from a friendly country and as allies to our comrades in arms. Now you will do the opposite if you give us the wrong sentence. Consider this: Pausanias buried them here because he thought it was friendly ground and that they would be among people who were friends; but if you kill us and turn Plataea into part of Thebes, won't you be leaving your fathers and kindred deprived of the honors they now have, in a hostile territory and among the very men who killed them? Won't you be subjugating the very soil on which the Greeks were liberated? Leaving the temples deserted, where they prayed before defeating the Persians? And abolishing the ancestral sacrifices set up by their founders?

[59] It will not add to your glory, Lacedaemonians, to do these things— not to violate the common laws of Greece, not to sin against your ancestors, not to destroy us because of someone else's hatred, when we are your bene-

---

154. "Evil to yourselves": here, probably, an evil reputation.

4. Justice and power: Plataea and Mytilene

factors and have done you no injustice ourselves. Only this will add to your glory: spare our lives, relent, and in your moderation take pity on us.[155] Fix your minds not only on the horror of what we would suffer, but also on the sort of people we are, who would suffer this fate. And remember the uncertainty of life, how disaster can strike anyone, even undeservedly.

It is right and absolutely necessary for us to beseech you and call upon the gods we all worship in Greece: listen to us. We have brought up the oaths your fathers made, and we beg you not to forget them; we have become suppliants at your fathers' tombs, and we call upon the dead not to fall under the rule of Thebans or let their best friends be betrayed into the hands of their worst enemies. We remind them of that day on which we won the most brilliant victory at their side—we who are now, on this day, in the most horrible danger.

To bring this speech to an end—which is necessary, but very painful for men in our situation, since it brings the danger to our lives even closer—we say in conclusion that it was not to the Thebans that we gave up our city (we would have preferred the most awful death by starvation to that). But we trusted you, and came over to you. And it is only justice, if you are not convinced by us now, for you to put us back where fortune had us, and let us choose our own fate. We lay on you this solemn charge: do not let us Plataeans, who were so zealous on behalf of Greece, be turned over to our worst enemies, the Thebans; do not violate our trust in you as suppliants by letting us out of your hands. Be our saviors, you who liberated the rest of Greece! Do not destroy us!

[60] So spoke the Plataeans. The Thebans were afraid the Lacedaemonians would give in to that speech, and so they came forward and said they also wished to speak, since the Plataeans had been allowed to give a longer speech than the short question required, contrary to the plan. When they were told to speak, they said:

SPEECH OF THE THEBANS

[61] We would not have asked permission to make a speech if these men had given a brief answer to the question, instead of turning against us with an accusation and at the same time defending themselves at length on points that are irrelevant, on which they were not charged, and praising

---

155. Moderation or self-control, *sōphrosunē*, was a virtue to which the Lacedaeminians laid special claim (i.84).

themselves for deeds with which no one has found fault. But as it is we must reply to these accusations and refute their defense, so that neither our 'wickedness' nor their 'glory' may do them any good. And you should hear the truth about both of these before you decide.

Our quarrel with them arose from this: we founded Plataea[156] after the rest of Boeotia, together with some other places which we had, once we had driven out the mixed peoples who were there; but the Plataeans would not allow us to be their leaders, as had been arranged at the start. Instead, they violated the traditions of their ancestors and took themselves outside the rest of Boeotia; and when we used force against them they went over to the Athenians and together they did us a great deal of harm, for which we made them suffer in return.[157]

[62] When the foreign king invaded Greece, they say they were the only Boeotians who did not join the Persians, and this is the point they use to glorify themselves and insult us. Now we admit they did not go over to the Persians, because the Athenians did not; by the same token, however, when the Athenians attacked the rest of Greece, they were the only Boeotians to go over to Athens. But you should consider what forms of government the two cities had when we did these things. Our city at the time happened to be governed neither by an oligarchy that is equally fair for all[158] nor by a democracy. Instead, we had what is most contrary to moderate lawful government, and nearest to tyranny: affairs were in the control of a small clique with absolute power. These few men hoped to increase their personal power even further if the Persian army was victorious, and so they held the majority back by force and brought the Persians in. The city as a whole was not master of itself at the time it did these things, and it does not deserve to be censured for mistakes it made when it was not governed under law.[159] But at least when the Persians were gone

---

156. If this is supposed to mean that Plataea was founded by Thebans, it is probably false, in view of Plataea's long independent tradition.

157. Herodotus v.77

158. "That is equally fair for all": *isonomos*. Elsewhere, *isonomia* is usually associated with democracy; this passage shows, however, that democrats could not make a unique claim to fairness for all, though *isonomia* here might refer to fairness for all aristocrats.

159. "A small clique with absolute power": *dunasteia*. Aristotle says that a *dunasteia* is the fourth stage of oligarchy, a hereditary clique that approximates monarchy and is the moral equivalent of tyranny (*Politics* 1292b7, 1293a31). Aristotle explicitly contrasts *dunasteia* with the rule of law. In this passage Thucydides anticipates the development by Plato in the *Laws* and Aristotle in

4. *Justice and power: Plataea and Mytilene*

and the city had regained its laws, look what happened: once the Athenians moved against the rest of Greece and tried to make themselves masters of our land, and had actually taken many places already with the help of internal divisions [*stasis*], didn't we fight at Coronea and liberate Boeotia with our victory? And aren't we now zealously helping to liberate the rest of Greece, and furnishing as many horses and as much other equipment as the other allies put together? That is our defense against the charge that we went over to the Persians.

[63] Now we will try to prove that you Plataeans have done more injustice to the Greeks than we have, and that you deserve severe punishment more than we do. You say you became allies and citizens of Athens to get back at us; in that case you should merely have called them in against us, instead of joining in their attack on other cities. That was open to you: if you had really been following the Athenians against your will, you could have fallen back on the alliance you already had with the Lacedaemonians against the Persians, which you keep bringing up. That would have been sufficient to protect you from us and, what is most important, to give you the security to do as you pleased. But no, you followed the Athenians of your own accord, you were not forced into it; you even chose to do so. And you say it would have been a shameful thing for you to betray your benefactors! It is far more shameful, and unjust as well, for you to have betrayed all the Greeks with whom you had sworn a treaty, than to betray the Athenians alone, especially since they are enslaving Greece, while the others are liberating it. Besides, what you are giving them in gratitude is out of proportion and quite shameful. You brought in the Athenians because of injustices that were done to you, as you say yourselves, and now you are cooperating with them in doing injustice to others. Yet it would be better to leave a debt of kindness unpaid than to return a good deed with an action that is unjust.

[64] In fact, you have made it clear that it was not for the sake of Greece that you alone did not join the Persians then, but because the Athenians did not. You wanted to do whatever they did, the opposite of the other Greeks; and now you claim the benefit of this, when it was only because of them that you did well. But that's unreasonable. You chose the Athenians; let them help you in this trial. And don't bring up that oath that was made

---

the *Politics* of the ideal of the rule of law. As for the value of the Theban excuse, we should not be impressed by their claim that the city was not master of itself; in fact, after the defeat of the Persians, Thebes withstood a siege by the Greek allies for 20 days rather than hand over their pro-Persian leaders for punishment (Herodotus ix.87).

in the past,[160] as if that should save you. You relinquished that oath, you see, when you violated it by helping the Athenians subjugate Aegina and others who were protected by the same oath, instead of preventing that. You were quite willing to help them then; you were governed then under the same laws as you are now, and no one had control of you by force, as happened to us.[161] Also, you rejected our last invitation, which we gave you before the siege, to be at peace with us and remain neutral. So whom could the Greeks all hate with more justice than you, when you are aiming at their destruction behind a screen of heroism? And as for those actions in which, as you say, you were of service for a time, you have made it clear that they were not your sort of thing at all. You have proved to us what it is that your nature truly inclines you to do: you have walked with the Athenians down the path of injustice. That is what we had to say about our going over unwillingly to the Persians, and your going over willingly to the Athenians.

[65] As for this last injustice you charge us with—our "unlawful entry into your city when a treaty was in effect and at a sacred time of the month"[162]—we do not think we are in the wrong as much as you are even on this point. If we had assaulted your city in combat or wasted your land as enemies, then we would have done you an injustice. But when men of your own city called us in of their own accord—top-ranking men in wealth and nobility,[163] who wanted to put a stop to your foreign alliance and bring you back to the ancestral customs that all Boeotians share—what is the injustice in that? "It is the leaders who break the law, not the followers."[164] In fact, however, they did not break the law, in our judgment, and neither did we. They are citizens as much as you are and had more at stake, and they opened their own gates and took us into their own city in a friendly spirit, not a warlike one. Their intention was to keep the bad people here from getting worse, and to give the better people what they deserve. The men who called us in are the arbiters of sensible policy; they were not trying to deprive the city of your persons, but to bring you back home to your kindred—not trying to make you anyone's enemy, but to arrange a settled peace for you with everyone.

[66] The proof that what we did was not an act of war is that we did no

---

160. Above, **iii.57**.

161. Above, **iii.62**.

162. Thucydides ii.2 and **iii.56**.

163. The "top-ranking men in wealth and nobility" are oligarchs. The passage that follows represents oligarchic thinking of the period.

164. Paraphrasing the Plataeans' remarks at **iii.55.4**

one an injustice, but proclaimed that anyone who wished to be governed by the ancestral customs of Boeotia should come to us. And you were peaceful at first; you were coming in readily and agreeing to our terms. But afterwards, when you realized how few of us there were, then you did not treat us as we had treated you (though perhaps we were a trifle rude in entering without the consent of the majority). Still, while we did nothing to cause a revolution in action, and used only speeches to urge you to leave, you attacked us contrary to our agreement. The ones you killed in the fighting do not upset us as much, for there was a kind of law governing their deaths. But the ones who held out their arms as suppliants, whom you captured alive and later promised not to kill—wasn't it a horrible thing for you to wipe them out lawlessly? You committed three injustices one after the other: first you broke the agreement, then you killed the men, and that broke your promise to spare them if we did no harm to your property in the fields. Yet you say that *we* are the lawbreakers and *you* do not deserve to be punished! No. And if these judges know what is right, you will be punished for all of your crimes.

[67] Now we have gone through this at length, Lacedaemonians, for your sake and ours alike: for yours, to let you see that your sentence will be just; for ours, to show that our vengeance is still more pious; and also to ensure that you are not moved by the recital of their virtues in the past (if they really had any). When victims of injustice have a record of virtue, that should count in their favor; but a good record should double the punishment for wrongdoers, because their crimes are so inappropriate for them.

And don't let them profit by weeping and appealing for pity when they bring up your fathers' tombs and their own lack of friends. On the other side, you see, we claim that our young men met a much more horrible fate when they were wiped out by these Plataeans—young men whose fathers either died at Coronea to bring Boeotia over to your side or are left in old age, bereft of family, to beg you for revenge, and they are suppliants with much more justice on their side.[165] People deserve to be pitied if they ought not have suffered as they have; if, on the other hand, justice requires that they suffer (as with these men), then their suffering ought to be a source of delight. As for their lack of friends, they have themselves to thank: they rejected their better allies of their own accord. They acted lawlessly before we had done them any harm, and condemned our men more out of spite than justice. And the penalty they are paying falls short of that, for they

---

165. At Coronea, in 447, Boeotian and other enemies of Athens defeated a substantial Athenian army and forced them to give up their attempt to expand into Boeotia (i.113).

will be sentenced under law—not holding out their arms in battle as they claim they are, but after consenting to put themselves on trial.

Therefore, Lacedaemonians, uphold the law of the Greeks, which these men have violated, and make them pay for their lawless actions against us—a just return for the zeal we have shown in your service. Do not let their words[166] make you reject us, but give the Greeks an example of a contest you decide not by words, but by deeds. If what they did is good, a brief report will suffice; if they are in the wrong, however, fancy speeches are merely smoke screens. But if those in authority do what you are doing now—summing up the issue in one question for everybody, and making judgments on that basis—then there will be much less searching for fine words to cover unjust actions.

[68] So spoke the Thebans. The Lacedaemonian judges still thought their question was the right one to ask—whether they had received any good service from the Plataeans in the war. This, they said, was because they had expected the Plataeans all along to keep the peace, in accordance with the old treaty of Pausanias after the Persian War; and later they had offered them neutrality on the same terms before the siege, and been refused. They held that they were released from the treaty, since their intentions were just, and they had been treated badly by the Plataeans.

So they brought each one forward and asked him the same question again: whether he had done any good service in the war for the Lacedaemonians and their allies.[167] And when they said they had not, they took them off and killed them without a single exception. They killed at least two hundred Plataeans there and twenty-five Athenians;[168] and they made slaves of the women. Then the Thebans gave the use of the city for a year to Megarians who had been driven out of their city by civil war, along with the surviving Plataeans who had supported Thebes. Afterwards, they razed it to the ground and used its foundations to build a hos-

---

166. "Words": *logoi*, which can mean words, speeches, arguments, or (as probably here) stories. In this context, each side is giving a speech and making arguments, and so using *logoi* in those senses. The point of difference is that since the Plataean case depends on history it depends on mere stories; whereas the Theban case depends on the current fact of the matter: that Plataea is allied with Athens. On the word-deed contrast here, see Parry (1957: 190 ff.).

167. See **iii.52**.

168. There had been four hundred eighty when the siege began, but about two hundred twenty had broken out and escaped in the meanwhile (iii.24).

tel[169] near the precinct of Hera two hundred feet around, with rooms in a circle upstairs and down, making use also of the Plataeans' roofs and doors. From the other materials in the Plataean wall, brass and iron, they made beds which they dedicated to Hera, for whom they also built a stone temple a hundred feet on a side. The land became public property which was rented on a ten-year lease and cultivated by Thebans. Virtually everything the Lacedaemonians did against Plataea they did for the sake of Thebes, which they thought would be useful to them in the war that was then afoot. So ended the business in Plataea in the ninty-third year of their alliance with Athens.[170]

---

169. The hostel would serve visitors to the Shrine of Hera, for the maintenance of the rites mentioned above.

170. The alliance lasted from 519 to 427 (Herodotus vi.108).

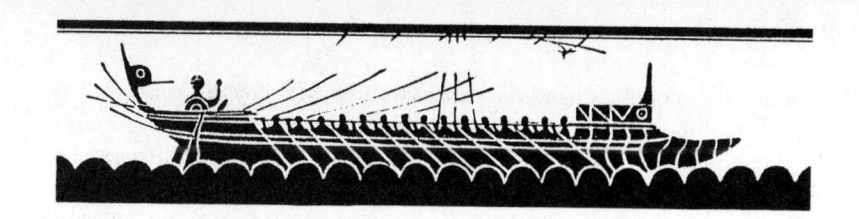

5. Human Nature Laid Bare in Civil War

a. The civil war in Corcyra [iii.81.2–85]

After describing the end of Plataea, Thucydides turns to other events of that summer, of which the most important was the civil war on Corcyra, an island off the western coast of Greece. Athens had been supporting Corcyra in the island's quarrel with Corinth, and this had been one of the provocations of the war, since Corcyra had been a Corinthian colony, albeit a highly independent one (p. 16).

In 427, the tension in Corcyra erupted in open civil war between democrats and oligarchs, and both sides called in allies from abroad. A Peloponnesian fleet arrived first and gave the democrats a fright; but the arrival of a large Athenian fleet under Eurymedon sent the Spartans packing and gave the democrats the confidence to begin a massacre of those who supported oligarchy, four hundred of whom had taken sanctuary as suppliants in the Temple of Hera. Others had been persuaded to help man the thirty ships they had expected to use in the defense of Corcyra against the Peloponnesians.

[81.2] When the people of Corcyra heard that the Athenian ships were approaching, and that the Peloponnesians were leaving, they brought in the Messenian soldiers[171] who had been outside into the city, and ordered the ships they had manned to come around into the Hyllaic port. While they were going around, the Corcyrean democrats killed all the opposing

---

171. The Messenians here were former helots (serfs) of the Spartans who had been resettled by Athens near Corcyra after the failure of their revolt against Sparta in 464. They had been brought to Corcyra by the Athenians to support the democrats there.

faction they could lay hands on; and as for the ones they had persuaded to man the ships, they killed them all as they disembarked. And they came to the temple of Hera and persuaded fifty of the oligarchic sympathizers who had taken sanctuary there to submit themselves to a trial; then they condemned them all to death. When they saw what was being done, most of the suppliants—all those who were not induced to stand trial by law—killed one another right there in the temple; some hanged themselves on trees, and everyone made away with himself by what means he could. For the seven days that the Athenian admiral Eurymedon stayed there with his sixty ships, the Corcyreans went on killing as many of their own people as they took to be their enemies. They accused them of subverting the democracy, but some of the victims were killed on account of private hatred, and some by their debtors for the money they had lent them. Every form of death was seen at this time; and (as tends to happen in such cases) there was nothing people would not do, and more: fathers killed their sons; men were dragged out of the temples and then killed hard by; and some who were walled up in the temple of Dionysus died inside it.

[82] So cruel was the course of this civil war [*stasis*], and it seemed all the more so because it was among the first of these. Afterwards, virtually all Greece was in upheaval, and quarrels arose everywhere between the democratic leaders, who sought to bring in the Athenians, and the oligarchs, who wanted to bring in the Lacedaemonians. Now in time of peace they could have had no pretext and would not have been so eager to call them in, but because it was war, and allies were to be had for either party to hurt their enemies and strengthen themselves at the same time, invitations to intervene came readily from those who wanted a new government. Civil war brought many hardships to the cities, such as happen and will always happen as long as human nature is the same, although they may be more or less violent or take different forms, depending on the circumstances in each case. In peace and prosperity, cities and private individuals alike are better minded because they are not plunged into the necessity of doing anything against their will; but war is a violent teacher: it gives most people impulses that are as bad as their situation when it takes away the easy supply of what they need for daily life.

Civil war ran through the cities; those it struck later heard what the first cities had done and far exceeded them in inventing artful means for attack and bizarre forms of revenge. And they reversed the usual way of using words to evaluate activities.[172] Ill-considered boldness was counted as loyal

---

172. "They reversed the usual way of using words": they applied terms of moral judgment in novel ways without changing their meanings, so as to commend

manliness; prudent hesitation was held to be cowardice in disguise, and moderation merely the cloak of an unmanly nature. A mind that could grasp the good of the whole was considered wholly lazy.[173] Sudden fury was accepted as part of manly valor, while plotting for one's own security was thought a reasonable excuse for delaying action.[174] A man who started a quarrel was always to be trusted, while one who opposed him was under suspicion. A man who made a plot was intelligent if it happened to succeed, while one who could smell out a plot was deemed even more clever. Anyone who took precautions, however, so as not to need to do either one, had been frightened by the other side (they would say) into subverting his own political party. In brief, a man was praised if he could commit some evil action before anyone else did, or if he could cheer on another person who had never meant to do such a thing.

Family ties were not so close as those of the political parties, because their members would readily dare to do anything on the slightest pretext. These parties, you see, were not formed under existing laws for the good, but for avarice in violation of established law. And the oaths they swore to each other had their authority not so much by divine law, as by their being partners in breaking the law. And if their opponents gave a good speech, if they were the stronger party, they did not receive it in a generous spirit, but with an eye to prevent its taking effect.

To take revenge was of higher value than never to have received injury. And as for oaths of reconciliation[175] (when there were any!), these were offered for the moment when both sides were at an impasse, and were in

---

what used to be thought evil and condemn what used to be thought good. Compare Plato's *Republic* 560d. See Nussbaum (1986: 404).

173. For this interpretation of a difficult sentence, I am grateful to Mark Gifford.

174. "Plotting for one's own security was thought a reasonable excuse for delaying action": this sentence is so sparing of words in the original that it allows a number of interpretations, of which these are a sample: *i. Long deliberation to avoid mistakes was considered a well-thought excuse for avoiding action (Gomme). ii. To plot against an enemy behind his back was perfectly legitimate self-defense (Warner). iii. Deliberation for one's safety was held to be a good excuse for abandoning one's party. iv. A man's plan for security gave others a reasonable pretext for defensive action, i.e. for a preemptive attack.*

175. "Oaths of reconciliation": oaths sworn between opposing parties, in contrast to the oaths party members swore to each other, which are treated in the preceding paragraph.

force only while neither side had help from abroad; but on the first opportunity, when one person saw the other unguarded and dared to act, he found his revenge sweeter because he had broken trust than if he had acted openly: he had taken the safer course, and he gave himself the prize for intelligence if he had triumphed by fraud. Evildoers are called skillful sooner than simpletons are called good, and people are ashamed to be called simpletons but take pride in being thought skillful.

The cause of all this was the desire to rule out of avarice and ambition, and the zeal for winning that proceeds from those two. Those who led their parties in the cities promoted their policies under decent-sounding names: "equality for ordinary citizens" [*plēthous isonomia politikē*] on one side, and "moderate aristocracy" [*aristokratia sōphrōn*] on the other. And though they pretended to serve the public in their speeches, they actually treated it as the prize for their competition; and striving by whatever means to win, both sides ventured on most horrible outrages and exacted even greater revenge, without any regard for justice or the public good. Each party was limited only by its own appetite at the time, and stood ready to satisfy its ambition of the moment either by voting for an unjust verdict or seizing control by force.

So neither side thought much of piety,[176] but they praised those who could pass a horrible measure under the cover of a fine speech. The citizens who remained in the middle were destroyed by both parties, partly because they would not side with them, and partly for envy that they might escape in this way.

[83]. Thus was every kind of wickedness afoot throughout all Greece by the occasion of civil wars. Simplicity, which is the chief cause of a generous spirit,[177] was laughed down and disappeared. Citizens were sharply divided into opposing camps, and, without trust, their thoughts were in battle array. No speech was so powerful, no oath so terrible, as to overcome this mutual hostility. The more they reckoned up their chances, the less hope they had for a firm peace, and so they were all looking to avoid harm from each other, and were unable to rely on trust. For the most part, those with the weakest minds had the greatest success, since a sense of their own

---

176. "Piety" : *eusebeia*. This evidently includes all of the virtues in which the Greek gods were supposed to take an interest.

177. "Simplicity, which is the chief cause of a generous spirit": literally, "simplicity (*to euēthes*), of which a generous spirit most takes part." This probably means that simplicity (or openness) is what best explains generosity. See my note on i.84.3 and Nussbaum (1986: 405 and 508, n.24).

5. Human Nature Laid Bare in Civil War

inferiority and the subtlety of their opponents put them into great fear that they would be overcome in debate or by schemes due to their enemies' intelligence. They therefore went immediately to work against them in action, while their more intelligent opponents, scornful and confident that they could foresee any attack, thought they had no need to take by force what might be gotten by wit. They were therefore unprotected, and so more easily killed.

Section 84 was not known to certain ancient authors who commented on the wider passage, and so is believed to be a work of imitation. I include it because it is thoroughly Thucydidean in thought and style, and of considerable interest in its own right:

[84] [Most of these atrocities, then, were commited first in Corcyra, including all the acts of revenge people take, when they have the opportunity, against rulers who have shown more arrogance than good sense, and all the actions some people choose unjustly to escape longstanding poverty. Most of these acted from a passionate desire for their neighbors' possessions, but there were also those who attacked the wealthy not for their own gain, but primarily out of zeal for equality, and they were the most carried away by their undisciplined anger to commit savage and pitiless attacks. Now that life had been thrown into confusion in the city, human nature—which is accustomed to violate justice and the laws—came to dominate law altogether, and showed itself with delight to be the slave of anger, the master of justice, and the enemy of anyone superior. Without the destructive force of envy, you see, people would not value revenge over piety, or profits over justice. When they want revenge on others, people are determined first to destroy without a trace the laws that commonly govern such matters, though it is only because of these that anyone in trouble can hope to be saved, even though anyone might be in danger someday and stand in need of such laws.]

Here Thucydides resumes:

[85] Such was the anger that the Corcyreans expressed in their city—the first against fellow citizens.

Eurymedon and the Athenians sailed away with their ships. Later, refugees from Corcyra—about five hundred of them had escaped—seized forts on the mainland and took control of the Corcyrean territory opposite the island, which they used as a base for plundering Corcyra, causing considerable damage and a severe famine that broke out in the city. Meanwhile, they sent ambassadors to Lacedaemon and Corinth about going home.[178] After a time, when nothing came of that, they got boats and hired mercenary soldiers, then crossed over to the island, about six hundred in all. There they burned their boats so that their only hope would be to take control of the land. They went up to Mt. Istone[179] and built a fort there; then they preyed on those in the city and took control of the land.

b. *The end of the Corcyrean insurgents [iv.47.3–48]*

In 425, the Athenian general Eurymedon returned to Corcyra and attacked the fort on Mt. Istone. The oligarchs there surrendered on condition that they be tried by the people of Athens. The Athenians, for their part, required that the oligarchs accept temporary imprisonment on an island, from which they must not try to escape.

The Corcyrean democrats were afraid Athens would pardon the oligarchs, so they enticed some of them to try escaping. The escape was discovered, and the Athenians, considering the treaty broken, turned their captives over to the Corcyreans. This is what happened next:

[47.3] When the Corcyreans took over the prisoners they shut them up in a large building and later brought them out twenty at a time, bound them together, and made them go down a path lined with hoplites drawn up on both sides. They were beaten and stabbed by the troops in the lines, whenever any of them was spotted as someone's personal enemy. And to speed up the laggards, men with whips followed them down.

[48] They took about sixty men from the building, drove them down the path, and killed them, while those inside the building thought they were only being moved to another place. When someone told them, and they saw the truth, they cried out to the Athenians and asked them to kill them if they wanted, but said that they were no longer willing to leave the building, and that, as long as they had the power, they would not allow anyone to come in.

The Corcyreans, however, had no intention of forcing their way in at the door; they climbed up on the roof of the building, tore off the roofing, and began throwing roof tiles and shooting arrows inside. The inmates defended themselves as well as they could, but most of them killed themselves either by stabbing their throats with arrows that had been shot at

178. I.e., asking for help in regaining power in Corcyra.
179. Mt. Pantocrator, the highest peak on the island.

5. Human Nature Laid Bare in Civil War

them or by strangling themselves with cords from beds that happened to be there or ropes they made from their own clothes.

This went on most of the night (for it happened at night); and so they perished either at their own hands by strangulation or else struck down from above. At daybreak the Corcyreans threw them criss-cross on wagons and carted them out of the city. The women they had captured at the fort were made slaves.

This is how the Corcyreans who had occupied the mountain fort were destroyed by the democrats; and at this point the civil war that had grown so large came to an end, at least as far as this war was concerned, since there was hardly anything left of one of the two sides.

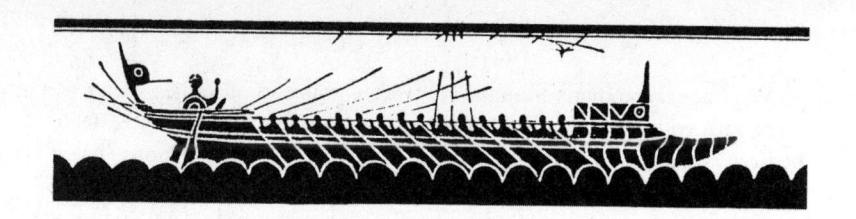

6. Justice and Power: Acanthus and Melos

a. The Spartans at Acanthus [iv.84.2–87]

In the summer of 424, the Lacedaemonian general Brasidas worked through Thrace (northern Greece) detaching cities from the Athenian empire wherever he could. Thucydides tells us that his virtue and good conduct made a positive impression on the cities there, winning many friends for Sparta. His arrival outside a city called Acanthus led to fierce argument in the city between the democrats (who favored Athens) and the oligarchs who had invited him:

[84.2] They let Brasidas address them, however, because the majority feared for their crops, which were still out in the fields; and so he persuaded them to let him in on his own and listen to him before they decided what to do. So Brasidas stood up before the people—he was a powerful speaker, for a Lacedaemonian—and spoke as follows:

THE SPEECH OF BRASIDAS

[85] My army and I were sent here, Acanthians, to make good the reason we Lacedaemonians gave for this war when we began it: to fight Athens for the freedom of Greece. If we were slow in coming it was because we underestimated the war back home, which we hoped would destroy Athens quickly without putting you at risk. So do not find fault with us for that. We are here now, as soon as we could get here, and we will try to bring down the Athenians with your help. But now I am astonished: Why are your gates shut against us? Why are you not glad to see us?

We Lacedaemonians thought we were coming to our allies—that we were with you in spirit before we actually got here, that you wanted us to be here. That is why, with all possible zeal, we took the enormous risk of marching many days through foreign territory. But if you people have a different plan—if you are standing against your own freedom and the freedom of the other Greeks—that would be terrible. And it's not only your opposition that concerns me, but the negative effect you will have on all the other cities I visit: they will all be less willing to join me if you, the first people I visit, with your reputation for strength and intelligence, refuse me. I will have no convincing explanation to offer, and they'll believe either that the freedom I bring is really injustice, or that my army is too weak and ineffective to protect you against the Athenians if they attack. And yet when I took this same army to relieve Nisaea, the Athenians did not dare risk battle, though they outnumbered us; and it is unlikely they would send as large an army as that against you.[180]

[86] As for me, I have come not to harm the Greeks but to free them; and I have bound the Lacedaemonians by the solemn oath that the allies I bring in will be autonomous. My purpose, moreover, is not to make you our allies by force or fraud; but, on the contrary, for us to be your allies against subjugation by Athens. Therefore I claim that, after the guarantees I have given, you have no reason to be suspicious of me or doubt that I am able to defend you; instead, you should join us with confidence.

Now if any of you are holding back for fear of certain people,[181] because you think we will turn the government over to them, take heart: you have my strongest guarantee that I did not come to take sides in civil war. I would not be bringing freedom in the strict sense, I think, if I set aside tradition and put the majority under the subjugation of the few or vice versa.[182] That would be worse than belonging to a foreign empire, and we

---

180. Here Brasidas is misleading the Acanthians. In fact the army he had at Nisaea had been larger than the one he now has, but even with that he had been reluctant to take on the Athenians. The Athenians had seized Nisaea (the port of Megara) earlier that year. Brasidas's army then came and occupied a position between Nisaea and Megara, to protect Megara. Seeing themselves outnumbered, the Athenians did not attack Megara. But they kept Nisaea. See iv.70–74 and iv.108.

181. "Certain people": oligarchs. The leading democrats no doubt feared reprisals from the oligarchs whom Sparta supported.

182. Again, Brasidas is misleading his audience. He had helped establish a narrow oligarchy in Megara earlier that year (iv.73–74).

Lacedaemonians would have no thanks for our trouble. Instead of honor and glory, we would be given the blame; and we would be openly guilty of just those offenses for which we are fighting Athens to the death—and it would be more hateful in us than in someone who had made no pretense to virtue. It is more shameful for men with a good reputation to overreach by means of an honest-looking fraud than to do so by an open use of force. Force moves with the justification of strength, which has been given by good fortune, while fraud works through the scheming of an unjust mind.

[87] That is how carefully we look after what matters most to us. The strongest assurance you could find, besides our oaths, lies in the facts: look at the facts behind our words and you will be compelled to see that it is to our advantage for us to do as I say.

Perhaps you will reply to my offer that it is beyond your power to join me, and you will protest that you wish us well and so should not be harmed by your refusal, that this freedom does not seem to you to be free of risk, and that though it is right to bring freedom to those who are able to accept it, justice forbids you to compel people to be free if they are unwilling. If you say that, I will call the gods and heroes of this place to witness that I came here to do good, but did not convince you; then I will try to force you over to our side by wasting your farmland.

Even so, I will not believe I am doing an injustice, since I have two utterly compelling reasons for this:[183] first, so that the Lacedaemonians will not be harmed by the taxes you will pay to Athens if, for all your goodwill, you do not join us; second, so that the other Greeks will not be prevented by you from escaping their subjugation. Otherwise, we Lacedaeminoians would have no good reason whatsoever for giving people freedom against their will, if it were not for the sake of some common good. Empire is not our goal; it is what we are working to stop in other people. And we would do an injustice to the greater number if we allowed you to stand against the autonomy we are trying to bring to all.

Think carefully about this. Strive to be the first in freedom for the Greeks and so win everlasting glory, save your personal possessions from destruction, and earn the name of highest valor for your entire city.

The people of Acanthus voted by secret ballot to rebel against Athens, persuaded by Brasidas' arguments and by their fears for their crops.

---

183. "Two utterly compelling reasons": *Kata duo anankas to eulogon.* Contrast this with Athenian appeals to *ananke*, which do not involve reasons, and do not issue, as these do, in justifications. See p. xxx.

b. Events leading to the Peace of Nicias [Summary]

Three main events led Athens and Sparta to come to terms: the Spartan defeat at Pylos, balanced by Athenian defeats at Amphipolis and Delium.

Pylos *(425)*. After the civil war in Corcyra, the war continued without major success or reversal for either side until 425. In that year an outpost of Athens in Sicily had been taken by Syracuse, and an Athenian fleet was sent out to Sicily. On the way, they seized and fortified the peninsula of Pylos on the west coast of the Peloponnesus and installed there a group of Messenian exiles who were trying to recover their homeland from Sparta. Sparta sent troops to recover Pylos, but a substantial number of them were isolated by the Athenians on the tiny island of Sphacteria and besieged there for some time. One hundred and twenty Spartan soldiers were captured when the Athenians finally attacked the island. This was such a blow to the Spartans that they offered terms of peace to Athens. Leaders such as Cleon, however, made the continuation of the war seem attractive to the Athenians, and the war dragged on until a series of reverses made the balance sheet more even.

Delium *(424)*. The Boeotians handed invading Athenian land forces a major defeat at a place called Delium north of Athens. This was one of the very few large-scale land battles of the period. It was at this battle that Socrates showed his famous courage in retreat (Plato, Apology *28e,* Laches *181b,* Symposium *221a ff.*).

Amphipolis *(424 and 422)*. In 424, our author Thucydides was a general with duties to protect Athenian interests in Thrace and elsewhere in northern Greece. While he was on the island of Thasos, the Spartans under Brasidas threatened the strategic Athenian colony of Amphipolis. Amphipolis had been founded by Pericles in 437/6 in a part of Thrace that was crucial to Athenian gold mining interests and also controlled access to timber reserves that were important to the Athenian navy. The new city had been settled with a mix of Athenian colonists and local people from northern Greece.

When the Spartan army arrived outside Amphipolis, the citizens who were loyal to Athens sent to Thucydides for help, but Brasidas offered terms that appealed to the majority of the citizens of Amphipolis, who surrendered the city to him and the Spartans. Thucydides arrived just too late to save the city. For this loss he was punished by exile from Athens. The story of Amphipolis is told in iv.104–8.

6. Justice and Power: Acanthus and Melos

This was a heavy loss to Athens. Cleon, the politician-general who was largely responsible for the success at Pylos, tried to regain Amphipolis in 422, but the attempt ended in defeat for Athens and death for Cleon. Although victorious, the Spartan general Brasidas was killed as well, and neither Athens nor Sparta had the will or the leadership to continue the war.

In 421 peace was sworn after negotiations led by the Athenian general Nicias, after whom the treaty is named. The Peace of Nicias was slightly more favorable to Athens than to Sparta, and was never really accepted by all of Sparta's allies. After describing the treaty, Thucydides tells us that it would not last, and that war would soon be resumed. In fact, he claims, warfare never really ended.

The Second Preface (v.26)

At this point in his History, Thucydides inserted a passage that is now known as his second preface:

This history also has been written by Thucydides of Athens in order as each event came to pass, by summers and winters, up to the time when the Lacedaemonians and their allies put an end to the Athenian empire and took the Long Walls and the Piraeus. At that point the war had lasted twenty-seven years in all.

As for the period of the treaty in the middle, anyone who thinks that this was not war is making a mistake. He should look at how the period was cut up by the actual events; then he'll find that it makes no sense to judge this a peace, when the two sides did not make the exchanges they had agreed on. Besides, there were violations on both sides in the Mantinean and Epidaurian wars, among other actions; and the allies in Thrace continued at war, while the Boeotians observed a mere ten-day truce.[184] So, counting the first ten-year war, the doubtful cessation of hostilities that followed it, and the war that grew out of that, you will find just that many years, if you add up the times, with only a few days left over. And for those who think there is some certainty in oracles, here is one case in which an oracle happened to be reliable.[185] I have remembered all along, from the beginning of the war right up to its end, that many people predicted it would last three times nine years.

---

184. Ten-day truce: probably a truce that either side could end on ten days' notice. Renewals every 10 days would have been impractical.
185. Thucydides looks down on those who trust oracles, soothsayers and the like (ii.54, v.103, vii.50, and vii.79).

I lived through all this at a good age to observe the war,[186] and I applied my mind to gaining accurate knowledge of each event. It turned out that I was living in exile for twenty years after my command at Amphipolis, and because I spent time with both sides (more time, in fact with the Peloponnesians, owing to my exile) I was able to observe things more closely and without distraction. So I will now discuss the quarrel that followed the ten-years' war, the dissolution of the treaty, and what came afterwards as they waged war.

c. The Melian dialogue [v.84–116]

[84] (In 416) the Athenians made war against the island of Melos, with thirty ships of their own, six from Chios, and two from Lesbos. The Athenian contingent was twelve hundred hoplites, three hundred archers, and twenty mounted archers, while the allies, including islanders, contributed about fifteen hundred hoplites. The Melians are a colony of the Lacedaemonians,[187] and so did not want to be subject to Athens as the other islands were. At the beginning, they had stayed at peace with both sides. Later on, however, when the Athenians drove them to it by wasting their land, they were openly at war.

Now the Athenian generals, Cleomedes and Tisias, set up camp in Melian territory with these forces. Before doing any harm to the Melian land, they first sent ambassadors to negotiate. The Melians refused to bring these ambassadors before the common people, but ordered them to deliver their message to a few officials and leading citizens. The Athenians spoke as follows:

[85] *Athenians:* Since we may not speak before the common people, for fear that they would be led astray if they heard our persuasive and unanswerable arguments all at once in a continuous speech—we know that is what you had in mind in bringing us to the few leading citizens—you who are sitting here should make your situation still more secure: answer every particular point, not in a single speech, but interrupting us immediately whenever we say anything that seems wrong to you. And first, tell us whether you like this proposal.

186. To be a general in 424 Thucydides should have been over thirty. If he was a very young general, he would have been born about 455, and would have been in his early twenties when the war began and in his early fifties when he wrote this sentence.

187. Herodotus viii.48.

6. Justice and Power: Acanthus and Melos

[86] *To this the Melian Council replied*: We would not find fault with the fairness of a leisurely debate, but these acts of war—happening right now, not in the future—do not seem to be consistent with that. We see that you have come to be judges of this proceeding, so we expect the result to be this: if we make the better case for justice and do not surrender because of that, we will have war; but if you win the argument, we will have servitude.

[87] *Athenians:* Well, then, if you came to this meeting to reason on the basis of suspicions about the future, or for any other purpose than to work out how to save your city on the basis of what you see here today—we should stop now. But if that is your purpose, let's speak to it.

[88] *Melians:* People in our situation can be expected to turn their words and thoughts to many things, and should be pardoned for that. Since, however, this meeting is to consider only the point of our survival, let's have our discussion on the terms you have proposed, if that is your decision.

[89] *Athenians:* For our part, we will not make a long speech no one would believe, full of fine moral arguments—that our empire is justified because we defeated the Persians, or that we are coming against you for an injustice you have done to us. And we don't want you to think you can persuade us by saying that you did not fight on the side of the Lacedaemonians in the war, though you were their colony, or that you have done us no injustice. Instead, let's work out what we can do on the basis of what both sides truly accept: we both know that decisions about justice are made in human discussions only when both sides are under equal compulsion;[188] but when one side is stronger, it gets as much as it can, and the weak must accept that.

[90] *Melians:* Well, then, since you put your interest in place of justice, our view must be that it is in your interest not to subvert this rule that is good for all: that a plea of justice and fairness should do some good for a man who has fallen into danger, if he can win over his judges, even if he is not perfectly persuasive. And this rule concerns you no less than us: if you ever stumble, you might receive a terrible punishment and be an example to others.

---

188. "Under equal compulsion": justice is relevant when both sides must feel the force of law; but when one side is more powerful, it does not apply. The Athenians are not saying that might makes right; merely that might supersedes right between unequals. For Brasidas' view see **iv.86**.

[91] *Athenians:* We are not downhearted at the prospect of our empire's coming to an end, though it may happen. Those who rule over others (such as the Lacedaemonians, who are not our present concern) are not as cruel to those they conquer as are a subject people who attack their rulers and overcome them. But let us be the ones to worry about that danger. We will merely declare that we are here for the benefit of our empire, and we will speak for the survival of your city: we would like to rule over you without trouble, and preserve you for our mutual advantage.

[92] *Melians:* But how could it be as much to our advantage to serve, as it is yours to rule?

[93] *Athenians:* Because if you obey, you will save yourselves from a very cruel fate; and we will reap a profit from you if we don't destroy you.

[94] *Melians:* So you would not accept a peaceful solution? We could be friends rather than enemies, and fight with neither side.

[95] *Athenians:* No. Your enmity does not hurt us as much as your friendship would. That would be a sign of our weakness to those who are ruled by us; but your hatred would prove our power.

[96] *Melians:* Why? Do your subjects reason so unfairly that they put us, who never had anything to do with you, in the same category as themselves, when most of them were your colonies, or else rebels whom you defeated?

[97] *Athenians:* Why not? They think we have as good a justification for controlling you as we do for them; they say the independent cities survive because they are powerful, and that we do not attack them because we are afraid. So when you have been trampled down by us, you will add not only to our empire, but to our security, by not staying independent. And this is especially true because you are islanders who are weaker than the others, and we are masters of the sea.

[98] *Melians:* But don't you think there is safety in our proposal of neutrality? Here again, since you have driven us away from a plea for justice, and are telling us to surrender to whatever is in your interest, we must show you what would be good for us, and try to persuade you that your interests coincide with ours. Won't this turn the people who are now neutral into your enemies? Once they've seen this, they will expect you to

attack them eventually also. And what would this accomplish, but to make the enemies you already have still greater, and to make others your enemies against their will, when they would not have been so?

[99] *Athenians:* We do not think the free mainlanders will be terrible enemies to us; it will be long before they so much as keep guard against us. But islanders worry us—those outside the empire like you, and those under the empire who resent the force that keeps them that way—these may indeed act recklessly and bring themselves and us into foreseeable danger.

[100] *Melians:* Yes, but if you would face such extreme danger to retain your empire, and if your subjects would do so to get free of you, then wouldn't it be great weakness and cowardice on our part, since we are still free, not to go to every extreme rather than be your subjects?

[101] *Athenians:* No, not if you think sensibly. Your contest with us is not an equal match of courage against courage; no honor is lost if you submit. This is a conference about your survival and about not resisting those who are far stronger than you.

[102] *Melians:* But we know that in war the odds sometimes are more even than the difference in numbers between the two sides, and that if we yield, all our hope is lost immediately; but if we hold out, we can still hope to stand tall.

[103] *Athenians:* Hope! It *is* a comfort in danger, and though it may be harmful to people who have many other advantages, it will not destroy them. But people who put everything they have at risk will learn what hope is when it fails them, for hope is prodigal by nature; and once they have learned this, it is too late to take precautions for the future. Do not let this happen to you, since you are weak and have only this one throw of the dice. And do not be like the ordinary people who could use human means to save themselves but turn to blind hopes when they are forced to give up their sensible ones—to divination, oracles, and other such things that destroy men by giving them hope.[189]

---

189. The application of this warning to the Sicilian Expedition is striking. In Sicily the Athenian armada was destroyed because their general, Nicias, had too much faith in divination. Again and again during the war, the Athenians were beguiled by hope into taking great risks. For the Athenian tendency to hope see **i.70, i.74, ii.42, ii.62, vii.77**. For the way hope leads to crime, see **iii.45**.

[104] *Melians:* You can be sure we think it hard to contend against your power and good fortune, unless we might do so on equal terms. Nevertheless, we trust that our good fortune will be no less than yours. The gods are on our side, because we stand innocent against men who are unjust. And as for power, what we lack will be supplied by the alliance we will make with the Lacedaemonians, who must defend us as a matter of honor, if only because we are related to them. So our confidence is not as totally unreasonable as you might think.

[105] *Athenians:* Well, the favor of the gods should be as much on our side as yours. Neither our principles nor our actions are contrary to what men believe about the gods, or would want for themselves. Nature always compels gods (we believe) and men (we are certain) to rule over anyone they can control. We did not make this law, and we were not the first to follow it; but we will take it as we found it and leave it to posterity forever, because we know that you would do the same if you had our power, and so would anyone else. So as far as the favor of the gods is concerned, we have no reason to fear that we will do worse than you.

As for your opinion about the Lacedaemonians, your trust that they will help you in order to preserve their own honor—we admire your blessed innocence, but we don't envy you your foolishness. Granted, the Lacedaemonians do show a high degree of virtue towards each other according to their local customs; but one could say many things about their treatment of other people. We'll make this as brief and as clear as possible: of all the people we know, they are the ones who make it most obvious that they hold whatever pleases them to be honorable, and whatever profits them to be just. So your plan will not support your hope for survival, and it now seems reckless.

[106] *Melians:* But on that point we most firmly trust the Lacedaemonians to pursue their own advantage—*not* to betray their colonists, the Melians, for in doing so they would benefit their enemies by losing the confidence of their friends among the Greeks.

[107] *Athenians:* Don't you realize that advantage lies with safety, and that the pursuit of justice and honor brings danger? Which the Lacedaemonians are usually least willing to face?

[108] *Melians:* But we believe they will take a dangerous mission in hand for our sake. They will think it safer to do so for us than for anyone else,

since we are close enough to the Peloponnesus for action, and we will be more faithful to them than others because our kinship gives us common views.

[109] *Athenians:* But the good will of those who call for help does not offer any security to those who might fight for them. They will be safe only if they have superior power in action. The Lacedaemonians are more aware of this than anyone else; at least they have no confidence in their own forces, and therefore take many allies along with them when they attack a neighbor. So while we are masters of the sea, you cannot reasonably expect them to cross over to an island.

[110] *Melians:* Yes, but they may have others to send. The Sea of Crete is wide; it is harder for its masters to seize ships there, than it is for people who want to escape to slip through. And if the Lacedaemonians failed in this, they would turn their arms against your own land or the lands of your allies that have still not been invaded by Brasidas.[190] And then you will be troubled about your own land, and that of your allies, and no longer about a country that does not concern you.

[111] *Athenians*: With your experience of what might happen, you are surely not unaware that Athens has never given up a single siege through fear of anyone else.[191] We are struck by the fact that though you said you would confer about your survival, in all this discussion you have never mentioned a single thing that people could rely on and expect to survive. Your strongest points are mere hopes for the future, and your actual resources are too small for your survival in view of the forces arrayed against you. Your planning will be utterly irrational, unless (after letting us withdraw from the meeting) you decide on a more sensible policy. Do not be distracted by a sense of honor; this destroys people all too often, when dishonor and death stand before their eyes. Many have been so overcome by the power of this seductive word, "honor," that even when they foresee the dangers to which it carries them, they are drawn by a mere word into an

---

190. Brasidas was the Spartan general who persuaded Acanthus and other cities to rebel from Athens in 424 and in 422 defeated an Athenian army at Amphipolis, where he was fatally wounded.

191. This was quite true at the time, and is borne out by the histories of Mytilene and Potidaea, both of which were taken after long sieges while Lacedaemonian forces were harassing Attica. The point foreshadows the siege of Syracuse, however, which the Athenians will be forced to abandon.

action that is an irreparable disaster; and so, intentionally, they fall into a dishonor that is more shameful than mere misfortune, since it is due to their own foolishness.

You must guard against this if you are to deliberate wisely, and you must not think it unseemly for you to submit to a city of such great power, which offers such reasonable conditions—to be our allies, and to enjoy your own property under tribute to us. You are being given a choice between war and survival: do not make the wrong decision out of a passion for victory. Remember what is usually the best course: do not give way to equals, but have the right attitude towards your superiors and use moderation towards your inferiors. So think about this when we withdraw from the meeting, and keep this often in your mind: you are considering what to do for your country—your only country—and this one discussion will determine whether it meets success or failure.

[112] So the Athenians withdrew from the conference, and the Melians, left to themselves, decided on much the same position as they had taken in the debate. Then the Melians answered as follows:

Melians: Athenians, our resolution is no different from what it was before: we will not, in a short time, give up the liberty in which our city has remained for the seven hundred years since its foundation. We will trust in the fortune of the gods, which has preserved it up to now, and in the help of men—the Lacedaemonians—and we will do our best to maintain our liberty. We offer this, however: we will be your friends; we will be enemies to neither side; and you will depart from our land, after making whatever treaty we both think fit.

[113] That was the answer of the Melians. As they broke off the conference, the Athenians said:

Athenians: It seems to us, on the basis of this discussion, that you are the only men who think you know the future more clearly than what is before your eyes, and who, through wishful thinking, see doubtful events as if they had already come to pass. You have staked everything on your trust in hope, good fortune, and the Lacedaemonians; and you will be ruined in everything.

[114] Then the Athenian ambassadors went back to their camp. When the generals saw that the Melians would not submit, they turned immedi-

ately to war and surrounded the Melian city with a wall, after dividing up the work with their allies. After that, the Athenians left a contingent of Athenian and allied troops there to guard the city by land and sea, and went home with the greater part of their army. The rest stayed behind to besiege the place.

[115] (About the same time, the Argives invaded the country around Phlious, where they were ambushed by Phlians and exiles from Argos, losing about eighty men. Meanwhile, the Athenians at Pylos brought in a great deal of plunder from the Lacedaemonians. The Lacedaemonians did not go to war over this, because that would have broken the treaty. Instead they proclaimed that any of their people could plunder the Athenians in return. The Corinthians were at war with the Athenians, but this was over certain disputes of their own, and the rest of the Peloponnesus kept quiet.)

The Melians, in a night attack, captured part of the Athenian wall opposite the market place, killed the men there, and brought in grain and as many supplies as they could. Then they went back and kept quiet. After that the Athenians maintained a better watch.

And so the summer ended.

[116] (The following winter, the Lacedaemonians were about to march into the land of Argos, but they returned when they found that the sacrifices for the border crossing were not favorable. The Argives suspected some of their own people of being involved in the Lacedaemonian plan; they captured some of them, and the rest escaped.)

About the same time, the Melians took another part of the Athenian wall, because there were not many men to guard it. After that another army came from Athens under the command of Philocrates. Now that the city was besieged in force, there was some treachery, and the Melians on their own initiative surrendered to the Athenians, to be dealt with as the Athenians decided: they killed all the men of military age and made slaves of the women and children. Later, they settled the place themselves, sending five hundred colonists.

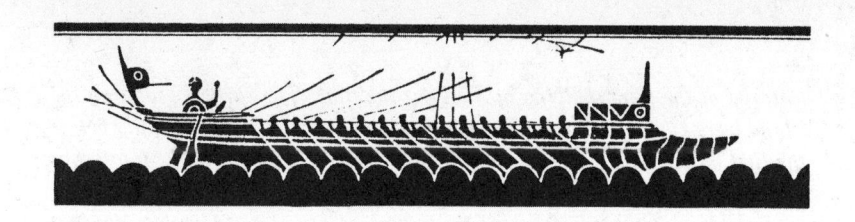

7. The Sicilian Expedition

That same winter, immediately after the destruction of Melos, Athens decided to attempt the conquest of the Greeks on Sicily, an enormous undertaking and a very dangerous one, as the Athenians were not well informed about the relative strengths of their allies and their enemies in Sicily. Athens had long wanted to establish bases on Sicily,[192] and evidently hoped also to establish sources of grain and timber in the western Mediterranean. Athenians in favor of returning to war thought that control over substantial parts of Sicily would increase Athenian power to the point at which the Peloponnesians would not be able to resist them. They wished, however, to make it appear that their expedition was merely a response to a call for aid from their allies.

Leontini, a Greek city in Sicily, had been an ally of Athens. In 422 its democracy was overthrown by an army from Syracuse and its people sent into exile, while its aristocrats took up residence in Syracuse. At the time, Athens had been unable to forge an alliance that would enable it to rescue the people of Leontini; but anti-Syracusan sentiment was strong in Athens, and many Athenians were itching for a chance to cut Syracuse down to size.

Conveniently, in 416, the Sicilian city of Egesta sought help from Athens. They had engaged in a war with their neighbor Selinus, which was being helped by Syracuse. A delegation from Egesta came to Athens asking for help; meanwhile, Athenian ambassadors who had been to Egesta to evaluate the situation there returned with glowing reports.

a. Sicilian antiquities [Summary of vi.2–6]

Thucydides begins his account of the Sicilian expedition by reviewing the

192. For earlier attempts by Athens see, for example, iv.1 and iv.24.

histories of the peoples living in Sicily at the time. The earliest people on the island were known as Sicels, who were said to have migrated from Italy before the first millennium B.C.E. They were later pushed mainly into the interior as Greeks settled along the eastern and southern coasts.

Egesta (sometimes known as Segesta) was a city of non-Greek origin that had adopted Greek culture. Syracuse, the largest and most powerful of the Greek cities, was Dorian in origin, as were most of the Sicilian Greeks. Catana and Leontini were exceptions, Ionian cities founded as colonies from Chalcis in Euboea, the long island that runs north of Attica. After taking over Leontini, Syracuse was riding high, and the potential friends of Athens in Sicily needed help more than ever. Athens therefore welcomed the offer of the Egestans to pay for the cost of a venture into Sicily.

[In fact, the situation was worse than the Athenians could have known. Egesta was lying about its resources, and would not be able to support an Athenian expedition. Leontini was defeated. The Sicels were naturally hostile to the Greek colonies on their island, but could not be relied upon to support the growth of the Athenian empire. Syracuse was now a city of mixed cultural heritage with a tradition of democracy; no doubt some of its citizens would support Athens, but this support would turn out to be much weaker than expected.]

A brief report of actions in Argos and Macedon brings Thucydides' account of the sixteenth year of the war to a close (vi.7).

b. Debate at Athens [vi.8–26]

[vi.8] Next summer, in early spring (in 415), the Athenian ambassadors returned from Sicily along with the ambassadors from Egesta, who brought sixty talents of uncoined silver as one month's pay for the sixty ships they wanted Athens to send.[193] The Athenians called an assembly and heard the same story from both sets of ambassadors, their own and those from Egesta. It was attractive but not true, especially the claim about the money—that they had a great store of it ready in their temples and in their public treasury.[194] On hearing this, the Athenians voted to send sixty ships to Sicily under the command of Alcibiades, Nicias, and Lamachus, with independent authority.[195] Their mission was to assist the people of

---

193. On the value of a talent, see glossary. This is the going rate for troops serving a long way from home (iii.17). There would have been two hundred men to a ship.

194. In fact, only thirty talents were available, as the Athenians discovered on their arrival in Sicily (vi.46). Thucydides says the ambassadors had been fooled by a false display of wealth. The temple at Egesta was begun on an elegant plan but never completed. The shell is still standing.

7. The Sicilian Expedition

Egesta against those of Selinus, to resettle Leontini if the war went well enough for them, and to carry out other actions in Sicily in whatever way they judged best for the Athenians.[196]

Four days later, the people assembled again to consider how to equip the fleet as quickly as possible, and to vote for whatever else the generals would need on the voyage. But Nicias had been put in command without his consent, for he thought the city had made the wrong decision to take on the conquest of all of Sicily—an enormous task—on a slight and specious pretext. So he came forward with the intention of changing their minds, and gave this advice to the Athenians:

SPEECH OF NICIAS

[9] Although this assembly was called to deliberate on the preparation we should make for the voyage of our fleet against Sicily, still it seems to me that we should once again consider whether it would be better not to send it at all, and not to draw on ourselves a war that is no business of ours, after so short a deliberation on so weighty an affair, and taking the advice of men who are not of our race.[197] For my part, I would gain honor from this expedition; and as for the danger to my life, I am less afraid than others, though I think one can be just as good a citizen by having a regard for one's own life and property: a person like that will want the city to prosper especially for his own sake. But as I have never before spoken anything that is against my conscience in order to gain higher honor for myself, I shall not do so now: I shall say only what I find to be the best. My speech would be too weak to prevail over your character if I advised you to save what you have and not risk what is in your hands for a gain that is uncertain and lies in the future. Still, I will let you know that your haste is unseasonable, and you will not easily achieve your goals.

[10] I say that you will leave many enemies here, and in sailing there you evidently want to draw new enemies towards you. Perhaps you think

---

195. The three generals could act without consulting the assembly. As the three generals shared power equally, it was necessary for at least two of them to agree on any decision.

196. The "other actions" consisted of the conquest of Syracuse, which, for diplomatic reasons, could not be part of the official mission.

197. Egesta, or Segesta, was a Hellenized city of northwestern Sicily. Its population, however, was not Greek by origin, but claimed to be descended from the Trojans.

that the peace treaty you made with the Lacedaemonians is firm;[198] in fact it will be a treaty in name only, even if you keep still (that is the result of what some of you—and some of the enemy—have done). But if a considerable force of yours ever fails, the attack our enemies make on us will be swift indeed. They only agreed to this treaty in the first place because circumstances compelled them to do so,[199] and they lost more face than we did; since then, many points in the treaty have come under dispute. Besides, there are some who utterly refuse to accept it, and they are by no means the weakest.[200] Some [the Corinthians] are at war with us already; others [the Thebans] are maintaining a ten-day truce with us because the Lacedaemonians are keeping still. But it is more than likely that if we divide our forces—as we're now in a hurry to do—they will be glad to join the Sicilians in an attack on us, since they preferred them as allies to many others in former times.

It behooves a man,[201] therefore, to consider these things, not to run into new dangers when the future of our city is up in the air, and not to seek a new empire before we have quite secured the one we have already. The Chalcideans of Thrace, after so many years of revolt, are still not tamed, and others on the mainland are of doubtful obedience.

We are rushing to the aid of Egesta, we say, because she is our ally and has been treated unfairly; but those who have done *us* an injustice by rebelling—well, we shall punish them some time in the future! [11] Yet if we subdue the Chalcideans, we could keep them down, while if we take control of Sicily, we would find it hard to rule so many people at such a distance. Now it would be foolishness for someone to attack people he can't hold down, when, if he fails, he will be in a very different condition from that in which he started.

As for the Sicilians, it seems to me, at least as things now stand, that they will be even less dangerous to us if they *do* fall under the rule of Syracuse. And yet that is what the people of Egesta are trying to use to frighten us. As things are, some individual cities may come in because they favor the Lacedaemonians; but there is no reason why one empire should attack the other. If Syracuse had an empire, then the same people would probably wipe it out, and on the same principle, as would apply to their

---

198. Peace of Nicias, 421–14.

199. See p. 100.

200. Corinth, Thebes, Megara and Elis were not parties to the Peace of Nicias.

201. The man in question is Alcibiades. Throughout the speech of Nicias, personal references to Alcibiades become progressively less indirect.

7. The Sicilian Expedition

pulling down our empire with the help of the Peloponnesians.[202]

The Greeks in Sicily will fear us most if we never come, and next to that if we show our power and then quickly withdraw. We all know, you see, that people are most impressed by a threat that is farthest away and least liable to have its reputation put to the test. But if we fail in any way, they will immediately despise us and join with our enemies here to attack us. That is just what has happened to you Athenians in regard to the Lacedaemonians and their allies: because you have done better against them than you expected (considering how frightened you were of them), you despise them now, and so you are turning against Sicily. You ought not to be puffed up by the misfortunes of your enemies; you should be confident only if your strategy is better than theirs. And don't think that the Lacedaemonians have set their minds on anything other than how they can repair their reputation after their recent disgrace. They are determined to overthrow us if they can—and all the more because they have been working so hard and so long to cultivate a reputation for excellence [aretē]. So if we are sensible we shall see that the real issue is not about the people of Egesta, who are not even Greek, but about how we may rush to our own defense against the insidious plots of a city that works through oligarchy [i.e. Sparta].

[12] We should also remember that we have only recently been given a rest from plague and war to allow our numbers and our money to increase; and it is only fair [dikaion] for us to spend this here, rather than on these refugees[203] who are begging for assistance; it is to their advantage to tell a specious lie and contribute only words, while their friends bear all the danger—they'll not thank their friends as they deserve if they win, and they'll destroy their friends for company if they lose.

Now there may be someone here who is delighted at being put in command and will advise you to sail—entirely for ends of his own, especially if he is rather young for such a command. He may wish to be admired for his horse-breeding and so, owing to his heavy expenses, he may aim at a profit from this command.[204] If there is such a man, do not let him purchase his personal splendor at this great risk to the city. Remember, men like that

---

202. The reasoning is odd, but consistent with Thucydides' view that people naturally want to tear down any empire.

203. The people of Leontini were refugees after their defeat in 422 by Syracuse.

204. Here Nicias plainly refers to Alcibiades, whose extravagance on horses had made him famous. Alcibiades was about thirty-six years old at the time.

defraud the people and waste their own money as well. Besides, this is an important matter; it is not the sort of thing a young man should decide, let alone take hastily in hand.

[13] When I see the supporters this man has mustered sitting here, I am afraid. You older men, I urge you if you are sitting next to one of those people: do not to be ashamed if they think you a coward for voting against war, and do not be sick (as they are) with yearning for what is not here. Keep in mind that the least success comes by way of desire, and the most by planning ahead. Raise your hands against this for the sake of your city, because it is running into greater danger now than ever before. Vote to observe the old boundaries between the Sicilians and us. There is nothing wrong with those boundaries—the Ionian Gulf if you sail along the coast, the Sicilian Sea if you sail directly across. Tell the Sicilians to manage their own affairs and settle their differences on their own. And to Egesta, send this particular answer: since they began the war against Selinus without the Athenians, they should end it in the same way, entirely by themselves. And tell them we will not make alliances after this as we used to do, with men whom we defend when *they* are in trouble, but who cannot give us any help when *we* are in need.

[14] And you, President of the Assembly, if you think it your job to take care of the city, and if you wish to be a good citizen, put this once more to the question, and let the Athenians speak to it again. If you are afraid to set aside custom by putting this to a second vote,[205] keep in mind that no one will blame you for doing this before all these witnesses. People will think that you are a physician to a city that has made a bad decision; and that good leadership is shown by one who does his best to benefit his city, or at least does no harm of his own will.[206]

[15] Nicias spoke along those lines, but most of the Athenians who took the floor advised against setting aside the earlier vote and urged them to make the expedition, while a few took the other side. Alcibiades made the most spirited case for the expedition partly out of his desire to cross Nicias (with whom he had been at odds on other points of state) and because Nicias had made a slanderous reference to him. Mainly, however, it was because he wanted to have a command and hoped to be the man who would take both Sicily and Carthage for Athens, and, with success, to increase his

---

205. "If you are afraid to set aside custom": *Luein tous nomous*. It was not against the law to put an issue twice to a vote, but it was unusual to do so.
206. Cf. Hippocrates, *Epidemics* I.xi.

own personal wealth and glory. Because he was highly esteemed by the citizens, he had desires that were too vast for his actual estate to support, for horse-breeding and other expenses as well. Later on this was one of the main causes of the destruction of Athens.[207] The people were alarmed by his highly unconventional personal life and by the ambitious plans he made for every little thing he did. So they thought he dreamed of being a tyrant, and they became his enemies. Even though his public management of the war was excellent, they were all so displeased with his private life that they put other people in charge. And this led to the defeat of the city not long afterwards.

At this time, however, Alcibiades came forward and gave this advice to the Athenians:

SPEECH OF ALCIBIADES

[16] Really, Athenians, I have a better claim than anyone else to have this command. (I am compelled to begin with this issue since Nicias raised it.) I consider myself quite worthy of this position, because what has made me notorious has also won glory for my ancestors and myself, and, besides, has helped my country. The other Greeks thought our city more powerful than it really was because of my elegant appearance at the Olympic Games, when before that they had hoped they'd beaten us down in the war. I entered seven chariots there (more than any one man had entered before); I won first, second, and fourth place; and in everything I displayed the magnificence of a winner.[208] Such actions ordinarily earn honor, but they earn a reputation for power as well.

As for my expenses in the city for dramatic festivals and my other splendid largesse, it is only natural that my fellow citizens feel envy; but outsiders see this as strength. And this so-called foolishness is really quite useful, when a man helps both himself and his city at private expense. There's no injustice in being above equality if you think well of yourself; since a person who is doing badly does not make anyone else a partner in *his* fortune

---

207. After a period of exile in which he collaborated with Sparta (415–12), Alcibiades redeemed himself by leading the Athenian war effort in the eastern Aegean with a great measure of success between 411 and 406. He was held responsible, however, for a mistake made by one of his subordinates that had resulted in significant losses. He was exiled again two years before Athens' final defeat in 404.

208. At the Olympic Games of 416. Only the very rich could afford to equip and train even one chariot.

either. If a man will not even greet us when we are down on our luck, then, when things go well for us, he should be equally content if we look down on him—or else, if he insists on equality, he should give the same in return. I know that all of those people who are as brilliantly successful as I am will cause pangs of envy as long as they live (especially to their peers, but also to everyone they meet); after their deaths, however, they will leave a legacy of people who claim a kinship with them that never existed, and a country that boasts of them not as strangers or sinners, but as their very own citizens who have done fine things.

That is what I aim at, that is what has made me notorious in my private life. Now consider whether I handle public affairs any the worse. Without great risk or expense to you I brought together the greatest powers of the Peloponnesus and made the Lacedaemonians stake everything they had on one day's battle at Mantinea and though they won the battle they have not yet recovered their confidence.[209]

[17] Here is the work of that youth and foolishness of mine, which is supposed to be unnatural: I dealt with Peloponnesian power by giving good arguments, my enthusiasm won their confidence, and I persuaded them. Don't be afraid of these qualities now, but make use of our services while I am still in my prime and Nicias is thought to be lucky.

Do not abrogate your decision about this voyage on the grounds that the power you will encounter there is great. The cities in Sicily are packed with a mixed rabble of various peoples, you see, and easily shift to admit newcomers as citizens. As a result, no one thinks of this as his own country, so they are not sufficiently armed to defend their own lives, and they do not have the usual fortifications for the defense of their land. Each person looks instead only to what he can get from the commonwealth either by a persuasive speech or by civil war, and keeps his property in readiness to move to another land if he should fail. It is not reasonable to expect that a crowd like this would either give ear to a single policy or adopt a common plan of action. If we say anything to please them, they will almost certainly come over one by one, especially if they are divided by civil war, as we hear they are.[210]

The truth is they do not have as many hoplites as they boast of; and the rest of the Greek population is not as large in each city as they say it is. Even

---

209. Alcibiades helped form an Athenian alliance with the Peloponnesian states of Argos, Elis, and Mantinea. These allies posed a threat to the Spartans but were defeated at Mantinea in 418.

210. Cf. the speech of Hermocrates, a Syracusan who called upon the Sicilian Greeks to unite against the Athenian threat in 424 (iv.59–64, esp. 61).

Greece has greatly falsified its numbers, and is scarcely armed enough for the current war.

So the situation there is as I have said, from the reports I have heard; and it will be even easier, since we will have a great many foreigners who will take our side through hatred of Syracuse,[211] and there will be nothing to hinder us at home if you make the right decisions. Our ancestors won the empire at a time when they had all the enemies we now say we would leave behind if we sail—and the Persians besides—and *their* only strength lay in their naval superiority. Besides, the Peloponnesians have never had less hope against us than now. Even if they were at full strength and even if we did not sail, they would be able to invade our land, but they can do us no harm by sea, since we are leaving a fleet behind us that is large enough to oppose them.

[18] What reasonable case could we make for holding back? What excuse could we make to our allies in Sicily for denying them assistance? We ought to defend them, if only because we have sworn to do so, without objecting that they have not aided us in return. We did not take them into our alliance so that they would come to our assistance, but so that they would trouble our enemies there and so prevent them from coming against us here.

This is how we got our empire—as did everyone else who rules—by eagerly coming to the support of anyone who calls on us, whether Greek or foreign. If we all sat still, or waited to decide which race of people we should help, then we would be adding little to our own empire, and therefore putting it at greater risk.[212] In dealing with a stronger power, one should not only defend oneself when it attacks; one should take advance action to preempt an attack. We cannot control the size of empire we want as we would a budget: in our situation we are compelled to plan new conquests as well as not to let our old subjects go free, because if we do not rule others we run the risk of being ruled by them ourselves.[213] You should not weigh peace in the same balance as others do unless you plan to change your way of life to match theirs.

Let us conclude, then, that sailing to Sicily will increase our power at home, and let us make the voyage, so that we may cast down the pride of the Peloponnesians and show them the contempt we have for the current

---

211. "A great many foreigners": these were Sicels, early settlers on Sicily most of whom resented the Greek colonies.

212. This is a reply to Nicias, who had opposed helping the Egestans because they were not Greek (vi.9).

213. Cf. **ii.62** and **63**.

peace by sailing against Sicily. And along with this we will either become masters of all of Greece by the addition of those cities, as we expect, or we will at least ruin Syracuse, to the benefit of ourselves and our allies. As for our safety, our ships will protect us whether we are successful and stay, or whether we leave; since we will be masters of the sea against all the Sicilians put together.

Don't give in to Nicias' arguments for his do-nothing policy. Don't let him distract you from this expedition by starting a quarrel between the young men and their elders. Follow the usual procedure instead, as our ancestors did when they brought us to our present height[214] by consulting young and old together. Try to advance the cause of our city by the same means now. And don't think that either youth or age has any power without the other: remember that the greatest strength comes from a mixture of the simplest people with the middle sort and those who make the most exact judgments, all together. Keep this in mind, also: that a city is like anything else: if it rests, it will wear itself out by itself. All human skills decay, but the waging of war continually adds to a city's experience and puts it in the habit of resisting the enemy in action, rather than making speeches. On the whole, I find that if a city which is used to being active grows idle, it will quickly be destroyed by this change; and the safest way for a people to live is to conduct civic affairs according to their current laws and customs for better or for worse, with the least possible change.[215]

[19] So spoke Alcibiades. Then the ambassadors from Egesta and the refugees from Leontini came forward, reminded them of their oaths, and begged them as suppliants to come to their help. When the Athenians had heard all this, they were far more earnestly bent on the expedition than they had been before. When Nicias saw that his earlier arguments would no longer sway them, he thought he might change their minds by insisting that the expedition be equipped on a very large scale. So he came forward again and spoke:

NICIAS' SECOND SPEECH

[20] Because I see you are entirely bent on this expedition, Athenians, I wish it the success we desire. I will, however, deliver my judgment on the matter as it stands now. From the reports I have heard, we are setting out

214. Cf. Pericles' remarks at **i.144**.
215. Cf. **iii.37**.

7. The Sicilian Expedition

against great cities that are not subject to one another and do not have the need for change that would make them welcome a shift from harsh servitude to easier masters, or give them any reason to prefer our empire to freedom.[216] Besides, there are a great many Greek cities for one island: in addition to Naxos and Catana (which I hope will join us because of their kinship with Leontini[217]) there are seven others armed in all respects mostly as we are.

The two we are mainly sailing against, Selinus and Syracuse, are the most powerful of these; they have many hoplites and archers and javelin-throwers, as well as many triremes and a mob of people to fill them.[218] They have a lot of money, some in private hands, some in the temples in Selinus; and the Syracusans have taxes coming in from some of the foreigners besides. Their main superiority to us is that they abound in horses and that they use their own grain rather than importing it.[219]

[21] Against a power like that we need more than a fleet with a small army; a large force of foot-soldiers must sail with them if we mean to do anything worthy of our plan and not be kept off the land by their many horsemen, especially if the cities there are terrified of us and join together, so that only Egesta proves to be our friend and furnishes us with cavalry to resist them. And it would be a disgrace to be forced to withdraw, or to send afterwards for help because our initial decision had been ill considered. So we should leave here with sufficient forces, realizing that we are going to sail far from home, and mount a different sort of campaign from when we went as allies to one of our subject peoples here, where we had easy access to the supplies we needed from our friends. But we are taking ourselves away to a land of strangers, from which a messenger could hardly reach us in four months during winter.

[22] Therefore my opinion is that we should take with us a great many hoplites of our own, our allies, and our subjects, as well as anyone we can get from the Peloponnesus by persuading them or offering them a fee. We should also take many archers and slingers to use against their cavalry, and

---

216. Nicias here speaks of Syracuse, which was both free of foreign influence and a democracy. Elsewhere in expanding her empire Athens had depended on exploiting local discontent (iii.62, see Dover).

217. Naxos was founded by people (most likely Ionians) from Chalcis in Euboea, who went on from there to found Leontini and Catana; Syracuse was founded by Dorians from Corinth.

218. Greek navies were manned by the lower social orders.

219. A weakness of Athens was her dependence on imported wheat.

we must be far superior in ships so that we can easily bring in what we need. We will also need grain in merchant vessels—both wheat and barley, and bread makers must be pressed into service and hired, a share from each mill, so that if the army is weather-bound it will have what it needs. (Because our army will be so large, not every city will be able to take it in.) We should provide everything else too, as much as possible, and not depend on others. Above all, we must take as much money as we can. As for the money they say is ready in Egesta, you should think of that as available only in speeches.

[23] Even if we go ourselves from Athens with a force that is not simply a match for theirs (except for their fighting troops, the hoplites) but superior in every way, we will hardly be able to overcome them and see to our own security. Remember that when people go to found a city among enemies of another race, they must take control of the land immediately, on the first day they land, or else they are sure to find everything hostile if they fail.[220] That is what I am afraid of, and I know that this business requires a great deal of good planning and even more good luck — a difficult matter, since we are only human. As for me, I want to set out with as little as possible left to luck, and to make the voyage with a force that can be expected to provide security. This, I think, will be the most reliable course for the whole city, and the safest for those of us who go on the expedition. If anyone is of a contrary opinion, I offer to resign my command to him.

[24] Nicias said all this in the belief that the Athenians would either be deterred by the magnitude of the undertaking or, if he had to sail, would at least provide him a large enough force for the safety of the voyage. But the difficulty of equipping the expedition did not wipe out their desire to make it; instead, it inflamed them all the more, and the result was the opposite of what he expected: they approved of his advice and thought there would be no danger now at all. Now everyone alike fell in love with the enterprise: the old men hoped to subdue the place they went to, or at least that such a large force would have no serious trouble; the young men were longing to see and study a far-off country and were confident they would be brought back safely; while the great mass of people, including the military, expected not only to gain their wages by it for the time being, but to win such power that their salaries would go on forever. The result of this vehement desire of the majority was that anyone who did not favor the expedition kept quiet out of fear that if he held up his hand in opposition he would be

---

220. Nicias here compares the expedition to a colony set down in a hostile territory, an experience well understood by his audience.

thought to harbor ill will against the city.

[25] In the end a certain Athenian[221] stood up and called on Nicias to make no further excuses or delays, but to declare right then before them all what forces the Athenians should vote to give him. To this he answered unwillingly that he would consider it at more length with his fellow commanders, but that his immediate judgment was this: they would need no fewer than one hundred triremes from Athens (of which a number to be determined would be troop-transports) and others to be sent for from the allies; with these should sail at least five thousand hoplites from Athens and the allies, more if possible. The rest of the force should be in proportion: archers from here and from Crete, slingers and anything else that was found necessary should be readied and taken along.

[26] Immediately on hearing this the Athenians voted for this decree: "the generals are to have independent authority to act as they see best both in regard to the size of the expedition and in regard to the entire voyage." After this they began their preparation by making lists of those who would serve and sending instructions to the allies. The city had just recovered from the plague and the continuous warfare: a number of young men had come of age and money had accumulated during the armistice, with the result that everything was more easily supplied. And so they were involved in preparations.

c. *Launching the expedition*

[Summary of vi.27–32]
Soon after, a gang of upper-class young men defaced most of the herms in Athens in a single night. (The herms were stone statues of religious importance scattered through Athens.) This caused great consternation, as it was felt that such a violation of sacred statues could bring the wrath of the gods upon the city. The ensuing investigation succeeded only in fanning people's fears of conspiracy and sacrilege. In this atmosphere of panic and rumor, accusations were made against Alcibiades. It was said that he had celebrated mock religious rituals in his house, and he was therefore suspected in the case of the Herms as well. Alcibiades denied all charges and offered to stand trial then and there, but his enemies decided to wait until he had left Athens before renewing their attack.[222]

---

221. Plutarch identifies him as Demostratus (*Life of Nicias*, 12); cf. Aristophanes, *Lysistrata* 387 ff.

222. A man named Andocides confessed involvement in the affair of the herms and was exiled. Later he wrote a detailed account of the matter in his *De Mysteriis*.

The expedition sailed in midsummer. All Athens turned out to see them off. After appropriate prayers and a stately exit from the harbor, the ships raced each other as far as the island of Aegina. There were a hundred Athenian triremes, of which forty were used for transport, thirty-four allied triremes, and two fifty-oared ships from Rhodes. Supplies were carried by thirty merchant ships and about a hundred smaller vessels. There were fifty-one hundred hoplites, of which fifteen hundred were Athenians of the hoplite class and seven hundred Athenians of the lowest property level who served as marines. The rest came from allied cities, as did more than a thousand lightly armed troops (archers and slingers). The main deficiency was in cavalry, as only thirty horses were taken across to Sicily (vi.43-44).

The Debate at Syracuse [Summary of vi.33–41]
When rumors of the Athenian preparation reached Sicily, the Syracusans called an assembly. The conservative leader Hermocrates warned the Syracusans to prepare for the attack from Athens, by mobilizing their allies and setting out to fight the Athenians before they crossed into Sicily. Hardly anyone believed him, however.

The democratic leader Athenagoras made light of the threat from Athens in a speech that is a model of rhetoric gone wrong. First, he argued that the idea that Athens would send an expedition was simply not reasonable (not eikos) in view (i) of the threat to Athens from the Lacedaemonians in their back yard, and (ii) of the great strength of Syracuse. (He was right, of course: it was unreasonable for the Athenians to launch their expedition. But they did so, nonetheless.) Second, (he says) the whole story appears to be a fabrication put forward to frighten the democrats into turning to the oligarchs for safety.

Athenagoras closed by promising to guard against a takeover by the oligarchs, and then gave these remarks in defense of democracy:[223]

> Some will say that democracy is neither intelligent nor fair [*ison*] and that the wealthy are best able to rule. But I answer first that the *demos* is the name for the whole people,[224] while *oligarchy* names only a part. Second, though the rich are indeed the best guardians of the city's money, the best

---

223. Since Athenagoras' advice is all bad, there is a bite to Thucydides' decision to join it to this defense of democracy, a form of government Thucydides tends to distrust.

224. In fact, *demos* has a number of meanings: although it can refer to the entire citizen body, it more often designates the poor or common people, and may mean simply a political group that claims to represent their interest. Athenagoras is

7. The Sicilian Expedition 125

councilors are the intelligent, and the best judges of what they hear are the many. Now in a democracy all three groups enjoy a fair share, both the groups and their members. But while an oligarchy allows the many their share of dangers; it takes more than its share of the profits—not only that, it runs off with everything. [vi.39]

An unnamed general then spoke, proposing the policy that eventually won the war for Syracuse, a policy very much in line with what we know of Thucydides' political views: the city should act together and forget its political divisions. First it should find out what was really going on, while making preparations for defense.

Arrival of the Athenians [Summary of vi.42–56]
On arrival, the Athenians and their Allies found that the treasure promised by Egesta amounted to only thirty talents. Uncertain how to proceed, they first delayed while Alcibiades tried unsuccessfully to persuade Messina to join them. After that they made a show of force at Syracuse and proceeded to Catana, where they settled an internal quarrel in their favor and drove out the faction that supported Syracuse. There they planned to set up camp for the winter.

At Catana they met a fast ship from Athens that had been sent to bring Alcibiades home to defend himself against a number of charges. He was suspected of having made secret arrangements with Sparta and also of various crimes against religion. Really, Thucydides believes, Alcibiades was in trouble because his loyalty to Athenian democracy was in doubt, and so the people did not carefully evaluate the rumors that were circulated against him. They had heard about the tyranny of Pisistratus and his sons, and were therefore in constant fear of a recurrence of tyranny. Thucydides thinks this fear of tyranny is irrational. He proceeds to explode one of the central myths of democratic Athens—that of the slaying of the tyrants by Harmodius and Aristogeiton.

Digression on the tyranny in Athens [vi.54.1–6]
In fact, Aristogeiton and Harmodius took this enormous risk as a result of a love affair. I shall tell the story at some length, to make the point that the Athenians are no more reliable than anyone else in reporting their own history or describing their own tyrants. When the reigning tyrant

---

using what is called a persuasive definition. His contemporaries would not have been moved; to most of them democracy meant mob rule, not rule in the interest of the whole people. See Glossary.

Pisistratus died as an old man [in 527], it was the elder brother Hippias who took power, and not, as ordinary people believe, Hipparchus. Now Harmodius was at that time glowing with youthful beauty, and the lover who had him was Aristogeiton, a citizen belonging to the middle class.[225] Harmodius was solicited by Hipparchus (the son of Pisistratus) but did not give in to him; instead, he told Aristogeiton all about it. Aristogeiton was struck with the anguish of jealousy, as happens to lovers, and also with the fear that Hipparchus might use his power to take the boy by force, so he immediately formed a plan to bring down the tyranny using the only means available to a man of his rank.[226] Meanwhile, Hipparchus made another attempt on Harmodius that was no more successful than the first. At this, although he was unwilling to use violence, the rejected suitor arranged to disgrace the boy in a subtle way that could not be traced to this event.[227]

In general, their government had not been hard on the people, and had consistently avoided arousing their anger. Tyrants though they were, the Pisistratids had cultivated virtue and wisdom to a high degree. Taxing only five per cent of Athenian income, they had adorned the city beautifully, fought their wars to the finish, and supported public religion. Meanwhile the city continued to enjoy all its former laws and customs, except that they always saw to it that one of their supporters held public office.

Assassination of Hipparchus [Summary of vi.55-59]
Thucydides corrects the popular myth on three points: first, the man who was assassinated was not the reigning tyrant, but the tyrant's younger brother; second, the motive was not politics but sex, really sexual harassment by a man in power; third, the assassination did not bring the tyranny to an end.

Harmodius and Aristogeiton planned to kill Hipparchus and Hippias at a religious procession. Fearing discovery, however, they acted in haste and were able to kill only Hipparchus, leaving the elder brother to continue his rule. Badly frightened by the episode, Hippias became increasingly repressive during the remaining three years of his reign. He was deposed by an army of Lacedaemonians in 510. Thucydides passes over without comment the splendid irony that it is Sparta that delivered Athens from tyranny and so

225. Greek men at this time sometimes had affairs with younger men or boys.
226. "The only means available to a man of his rank": assassination. An aristocrat or a man of wealth could presumably have organized a more subtle *coup d'etat*.
227. We learn in vi.56 what Hipparchus did to disgrace Harmodius: he invited the boy's young sister to participate in a religious procession and then threw her out on the grounds that her family were not citizens of good standing.

7. The Sicilian Expedition

prepared the way for democracy in Greece.

Alcibiades' escape [Summary of vi.60–61 and 88–93]
The attempt to arrest Alcibiades failed when he escaped and took refuge in Sparta. The advice he subsequently gave to the Spartans was excellent. First, he advised them to take immediate steps to save Syracuse by sending fresh troops and a crafty general to lead them. Second, he advised them to fortify a hilltop in Attica (Decelea) and maintain a force there year in and year out; this would be far more damaging to Athens than the annual invasions Sparta had been sending at harvest time (vi.91). The Spartans took Alcibiades' advice.[228]

In order to win the confidence of the Lacedaemonians, Alcibiades explained in his speech why he was willing to help them now after years of service to the Athenian democracy:

> If anyone thought worse of me for siding with the people, he should realize that he is not right to be offended. We[229] have always been in disagreement with tyrants, you see. Whatever is opposed to an autocrat is identified with the people (*demos*) and because of this we have continued as leaders of the majority party. Besides, in a city governed by democracy, we were generally compelled to conform to prevailing conditions; we have tried, nevertheless, to be more moderate in politics than the headstrong temper that now prevails. There have been others in the past—there still are some—who have incited the mob to worse things. These are the ones who have driven me out. But as for us, we were leaders of the city as a whole, and we thought it right to join in preserving the city in the same form in which it turned out to be greatest and most free—the form in which we had received it. We did this even though anyone with any sense knows well enough what democracy is—I as well as anyone (that's why I could lambaste it if I wanted, although there is nothing new to say about a form of government that everyone agrees is foolish). Besides, we thought it was not safe to change our government when you were bearing down on us as enemies. [vi.89.3-6]

* * *

> Now in my judgment no one should think worse of me because I, who was once thought a lover of my own city, am now of my own power going against her with her greatest enemies; and I do not think you should distrust my word as coming from the zeal of a fugitive. For though I am fleeing from the

---

228. Either the idea was an old one, or else Thucydides foreshadowed this development in the debate at Sparta (i.122, **142**).

229. Alcibiades' noble family, including Pericles.

malice of those who drove me out, I shall not, if you take my advice, flee from helping you. Those who have merely harmed their enemies, as you have, are not so much enemies as are those who have compelled their friends to become enemies.[230] I do love my city, but as a place where I could safely engage in public life, not as the site of injustice to me. I do not think the city I am going against is my own; it is much more a matter of my recovering a city that is not mine. A true lover of his city is not the man who refuses to invade the city he has lost through injustice, but the man who desires so much to be in it that he will attempt to recover it by any means he can. [vi.92.2–4] [231]

The Athenians at Syracuse [Summary of vi.62–88 and 94–105]
On the Helorus Road the Athenians won a brilliant victory over the Syracusans (vi.65–71). Up to now they had been avoiding a confrontation with Syracuse because they lacked sufficient cavalry to face the Syracusans on open ground. Now they lured the enemy cavalry north towards Catana, then sailed to Syracuse, landed, and dug in. The Syracusans showed their inexperience in the battle that followed and took considerable losses.

After the battle of the Helorus Road, the Athenians sailed back to Catana for the winter, and the Syracusans began to improve their defenses. Meanwhile, the citizens of Camarina (on the southwest coast of Sicily) listened to a debate between representatives of Syracuse and Athens, who were each trying to win

230. That is, in harming the democrats (the true enemy) the Lacedaemonians have not played the part of an enemy to Athens; the democrats, on the other hand, in making Alcibiades their enemy, have made themselves the enemies to Athens.

231. A frequent theme in this *History* is the readiness of exiles to ally themselves with the enemies of their home cities, in return for which the enemies support the political causes of the exiles. "My country right or wrong" is a sentiment that would have meant little to Thucydides or his contemporaries. All the more strange in its context, then, is the attitude of Socrates in Plato's *Crito,* who says he has an obligation to obey the city that has—wrongly in his view—condemned him. Contrast the case of Themistocles, who went over to the Persians when he was exiled by the Athenians. Thucydides finds nothing to censure him in this, and indeed praises him for the high quality of the advice he gave to the Persians in their continuing war against the Greeks (i.138). We know that Thucydides had been in exile from Athens after the loss of Amphipolis in 424 (which was not his fault) and that he had also spent some of his exile in the Peloponnesus. It is tempting to believe that the speech he gives here to Alcibiades reflects some of his own sentiments toward the city that had rejected him on such slender grounds.

7. The Sicilian Expedition

Camarina over to their side in the war (vi.72–88). The debate is worth reading as a whole, but one passage stands out from the Athenian representative's defense of their empire (vi.83.4): "As we told you, it is out of fear that we hold onto our empire in Greece; and we came to Sicily for the same reason, to make arrangements with our friends for our own safety—not to enslave anyone, but rather to see that no one is enslaved."[232] The Camarinans were not convinced; in equal fear of both sides, they declared neutrality.

In the spring of 414, the Athenians nearly brought the war to a successful conclusion. They seized the heights behind Syracuse (known as Epipolae), built a circular fort there, and began to run lines of fortification around the city, down both sides towards the sea. Once the walls were completed, it would only be a matter of time before Syracuse surrendered. The Syracusans countered by trying to build fortified walls across the advance of the Athenian fortifications (see map), but the Athenians foiled two such attempts and cut off the Syracusan water supply. The Syracusans attempted to storm the circular fort while most of the Athenians were away. Nicias happened to be in camp at the time, nursing an illness. He saved the fort by setting fire to the equipment, which drove off the enemy. Lamachus had been killed the same day in an earlier engagement, and Nicias—who was chronically ill and had opposed the business from the start—became sole commander of the expedition for the time being.

d. Defeat of the expedition

Sparta Joins the War [Summary of vii.1–41][233]
Syracuse was now on the edge of surrender, but in the nick of time the Lacedaemonian general Gylippus stole into Syracuse by sea with a small force. He quickly put new heart into the Syracusans, seized the heights of Epipolae, and ran a line of fortification across the advance of the Athenian siege-wall. It now appeared that the Athenians would not be able to complete their siege-wall and had lost their best chance to take Syracuse. Nicias then went into a defensive posture. He saw how grave the situation was and realized that the army would have to be withdrawn or substantially reenforced. Fearing that the Athenians would not believe a messenger, he sent the bad news to Athens in the form

---

232. See the similar Athenian defense at **i.75** and contrast the speech of Brasidas at **iv.87**.

233. "I do assure you that there is no prose composition ... which I place so high as the seventh book of Thucydides. It is the *ne plus ultra* of human art." Macauley to Ellis, 25 August 1835.

of a letter *(vii.11–15)* in which he said that the Athenian army was now under siege itself. He went on to point out that his force was losing its effectiveness: ships and their rigging were wearing out, slaves were running away, and foreign troops were deserting. Nicias insisted that the army either be called back to Athens or reenforced by a number of troops and ships equal to the original expedition. At the end of the letter he asked to be relieved of the command.

The Athenians decided not to relieve Nicias. They would, however, send reinforcements under Demosthenes and Eurymedon, who would be joint commanders with Nicias. Eurymedon came right away with a few ships, while Demosthenes stayed back to muster the new expeditionary force.

That winter (414–13), the Lacedaemonians decided to go to war against Athens *(vii.18)*. Perhaps they had been at fault in 431, when they started the original ten-year war. This time, however, there was no doubt in their minds: Athens had broken the Peace of Nicias[234] and would have to bear the consequences. In the spring of 413, the Lacedaemonians invaded Attica and fortified Decelea as Alcibiades had advised them to do. This was a serious threat to Athens, for it kept the farmland of Attica under constant threat of attack and virtually put Athens under siege. Still, the Athenians were determined to wage war both at home and in Sicily, and they imposed new taxes on their empire in order to support the war.

Meanwhile, Gylippus brought new troops to Syracuse from various allies in Sicily. He captured Plemmyrium (the point of land across the great harbor from the city), and subsequently strengthened the Syracusan navy. Then a series of battles in the great harbor gave naval superiority to the Syracusans for the first time.

Night battle for Epipolae *[vii.42–46]*

[42] But just as the Syracusans were preparing to follow up on their victory with attacks by land and sea, Demosthenes and Eurymedon arrived with reinforcements from Athens: about seventy-three ships (including foreign ones) and five thousand Athenian and allied hoplites, along with a good number of javelin throwers, both Greek and foreign, slingers, archers, and enough supplies. The Syracusans and their allies were quite dismayed at first, with no end in sight and no respite from danger, seeing that in spite of the fortification at Decelea there had come an army almost

---

234. During the winter of 415/14 the Athenians had supported Argos against Sparta and, in the process, attacked Epidaurus, Prasiae, and various other cities of the Peloponnesus. This was regarded by the Lacedaemonians as a clear violation of the Peace of Nicias, and Thucydides agreed (vi.105).

as large as the first, and the power of Athens seemed great on all sides. Meanwhile, a sort of confidence returned to the first Athenian army in the wake of its misfortunes.

When Demosthenes saw how things stood, he decided he should not waste time and fall into Nicias' situation. (The fear Nicias inspired on his first arrival had turned to contempt when, instead of attacking Syracuse at once, he had spent the winter at Catana.[235] At the same time, he had allowed Gylippus to reach Syracuse with his army of Peloponnesians—which the Syracusans would not even have sent for if he had attacked directly, since they thought they were strong enough alone, and would not have learned of their weakness until surrounded by a siege-wall, with the result that even if they had sent for aid it would not have been as helpful.)

So Demosthenes thought all this over and realized that like Nicias he would be most frightening to the enemy right now on the first day. He therefore decided to put the present shock-value of his army to use as quickly as he could. He observed that the cross-wall by which the Syracusans had kept the Athenians from encircling the city with their siege wall was only a single one, and that if anyone took control of the way up to Epipolae and then seized the camps there he would easily capture the cross-wall (since no one would even wait for the attack). He therefore hurried to put this to the test, as he thought it his quickest way to end the war: either he would succeed and take Syracuse, or he would lead the army away and prevent any further attrition to the Athenians who were there with him or to Athens as a whole.

First, then, the Athenians went out and wasted the land of the Syracusans around the Anapus River, and they were the stronger, as at first, by land and by sea, since the Syracusans dared not go out against them either way, except for horsemen and javelin-throwers from the Olympeion. [43] After that, Demosthenes decided to try to take the cross-wall with battering rams [*see ii. 77*]. But the rams he brought up were burnt by the enemies who were defending the wall, and his other attacking forces were repulsed at many points; so he decided to waste no more time, and persuaded Nicias and the other generals to make the attempt he had planned against Epipolae. It was considered impossible to approach and make the ascent secretly by day, so he ordered them to take five days'

---

235. After their initial victory on the Helorus Road in 415, Nicias and Lamachus had decided to sail away. As this was a joint decision it does not seem entirely fair to blame Nicias for it.

rations, all the stone-masons and builders, a supply of arrows, and whatever else they would need to build a fort if they took the hill. Then he and Eurymedon and Menander marched against Epipolae with the whole army after the first watch, leaving Nicias in the camp.[236]

When they reached Epipolae at Euryalus, just where the earlier army had made their first ascent,[237] they were unseen by the Syracusans who kept watch. They then advanced and seized the Syracusan outpost that was there, killing some of the guard. Most of them, however, escaped and ran straight to the camps, of which there were three on Epipolae, all fortified: one for the Syracusans, one for the other Sicilians, and one for their allies. They reported the attack there and also informed the six hundred Syracusans who had originally guarded this part of Epipolae. They came immediately to the defense, but Demosthenes and the Athenians ran into them and put them to flight, though they fought with spirit. The main body of Athenians continued to advance in order to finish what they had come for in one rush, without losing their momentum. Meanwhile, another party had taken the Syracusan cross-wall right away—the troops guarding it had not even stayed to fight—and were pulling down its battlements.

The Syracusans and their allies, along with Gylippus and his forces, came to the defense from the fortified camps. Because they had not expected so daring an attack, and at night too, they were in a state of panic when they joined battle with the Athenians and at first they were forced to pull back. But the Athenians were rushing forward in greater disorder, thinking they had won and wanting to get through all of the enemy forces that were not yet engaged in the battle as quickly as possible, to prevent their regrouping during a lull in the attack—and while the Athenians were advancing in disorder, the Boeotians were the first to offer them any resistance: the Boeotians charged, routed the Athenians, and put them to flight.[238]

[44] And then the Athenians were thrown into great perplexity and confusion, which it was not easy to sort out by asking both sides how the

---

236. The plan was to go around the end of the cross wall and seize and fortify the heights that commanded the wall and the Syracusan camps.

237. After the first winter the Athenians had taken Epipolae by this route (vi.97); their enemy Gylippus used the same approach when he took the hill and began the successful cross wall (vii.2).

238. Boeotia had sent a force of three hundred hoplites while Decelea was being fortified.

7. The Sicilian Expedition

particular events fit together.[239] Battles are easier to understand in daylight, but even then soldiers who are present scarcely know more than their own particular experiences. So in a night battle—and this the only one in the war to involve large armies—how could anyone know anything for certain? Though the moon was bright, they saw each other as you'd expect in the moonlight: bodies were visible, but there was no way to know whether they were friends or enemies. And there were a great many hoplites on both sides, maneuvering in a very tight space. Some of the Athenians were beaten already; others, undefeated, were still moving ahead in the original direction of attack. Also, a great part of the rest of the army either had just got to the top of the hill or were on their way up, and did not know which way to go. Once the rout had begun, all the forward troops were in confusion, and the shouting made it hard to tell what was happening. The Syracusans and their allies were cheering each other on as victors with great clamor, as that was their only means of communication at night, and at the same time they were holding off anyone who attacked.

Meanwhile, the Athenians were trying to find each other and were taking everyone who was going the other way as an enemy, including friends who were already running back for safety. They were constantly asking for the password, since they had no other means of recognition. As they were all asking at the same time, this produced a great racket, and gave away the word to the enemy. The enemy password, however, they could not learn as easily, since the enemy, who were keeping together in their victory, had fewer problems of recognition. The result was that when the Athenians met enemies whom they outnumbered, they let them go because they knew the password; but they—if the situation were reversed—could not answer and were killed. By far the worst damage, however, was caused by the singing of the Paean ("battle-hymn");[240] coming from both sides right near them—it drove them to their wits' end. The Argives and Corcyreans, along with all the other Dorians who sided with Athens, put fear into the Athenians whenever they sung the Paean, and the enemy had the same effect. The final result of all this was that men from various parts of the army kept running into each other, once they were in total confusion—friends against friends and citizens against fellow citizens. They not only terrified each other but even came to hand-to-hand fighting and could scarcely be parted without difficulty. And as they were being chased along the cliffs—since

---

239. Here Thucydides describes one of his methods. See **i.22, v.26**, and v.68.
240. Battle hymns were sung by all Greeks before and after battle, but only Dorians used them during an actual fight.

the way down from Epipolae is narrow—many of them threw themselves off the rocks and died. And when the survivors got back down to level ground, many of them, especially members of the first army, knew the country well enough to find safety in the camp. Some of the second army, however, lost their way and wandered into the fields; these were rounded up and killed by Syracusan horsemen at daybreak.

[45] Next day the Syracusans put up two trophies, one in Epipolae, where the Athenians had come in, the other at the place where the Boeotians had made the first stand. Meanwhile, the Athenians retrieved their dead during a ceasefire. Many Athenian and allied troops were killed, and more weapons were lost than were taken from the dead, since those who were forced to leap from the cliffs left their armor behind, and though some of them perished, others survived.

[46] After this the Syracusans recovered their former confidence from their unexpected success and sent fifteen ships under Sicanus to Agrigentum, which was in a state of civil war, to bring the city over to their side if possible, while Gylippus went around the rest of Sicily by land again to raise another army in the hope of taking the Athenian lines by force, considering how the battle of Epipolae had turned out.

The Athenians delay their departure [vii.47–56]
[47] Meanwhile, the Athenian generals met to discuss the disaster that had struck them, as well as the general weakness of the whole army at the time. They saw that their plans had failed and that the soldiers were angry at staying on. They were troubled by sickness from two causes: this was the season of the year in which people are most susceptible to disease, and the site of their camp was swampy and unpleasant.[241] Besides, everything seemed hopeless to them. Demosthenes said he thought they should stay no longer; they should follow the plan he made when he took the chance on Epipolae. Since this attack had failed, he voted to leave and waste no more time while they were still able to cross the sea and the expedition could at least win a battle with the ships that were newly arrived. He also said that it would be more effective for the city to wage war against those who were setting up fortifications on her own soil than against the Syracusans, who could no longer easily be defeated, and that they had no reason to spend any more money on the siege.

[48] That was Demosthenes' conclusion. As for Nicias, however, although he personally felt that their position was poor, he did not want this

---

241. The season was summer, and the disease was possibly malaria.

weakness to be made public in discussion. He did not want to announce their departure to the enemy by putting it openly to the vote of many soldiers, for then they would be much less likely to surprise the Syracusans when they did decide to go. As for the situation of the enemy, with which he was much better acquainted than the others, he still held out hope that Syracuse would be in poorer shape than the Athenians if only they would continue the siege: the Athenians would wear them out by lack of money, especially since with their present fleet they had greater control of the sea. Besides, he said, there was an element in Syracuse that wanted to turn the city over to Athens and kept sending him messages not to let them raise the siege. Knowing all this, he said in his public speech at that time that he would not take the army away (though in fact he was wavering and making time for further consideration). For he said he was well aware that the Athenians would not accept their departure unless they had voted for it themselves. And the people who would pass judgment on them had not seen matters at first hand, as they had, but would base their votes on the reports of others and would believe any slander they heard from a fine speaker. As for the soldiers now present, he said, many, indeed most, of those who were now wailing about their misery would wail on the other side when they got home and complain that the generals had sold out and left for a bribe.[242] So, for his part, he knew too much about the nature of the Athenians to want to be killed unjustly by them on a dishonorable charge. If he had to die, he'd prefer to do so at the hands of the enemy—a risk he'd be taking on his personal initiative. Besides, in spite of everything, the Syracusans were in a condition even worse than their own: the cost of keeping mercenaries, along with paying for outlying ports and maintaining a large fleet for a full year now, had made them poor and would soon cripple them. They had already spent two thousand talents and were heavily in debt as well. If the Syracusans lost even a small part of their force through not supplying it, their troops would drift away, since they were allies and not compelled to fight, as ours were, by their situation. Therefore, he said, the Athenians should hang on and continue the siege, rather than go away in defeat over money, in which they were far superior.

[49] Nicias said all this forcefully because he saw exactly how things were in Syracuse and knew they had run out of money. Besides, he knew how many Syracusans wanted the Athenians to win and were sending him messages not to raise the siege. At the same time, he placed special confi-

---

242. The generals in command of an earlier expedition to Sicily had been convicted on such a charge in 424.

dence in the navy, just as he had before, in spite of their defeat.[243]

Demosthenes, however, would not hear of continuing the siege at all. If they could not take the army away without a vote's being taken in Athens—if they had to wear down the Sicilians—then, he said, they should move up to Thapsus or Catana and stay there, where their land forces could subsist by overrunning a large territory, plundering their enemies' land and so weakening them. Meanwhile, he said, they should use their ships for combat in the sea, rather than in the narrow harbor that favored the enemy. In the open water they could use their skill in pulling away and charging without rushing up and pulling back within narrow, circumscribed limits.

All in all, he said, there was no way he would want to stay any longer where they were: they should get out of there as quickly as possible, without delay. Eurymedon gave the same advice, but as Nicias was still opposed, delay and hesitation began to grow, along with the suspicion that Nicias' confidence came from knowing more than the others. In this way the Athenians procrastinated and stayed in that place.

[50] Meanwhile Gylippus and Sicanus returned to Syracuse. Sicanus' plan for Agrigentum had failed when the faction that was friendly to Syracuse there got driven out while he was still at Gela. But Gylippus came with another large army raised in Sicily and with the Peloponnesian hoplites that had been sent by transport ships in the spring and had arrived at Selinus from Libya. (A storm had driven them to Libya, and the Cyreneans there had given them two triremes with pilots. In sailing along the coast they had sided with the Euesperides, who were besieged by the Libyans. After defeating the Libyans, they had sailed along to Neapolis, a Carthaginian trading post, where there is the shortest route to Sicily—two days and a night of sailing. From there they had crossed to land in Sicily at Selinus.[244])

As soon as these reinforcements arrived, the Syracusans immediately prepared to attack the Athenians both on sea and on land. The Athenian generals saw that a fresh army had reinforced the enemy, while their own situation, far from improving, was getting worse every day on every point, especially owing to the sickness that weighed on the men. Now the generals were sorry they had not moved out earlier, and since even Nicias had

---

243. The text is difficult and has been emended by all editors. I have translated the simplest emendation, that of Classen.

244. Euesperides is modern Benghazi; Neapolis is Nabeul. The distance from Nabeul in Africa to Selinus in Sicily is about 140 miles.

7. The Sicilian Expedition

withdrawn his earlier opposition, provided there was no public vote on the matter, the generals gave word as secretly as they could and told everyone to be prepared to sail from the camp on a certain signal. And they were going to do it, but just when they were ready to sail, the moon had an eclipse, since there was a full moon that night. Then most of the Athenians took the eclipse to heart and called on the generals to stop, while Nicias—who put too much faith in divination and such practices—said he would not even consider moving now until they had waited the twenty-seven days prescribed by the soothsayers. That is why the Athenians put off their intended departure.[245]

[51] The Syracusans found out about this on their own and it encouraged them more than ever not to let up on the Athenians, now that the latter had acknowledged that they were no longer stronger on land or sea—otherwise they would never have planned to sail away. Besides, they did not want them settling down anywhere else in Sicily, where they would be harder to fight, but wished to compel them to give battle at sea as soon as possible in a place where Syracuse would have the advantage. So they manned their ships and trained as many days as they thought sufficient. When the time was right they assaulted the Athenian walls on the first day, and when a small number of hoplites and cavalry sallied out by a gate, they cut off some of the hoplites, routed them, and chased them back. Because the entrance was narrow, the Athenians lost seventy horses and a small number of hoplites.

[52] On that day, the Syracusan army withdrew, but on the next they sailed out with seventy-six ships while their infantry advanced to the walls. The Athenians went out against them with eighty-six ships and engaged them in battle. Eurymedon had charge of the right wing of the Athenians, and drew his ships closer to the shore, in hopes of surrounding the enemy; but the Syracusans and their allies first defeated the Athenian center and then cut him off in the inmost hollow of the harbor, where they killed him and destroyed the ships he had with him.[246] After that they chased down all the Athenian ships and drove them ashore.

---

245. For Thucydides' attitude toward divination, etc., see **ii.54**, **v.103**, **vi.26**, and **vii.79**.

246. This extraordinary sentence telegraphs its disturbing ending by putting the name of its main figure, Eurymedon, as the first word, but in the accusative case, and then letting the reader wonder about his fate until the last phrase. So swift and telling is the turning point of this battle. Eurymedon was cut off in the northern part of the harbor, close to Ortygia (the old city).

[53] When Gylippus saw his enemies' navy vanquished and carried past the stockade of their own camp, he ran down to help with part of his army along the causeway,[247] intending to kill those who landed and made the shore there friendly to the Syracusans, so they could tow the ships away more easily. But the Etruscans[248]—they were the ones who were guarding this area for the Athenians—saw them coming on in disorder, so they rushed out to attack and routed the Syracusans who were in front, hurling them into the marsh called Lysimeleia. Later, when the Syracusans and their allies arrived in greater strength, the Athenians came to the rescue in alarm for their ships and engaged them in battle. After beating them, the Athenians chased the Syracusans away and killed a few hoplites, while saving most of their ships and bringing them around to the camp. But the Syracusans and their allies took eighteen Athenian ships and killed all the men in them. Intending to set fire to the rest of them, the Syracusans loaded an old hulk of a boat with brush wood and pine torches—the wind was running right towards the Athenians—set it afire and aimed it at them. Then the Athenians, in alarm for their ships, devised ways of putting out the flames and escaped the danger by quenching the fire and preventing the approach of the hulk.

[54] After that, the Syracusans put up a trophy for the naval battle and also for the previous day's interception of hoplites, when they had taken the horses as well. The Athenians put up a trophy of their own for the Etruscan victory that drove foot soldiers into the marsh, and for their own success with the rest of their army.

[55] Now that the Syracusans had won a brilliant victory—and had won it at sea, where they had formerly been afraid of the ships that had come with Demosthenes—the Athenians were totally downhearted. Their surprise was great, but their regret at having made the expedition was even greater.

These were the only cities they had come against that were like them in character—that were governed as they were by democracy[249] and had ships and cavalry, along with substantial resources. The Athenians had not been able to bring any advantage to bear on them: they could not bring them to

---

247. The causeway separated the harbor from the swamp to its west.

248. The Etruscans, a people of northern Italy, were longstanding enemies of Syracuse and had volunteered to help the Athenians.

249. Syracuse was at the time a moderate democracy; a more extreme government would take over after the Syracusan victory over Athens. See Aristotle, *Constitution of Athens* 1304a27.

surrender either by offering them a change in constitution[250] or by bringing superior force down on them; and now that they had failed in most of their plans, they were at their wits' end—especially since they had been vanquished even at sea, which they had never expected, and which made them more dejected than ever.

[56] And now the Syracusans started sailing around the harbor without fear and planned to shut off its entrance, so that the Athenians could no longer sail out secretly at will. Indeed, the Syracusans were no longer concerned merely to save themselves, but were designing ways to block the escape of the Athenians, since they correctly believed that their strength was now much greater than the Athenians', and that if they could overcome the Athenians and their allies both at sea and on land, they would win great glory among the Greeks. Of the other Greeks, they hoped, some would be set free immediately, while others would be liberated from fear, since it would be impossible for Athens, with her remaining strength, to sustain any longer the war that would be brought down upon her. And they would be given the credit for this, so that everyone else—even generations to come—would admire them greatly. And indeed the contest was an important one, for more than the reasons given above: besides defeating the Athenians, they would defeat all of Athens' many allies as well, and they would do this not alone but as leaders of the Corinthians and Lacedaemonians who had come to their aid, while they had been the first to expose their own city to danger and had opened the way for most of their naval success.

Forces on both sides [Summary of vii.57–59]
Here Thucydides interrupts the story to give a list of the allies on both sides. In this he follows the tradition set by Homer in Book II of the Iliad, *but goes beyond it by providing political explanations for the presence of each ally. On the Athenian side were:*

(1) willing allies from Athenian colonies,

(2) unwilling allies who came from subject states within the empire,

(3) a few independent allies, such as Chios, that were obliged by treaties to support Athens, and

(4) more willing forces who came from states that were not in the empire, either for mercenary reasons or out of hatred of Sparta.

250. Nicias had predicted this problem (**vi.20**)

Of the entire allied force, most were Ionian, although the fourth category included a number of Dorians, such as those from Argos, an enemy of Sparta. There were also a number of non-Greeks, such as the Egestans (who had invited the Athenians in the first place), the Etruscans, and a few Sicels.

Syracuse, a Dorian city, was aided by:

(1) neighboring states such as Selinus,

(2) some Sicels, and

(3) allies from the Peloponnesian League (Spartans, Boeotians, and Corinthians). As the Syracusans were already quite numerous, the most valuable contribution of Sparta was the excellent leadership provided by their general, Gylippus.

Preparations for the battle in the Great Harbor, September 9, 413 [Summary of vii.59–68]
The Syracusans proceeded to block the mouth of the harbor—nearly a mile wide—with a string of transports and triremes at anchor. When they saw this, the Athenians realized that their position was untenable. Before the eclipse, they had told their allies in Sicily to suspend shipments of supplies by land; now they would be cut off completely if they lost communication by sea. So they decided to pull in their ground forces to defend the smallest possible compound, and then to man every available ship in an attempt to break out of the harbor. If they failed, they would leave Syracuse by land.

Before the battle, Nicias encouraged his forces with a speech in which he reminded them of their advantages, warned them of the danger to Athens if they failed, and gave them tactical advice—to grapple with Syracusan ships whenever possible and sweep their decks clear of defenders.

On the other side, the Syracusan generals and Gylippus prepared their ships to ward off Athenian grappling irons, and encouraged their forces with a speech. They pointed out that the Athenians had overloaded their ships with land soldiers who would not be effective at sea, reminded their troops of earlier victories, and exhorted them to be as hard on the Athenians as the Athenians would have been on them, implying that Athens would have treated Syracuse as it had treated Melos (p. 109). They concluded:

> No one should go soft and think that we would gain if they broke out safely. That's what they will do just the same, even if they defeat us; but we will have a fine victory if we carry out our plans—as is to be expected—of punishing the Athenians while restoring liberty to all of Sicily with greater

stability and productivity than before. This is the rarest kind of jeopardy: if we lose we'll come to little harm, but if we win the benefits will be enormous. (vii.68.3)

BATTLE IN THE GREAT HARBOR

September 9, 413 [vii.69–74]

[69] The Syracusan generals and Gylippus gave this encouragement to their soldiers; then they manned their ships as soon as they saw the Athenians doing the same. Nicias was terrified by the present state of affairs, realizing how great the danger was and how near, now that they were on the point of departing, and thought—as happens in a great crisis—that when all has been done there is still something missing, and that when everything has been said it is still not enough. In this state he once again called on each ship captain, one by one, addressing him by his father's name, his own, and that of his tribe, and entreated each one if he had a brilliant reputation not to betray it now, and not to tarnish the ancestral virtues that had distinguished their forefathers. He reminded them also of their country with its great liberty and the untrammeled freedom it gives everyone to live as he pleases;[251] and he said whatever else people say at such a time when they are at the point of action and don't mind sounding old-fashioned, using words that fit nearly any occasion, bringing in wives and children and ancestral gods, crying out in the hope that such speeches will be helpful in the terror of the moment.

When he had exhorted them as long as he thought he could (which was less than he thought he should), Nicias withdrew and led his land forces along the shore, placing them as widely as he could so as to give the maximum benefit of their encouragement to those on board the ships. Meanwhile, Demosthenes, Menander, and Euthydemus—these men had embarked as commanders of the fleet—put out from their camp and sailed straight to the barrier at the mouth of the harbor, to the passage that had been left open, with the intention of forcing their way out.

[70] The Syracusans and their allies had already put out with about as many ships as before, some of them guarding the outlet and the rest forming a circle around the harbor so they could attack the Athenians from all sides at once. At the same time, their land forces came along to support

---

251. For a similar thought, see the Funeral Oration, **ii.37**.

them wherever their ships might put ashore. The Syracusan navy was under the command of Sicanus and Agatharchus, each of whom had charge of a wing, while the Corinthians under Pythen held the center. When the Athenians first reached the barrier, their initial charge overwhelmed the ships assigned to guard it, and they tried to break open the bars. But after that, when the Syracusans and their allies hit them from all sides, the battle spread from the barrier throughout the harbor and was more fiercely fought than any naval battle in history. The sailors were full of enthusiasm to row wherever they were ordered; the steersmen were full of ingenuity and there was great mutual rivalry among them. The soldiers on board did their utmost when one ship came alongside another to see that their fighting from the decks was not outdone by the sailors in other tasks. Each and every one of them, in fact, pushed himself eagerly to be the best at his assignment.

But with so many ships engaged in a small area (this was the largest sea-battle in the narrowest quarters, for there were almost two hundred ships altogether) they could not ram each other very often, since there was no room to back up and charge; but they had frequent collisions, as one ship would run against another by chance while it was fleeing or attacking a third vessel. While a boat was approaching, the soldiers on the decks pelted it with javelins and arrows and stones in abundance; but once they were alongside they fell to hand-to-hand fighting as the marines tried to board each other's vessels. In many places, owing to the lack of room, it happened that one ship would be charging another while being charged itself, and that two ships, or sometimes more, would be forced against one, and the captains wound up having to defend on one side while preparing to attack on the other, not just one ship at a time but many from all directions. Meanwhile the great din of so many ships in combat was terrifying and drowned out orders coming from the officers. Officers were shouting out instructions and encouragement on both sides, of course, going beyond their normal duties in the excitement of battle: the Athenians were crying out to their men to force the passage and now if ever to show their spirit and secure a safe return to their country; the Syracusans and their allies were shouting about how fine it would be to prevent the Athenian escape and to bring honor to each country by their victory. The generals on both sides were shouting as well: if they saw anyone backing to stern unnecessarily they called on the ship-captain by name. The Athenians would ask if he was retreating because he thought he'd be more at home here, where the land was so terribly hostile, than on the open sea, which they had won at such cost. The Syracusans would ask why he was running away, since he knew perfectly well that the Athenians were desperate to escape any way they could.

[71] While the naval battle hung in the balance, the land forces on both sides were in an agony of suspense and conflict of mind, the local troops eager to win more glory than before, the invaders afraid that their situation might get even worse. Since everything depended on their ships, the Athenians were in the most extraordinary fear of what might happen, and since the battle was uneven in different parts of the harbor, the watchers on shore could only get uneven impressions of it. They were watching at close range and not all seeing the same thing at the same time. Those who saw their side winning took heart and fell to calling upon the gods not to take away their chance of escape; meanwhile, those who caught sight of defeat were wailing, even shrieking outright, and they were more overwhelmed in their minds by the sight of the battle than the actual combatants were. Others could see a part of the fighting that hung in the balance, and the protracted indecision of the struggle was agony for them as their bodies reflected their fears. These watchers had the hardest time of all, as they were always on the brink between escape and destruction. So it was that in one and the same army, while the sea battle was in doubt, you could hear all this at once: wailing, cheering, "we're winning," "we're losing," along with all the other confused shouting that has to come from a great army in serious trouble.

Much the same happened to the men on the ships, until at last, after a long-drawn out battle, the Syracusans and their allies clearly got the upper hand, forced the Athenians to retreat, and chased them back to land with a lot of shouting and cheering. Then the troops from the ships landed helter skelter—if they hadn't been taken at sea—and rushed to the camp. And now the soldiers on land were no longer of two minds: they all wailed and groaned from the same impulse, all unable to bear what had happened. Some of them ran to help the ships, others rushed to guard what was left of the wall; most of them, however, were only looking for a way to save their own skins. The panic at this point was greater than it had ever been. Their disaster was comparable to the one they had inflicted on the Lacedaemonians at Pylos: when the Lacedaemonians lost their ships there they also lost the men they had put on the island; and now the Athenians had no hope of escaping over land unless by a miracle.

[72] After this cruel battle, which consumed many ships and men on both sides, the victorious Syracusans and their allies picked up their dead and the wreckage of their ships, sailed back to the city, and put up a trophy. The Athenians, however, were so cast down by the enormity of the present

disaster that they never thought to ask permission to pick up their dead or their wreckage; all they wanted was to get away that very night. Demosthenes went to Nicias and proposed that they man the remaining ships and, if possible, break out at dawn, since, as he said, they still had more serviceable ships than the enemy. The Athenians had sixty ships remaining, while the enemy had fewer than fifty. Nicias accepted this proposal, but when they asked the sailors to man the ships they refused to go aboard. They were in such a panic from their defeat that they thought they could never win a victory ever again.

[73] And so they all resolved to break out by land. Hermocrates of Syracuse suspected they had such a plan, however, and thought it would be terrible if an army of that size withdrew by land, found a base somewhere in Sicily, and planned a new campaign against them. So he went and told the authorities what he was thinking, and urged them not to let the Athenians slip away by night, but to send out all the Syracusan and allied forces to occupy the roads, seize the narrow passes, and keep watch. The authorities agreed with him and felt as strongly as he did that this should be done, but they were afraid that they could not easily get the soldiers to obey, since they were now happily resting after the great battle and enjoying a festival besides (by coincidence this was the day for worshipping Heracles). Most of the men had been celebrating their victory by drinking heavily at the festival, and now the very last thing they would agree to do would be to take up their arms again and sally out to fight. Hermocrates saw that the authorities were convinced his proposal was impossible, and, because he could not persuade them, he came up with this stratagem on his own: he was afraid the Athenians might easily get a head start during the night and cross over the most difficult terrain, so as soon as it grew dark he sent some of his friends on horses to the Athenian camp. They rode up within earshot and called to a few Athenians, pretending to be friendly to their cause (Nicias did have some informants inside the city); then they instructed them to tell Nicias not to take the army out at night, since the Syracusans were guarding the roads, but to prepare for an easy departure the next day. The horsemen said this and rode off, while those who heard them took the message to the Athenian generals.

[74] It never occurred to the generals that this message was a fraud, so they decided to stay the night. Then, since they had not set off immediately after their defeat, they decided to wait another day to give the soldiers time to pack as well as they could, taking what they needed the most and leaving all the rest behind. Their aim was to take only what was necessary for physical survival.

Meanwhile the Syracusans and Gylippus took their land forces out ahead of them and blocked the roads in the area the Athenians were likely to cross; they also guarded the river and stream crossings and posted troops to receive and hold the Athenian army where they thought best. They also sailed up and dragged the Athenian ships off the beach. They burned some of these (as the Athenians would have done) and easily tied up the others wherever they lay and towed them into the city, since there was no one to stop them.

THE ATHENIAN RETREAT

Retreat and destruction of the Athenian force [vii.75–viii.1]
[75] Later, two days after the sea-battle, Nicias and Demosthenes decided they were ready enough, and the army began its withdrawal. It was a lamentable departure, and not just because of the single fact that by losing all their ships they had dashed all their great hopes and put themselves and their city in danger: as they left the camp each one of them was struck by the sight or the thought of some great grief. The dead were lying about unburied, and when anyone saw the body of a friend on the ground he was seized with fear and horror, while the living who were left behind sick or wounded were a more horrible sight than the dead and were far worse off than those who had passed away. Their continual pleading and wailing brought home the utter helplessness of the army; they begged to be taken along, and if any of them saw a friend or relative he'd call on him by name, and they would hang on the necks of their departing tent-mates, or follow them as far as they could, till strength or life failed them and they were left behind with no shortage of prayers and lamentations.

As a result the entire army was full of tears, and in this state of helplessness it was not easy for them to start their retreat, though they were leaving a hostile place and had already suffered more than tears could express; still, they were afraid of the suffering their unknown future might bring them. They hung down their heads and many thought themselves worthless. They seemed like a whole city of refugees trying to escape from a siege, and not a small city either, as there were no fewer than 40,000 people in the entire crowd that was on the march. Each of them carried whatever provisions he could; even hoplites and horsemen did this, although it went against custom for them to carry their own rations while under arms; some did so because they'd lost their servants, others because they did not trust them, since they had been deserting for a long time and now most of them had just run away. Even so, they did not carry enough, since the army was running out of food. And the other indignities they bore were too great for them to take lightly at this point, even though sharing troubles equally with many other people usually lightens the load. The worst part was that they had come down from such a height of splendor and glory to this miserable end—the greatest reversal that had ever happened to a Greek army: these men who had come to enslave other people now had to leave in fear of being enslaved themselves; in place of the prayers and battle-hymns with which they had sailed out they now left with the omens against them; besides, this force that had travelled by sea was now reduced to footsoldiers, depending on hoplites more than on sailors. Still, in view of the great danger hanging over them, they felt they had to bear all this.

[76] When Nicias saw that the army had lost its spirit and was so greatly changed, he passed through the ranks and gave them whatever encouragement and comfort he could in the circumstances, his voice rising higher and higher as he went along because he was so serious and so eager that his exhortation should benefit as many men as possible.

NICIAS' EXHORTATION

[77] "Even now, allies and Athenians, we should keep hope alive. People have been saved ere now from greater dangers than these. You should not think too badly of yourselves, either for your past losses or present suffering, which is undeserved. I may have less strength than any of you—you see how sick I am—but I have as good a reputation as anyone for success in both private and public life, and I am now in the same danger as the worst men here. Still, I have passed my life in the great piety that is ordained towards the gods, while towards men I have shown great justice and given no offense. In view of this my hope for the future is still confident, and these losses cause me no anxiety so far as our merit is concerned; indeed, we may well have some relief from them. Our enemies have now had their share of good luck, and if we have offended any of the gods in this campaign we have already had enough punishment. Others have invaded their neighbors before we did, and what they suffered for doing what human beings do[252] has been bearable. And now we have a reason to hope for milder treatment from the gods, since we have come to deserve their pity more than their anger. And just look at yourselves: with so many fine

---

252. Cf. **i.76** and **v.105** where the Athenians also defend their expansionist policy as normal for human beings.

7. The Sicilian Expedition

hoplites, marching in good order, you shouldn't give way to panic. Wherever you settle down you will immediately be a city, and no other force in Sicily will be able to withstand your attack or force you out once you're established.

As for the journey, you must take care that it be safe and orderly. And each of you keep this thought above all: that whatever place you are forced to fight in will be your country, with your walls. We will hurry along our way equally by night and day, since our supplies are short. If we can reach a friendly town of Sicels, then you should consider yourselves secure. A message has been sent to them telling them to meet us and bring food.

To conclude, soldiers, you must see that your only choice is to be brave; there is no place of safety near enough for cowards to reach. But if you now escape our enemies, you will all see what you desire, and those of you who are Athenians will restore the fallen power of Athens to its former greatness. It is the men, you see, and not the walls or empty ships, that are the city."

[78] As Nicias made this exhortation he went along the troops, collecting any stragglers he saw out of position and putting them in their places. Demosthenes did no less for his troops and said much the same things. Then they marched out in hollow rectangle formation, Nicias commanding the front and Demosthenes the rear, hoplites on the outside and baggage carriers and general rabble inside. When they came to the crossing of the Anapus River they found a unit of Syracusans and their allies drawn up on the bank. These they put to flight, took control of the ford, and marched forward, harassed by the pressure of the Syracusan cavalry and the javelins of their light-armed troops. On that day they advanced about four miles and a half and spent the night by a certain hill. The next day they left at dawn and went about two miles further, reaching a flat place where they set up camp, planning to get food from the houses (for the place was inhabited) and to take water from there along with them, since it was scarce for many miles ahead of them on their intended route. But the Syracusans got ahead of them and walled off the passage in front of them where there is a steep hill with precipitous ravines on either side, called the Acraean cliff. The next day the Athenians went on, while great numbers of Syracusan cavalry and javelin-throwers pressed them from both sides by charging them or throwing javelins. The Athenians fought for a long time and then returned to their camp. They had less food than before, now that the Syracusan cavalry would no longer let them leave their position.

[79] Early in the morning they set off on their way up to the hill that

had been fortified by the enemy. In front of them, below the wall, they found the enemy footsoldiers lined up many shields deep, as the place was narrow. The Athenians charged and attacked the wall under heavy fire from the soldiers on the steep hill above them, who could easily reach their targets since they were throwing their javelins from above. When the Athenians could not force through, they backed down and rested. Just then a small thunderstorm blew up and drenched them, as often happens when autumn is near. At this the Athenians lost heart still more and thought that all these events were meant to destroy them. [253] While they were resting, Gylippus and the Syracusans sent a detachment to dig in behind them where they had entered the gorge; but the Athenians sent some of their own men in response and stopped them. After that the Athenians took their whole army down to more level ground and camped.

The next day they went on[254] while the Syracusans pelted them with javelins from all sides in a circle and wounded many of them. And when the Athenians went after them, they withdrew, but when the Athenians backed off they attacked. They were especially fierce in attacking the Athenians at the rear, in hopes that routing a small number of them would throw the whole army into a panic. The Athenians held out against this for a long time, and after advancing a little over half a mile they rested on the plain while the Syracusans retired to their own camp.

[80] That night Nicias and Demosthenes made a decision. The army was in terrible shape: they had run out of all their supplies and many of them had been wounded in all those encounters with the enemy. So they decided to light as many fires as they could and take the army out of there, not the way they had originally planned, but towards the sea—the opposite direction from the route guarded by the Syracusans. (All along, they had been marching not towards Catana but towards the other part of Sicily, around Camarina and Gela and the Greek or foreign cities in that area.[255]) And so, when they had lighted a good many fires, they moved off in the night. And then—well, in any army, especially a large one, fear and terror are likely to strike, and more so at night, in enemy territory, and when the

---

253. Thucydides is scornful of superstitions. See also **ii.54**, **v.103**, **vi.26**, and **vii.50**.

254. They must have taken a new direction now, in an attempt to get around the gorge.

255. They would have been expected to head for Catana, since that was the nearest friendly city. The other cities were not friendly to Athens, but at this point the generals wanted simply to get out of range of the Syracusan army.

7. The Sicilian Expedition

enemy is not far off—*then* they fell into a total panic. Nicias' unit, which led the way, stayed together and made good progress, while Demosthenes' troops, much more than half the army, got separated and went on without much order. Still, they reached the sea at dawn and set off on the Helorus Road towards the Cacyparis River, which they planned to cross so they could head for the interior. There they hoped to meet the Sicels whom they had sent for. When they got to the river they found another unit of the Syracusan guard digging in and putting stakes across the ford. They forced their way across and went on to the next river, the Erineus, on the advice of their guides.

[81] Meanwhile, when the Syracusans and their allies realized at daybreak that the Athenians had gone, many of them accused Gylippus of letting them go intentionally, and went after them in hot pursuit. Their route was easy to follow, and they caught up around lunchtime. First they found Demosthenes' troops, who were in the rear and had moved more slowly and in greater disorder because of that panic during the night. Immediately, the Syracusans attacked and surrounded them with cavalry—which was easy since they were divided—and herded them into one place. Nicias' troops, however, were almost six miles further on; he was moving faster because he thought that their safety lay in not willingly staying to fight at this point and that they should retreat as quickly as possible and fight only where compelled to do so. But Demosthenes was having a much worse time of it, under constant pressure from the enemy because he was in the rear where they attacked first. When he saw that the Syracusans were in pursuit, he stopped his advance and went into battle formation. During this lengthy process, however, he got surrounded by enemy cavalry, and then he and his Athenians were in serious trouble. They were huddled up in a place with a wall around it, roads on this side and that, and a good many olive trees; and they were being hit by javelins from all sides. The Syracusans had a good reason for attacking them in this way rather than at close quarters: it would only have helped the Athenians for them to expose themselves to danger at the hands of such desperate men. Besides, now that victory was assured, everyone felt a certain reluctance to throw away his life, and they hoped that their tactics would enable them to subdue the Athenians and take them alive.

[82] After hitting them all day from all sides, Gylippus saw that the Athenians were worn out with wounds and other troubles, so he and the Syracusans and their allies made a proclamation: any of the islanders with the Athenians could freely come over to their side if they wished (and

troops from a few cities did cross over).[256] Afterwards they made an agreement with all the rest of Demosthenes' troops: if they laid down their arms, no one would be killed by violence or imprisonment or starvation. So they surrendered, six thousand of them in all;[257] and they threw all the money they had into the hollow of some shields, filling up four shields. They were then taken immediately to the city.

Meanwhile, Nicias and his army reached the Erineus River that day, crossed, and set up camp on high ground. [83] Next day the Syracusans caught up with him and told him that Demosthenes' troops had surrendered. They ordered him to do the same. Nicias did not trust them, so he sent a horseman under truce to find out. When the horseman brought back word of the surrender, Nicias sent a herald to Gylippus and the Syracusans to say that he was ready to agree on behalf of the Athenians to repay Syracuse for the cost of the war if they would let his army go away. He also promised to give them Athenian hostages till the money was paid—one man for each talent. But the Syracusans and Gylippus did not accept the terms. They attacked and surrounded the Athenians, hitting them with missiles from all sides, as they had the others, till evening. Then, although they were pinched by their lack of food and supplies, they kept watch that night intending to leave as soon as it was quiet. But when they took up their weapons the Syracusans heard them and raised the battle-hymn. The Athenians realized they had been found out and returned to camp, all but about three hundred of them who forced their way through the Syracusan guards and went as far as they could that night.

[84] When day came, Nicias led his army forward, while the Syracusans and their allies laid into them as before, hitting them from all sides with javelins and other missiles. The Athenians hurried on to the Assinarus River, partly because they were under pressure on all sides from attack by the cavalry and the rest of the mob (which they hoped would ease off once they had crossed the river), and partly because they were exhausted and desperate for water. As soon as they were there, they rushed in without any order, each man wanting to be the first to cross, while the enemy laid into them and made the crossing even harder. They were forced to go into the river in heaps, and so they fell upon one another and got

---

256. The islanders with the Athenians were allied troops. Their weak response to this invitation shows that such troops felt some loyalty to Athens. See p. xiv.

257. "Six thousand": the casualties had been heavy. The tearful army that had left Syracuse seven days earlier had numbered forty thousand, and Demosthenes had started out with more than half of the total (**vii.75**).

7. The Sicilian Expedition

trampled under foot. Some died immediately on each other's spears, others got tangled in the baggage and were washed away. On the other side of the river were Syracusans who stood on the steep bank and threw javelins down at the Athenians while most of them were drinking greedily or getting in each other's way in the river hollow. The Peloponnesians also came down and killed them in the river. This immediately fouled the water, but they went on drinking it nonetheless; and though it was full of mud and blood, many of them even fought over it.

[85] In the end, when many dead lay heaped in the river, and the army was utterly defeated, partly at the river, and partly by horsemen who chased down those who ran away, Nicias personally surrendered to Gylippus because he trusted him more than he did the Syracusans. He told Gylippus and the Lacedaemonians to do whatever they liked with him, but to stop slaughtering the other soldiers. After that, Gylippus ordered his troops to take live captives. The remaining soldiers were brought to the city alive (except for the many who were hidden away)[258] while the three hundred who had broken through the guard during the night were chased down and captured also. The number of Athenian captives collected as public property was not large, but a great many were secretly stolen away and all Sicily was filled with them. (That was because there had been no agreement in their case, as there had for those captured with Demosthenes.) A large part of the army was dead, for the slaughter at the river had been dreadful, exceeding that of any other action in this war, while a good many had been killed earlier during those frequent attacks along the way. Still, many escaped. Some got away then and there, while others were made slaves and ran away later. All these fugitives made their way towards Catana.

[86] The Syracusans and their allies formed up and returned to the city with their booty and as many prisoners as they could take. The remaining Athenian and allied captives were sent down into the stone quarries, which they considered the easiest place to guard safely; but Nicias and Demosthenes were executed, though Gylippus was opposed to this, since he thought it would be a fine prize for him if he could deliver the enemy generals to the Lacedaemonians on top of everything else. One of the two happened to be their worst enemy—Demosthenes, for what he did on the island and at Pylos; while the other had been extremely helpful to them over the same affair. Nicias had worked hard on behalf of the

---

258. Syracusan soldiers hid some captives so that they could ransom them for personal profit.

Lacedaemonians on the island; it was he who had persuaded the Athenians to make the treaty that released them.[259] For this the Lacedaemonians were friendly towards him, and that was the main reason he had trusted Gylippus enough to surrender to him. Some of the Syracusans, however, had conspired with him earlier (so it is said) and were afraid that he would speak out under torture and so get them into trouble just when all was going well. Others, mainly Corinthians, were afraid that with his great wealth he would bribe certain people, make his escape, and be the cause of some fresh mischief to them. So they persuaded the allies to kill him. This or something like it was the cause of his death, though of all the Greeks in my time he was the one who least deserved such a misfortune, since he had regulated his whole life in the cultivation of virtue (*aretē*).

[87] The Syracusans treated the men in the quarries badly at first. They were crowded together in a small sunken area without a roof where they were tormented by the sun's heat and stifling air, followed by cold nights, as autumn was coming on—a change that gave them new diseases. They had to do everything in the same narrow space, and besides that [i.e. the excrement] the carcasses of the dead, who had died of their wounds or the change in temperature or some such cause, were heaped up together and the stench was unbearable. All the while they were afflicted with hunger and thirst, for during an eight-month period they fed each man a cup of water and two cups of grain each day.[260] In short, they were not spared a single one of the miseries you'd expect when men are thrown into a place like that.

For seventy days they lived like this all together. After that they kept the Athenians, along with the Sicels and Italians who had joined them, but sold all the rest. It is hard to say how many men were captured altogether, but there were at least seven thousand.

This was the greatest action of the war—in my opinion, the greatest in all Greek history—the most glorious victory for the winners, and the worst calamity for the losers. They were utterly vanquished on all points,

---

259. The island is Sphacteria, off Pylos, where Demosthenes had cut off the hundred twenty Lacedaemonian soldiers whose loss helped bring Sparta to agree to the Peace of Nicias. Nicias had brought about the release of the Spartan soldiers besieged at Sphacteria and arranged the peace of 421 that bears his name.

260. A cup: a *kotyle* held about 0.27 liters. When the Lacedaemonian soldiers were cut off on Sphacteria, the Athenians allowed each of them two cups of wine, eight cups of grain, and a piece of meat, plus an additional half ration for each slave. The grain was probably wheat.

7. The Sicilian Expedition

and none of their losses was small. It was "total destruction" as the saying is,[261] for the army and navy alike. There was nothing that was not lost, and few out of many returned home.[262] That is what happened on Sicily.

[viii.1] When the news was told in Athens, even though the messengers were actual soldiers who had fled from the scene itself, and gave a clear report, people refused for a long time to believe that the loss had been so utterly complete. When they did realize the truth, they were furious with the orators who had joined in promoting the expedition (as if they had not voted for it themselves!).[263] They were also angry with the prophets and soothsayers and all those who had claimed to give them assurances from the gods that they would take Sicily. Everything from every side was a grief to them, and on top of this overwhelming loss they were stricken with fear and panic, the worst ever. It was bad enough that every private family, and the city as a whole, was burdened with the loss of so many hoplites and cavalry and men of military age for whom replacements were nowhere to be seen. But when they did not see enough ships in the boathouses, or money in the treasury, or officers to staff the ships, then they lost hope of surviving this crisis altogether. They thought their enemies from Sicily would immediately sail a navy into the Piraeus,[264] especially after such a great victory, while their enemies in Greece would double all their preparations and lay into them fiercely by land and by sea with the support of their former allies, who would now rebel.

Nevertheless, they decided they ought not to give in while they still had resources. They voted to build a fleet using wood and money from wherever they could find it, and also to make sure of their allies' loyalty, espe-

---

261. "Total destruction": *panōlethria*, a word Herodotus uses for the sack of Troy, ii.120.5.

262. According to Isocrates, forty thousand soldiers were lost along with two hundred forty triremes, an enormous loss even for an alliance of Greek city states. Athens alone lost three thousand hoplites, nine thousand of the lower class of citizens, and at least a hundred sixty triremes. Since Athens had begun the war in 431 with only thirteen thousand hoplites of prime military age, and had since lost many of these to war and plague, the loss of three thousand hoplites would have been devastating.

263. See iii.43 for a similar complaint. The whole city had been committed to the expedition (vi.31). Aside from Demostratus (see note on vi.25) we do not know who these orators were.

264. The Piraeus: the harbor of Athens.

cially those on Euboea.[265] Then they decided to slash public expenses and to select a committee of senior men to advise them on the crisis as the situation demanded. Now that they were face to face with real danger, the people were ready—as often in democracy—to turn over all their affairs to good management.[266] Then they carried out the decisions they had made. And so the summer ended.

265. Euboea: the long island running north of Attica, an important source of farm products for Athens.

266. The selection of such a committee smacks of oligarchy. It is a sensible move, to Thucydides' way of thinking, but a move the *demos* would take only in a crisis, and shows that Athens was swinging toward the conservative revolution that would give it an oligarchy in 411. Syracuse, meanwhile, moved in the opposite direction. A group of radical democrats including Athenagoras came to power in the wake of the victory over Athens in 412. Their triumph was brief. In 409 Carthaginians swept into a Sicily weakened by war; they destroyed Selinus, Himera, and (a few years later) Acragas. To meet the continuing threat of attacks from Carthage, Dionysius seized power in Syracuse, overthrew the democracy, and became tyrant in 405.

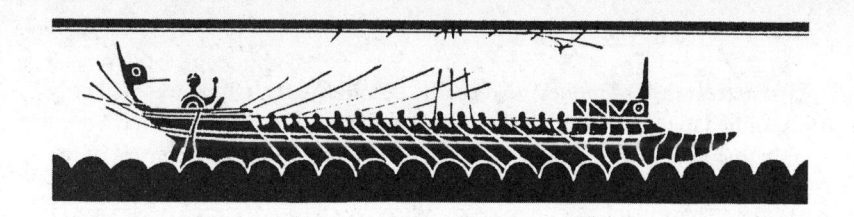

8. Aftermath of the Sicilian Expedition[267]

The collapse of the Sicilian expedition was a major turning point for Athens. The tragedy of its imperial ambitions was complete, and the remaining years of the war are a tale of survival against tall odds. "The following winter," continues Thucydides, "all the Greeks immediately rose up against Athens in view of their overthrow in Sicily" (viii.2.1). This was what the Athenians most feared, and it may have been what Thucydides thought they deserved. What actually happened was less dramatic. A number of allied or subject cities turned against Athens, but many apparently remained loyal.[268] The most damaging defection was that of the island of Chios in 412, which arose from a turn toward oligarchy there that was encouraged by the Spartans. Meanwhile, another important island, Samos, went the opposite way: with radical democrats firmly in control, it became the main base for Athenian operations in the Aegean Sea.

The greatest change in the war at this time came from the intervention of Persia, which began to finance Spartan naval operations. Greek navies

---

267. This section is meant as a sketch for those who want only to know what happened next in broad terms. Readers interested in the political history of Athens and the fall of the empire should read Book VIII entire along with Donald Kagan, 1987.

268. Why did they remain loyal? Athens was too weak at this point to frighten them into loyalty by a show of force. Probably the best explanation is the one Thucydides consistently ignores: that without Athenian support, many cities in the empire would not have been free from the Persians, and would not have been able to maintain democratic governments in the face of internal opposition from conservatives. For other evidence of allied loyalty to Athens, consider the troops who stayed with Demosthenes when they could have surrendered safely (**vii.82**).

cost a great deal of money to keep afloat, and Sparta, which was rich only in trained manpower and agricultural land, would not otherwise have been able to compete in this area. The Persians wanted to regain control of the Greek cities and islands along the western coast of Asia Minor,[269] and to do this they were willing to weaken the Athenians without giving the Spartans very much power. They therefore initiated a delicate game of diplomacy in which Athens and Sparta competed for financial support from Persia. Athens never got anything but a few messages to raise their hopes and throw their internal politics into confusion; the Spartan navy got less than they wanted but enough to make them a serious threat to the Athenians.

Oligarchy in Athens
Athenian conservatives believed that if they could set up a stable oligarchy in Athens they would earn the confidence of the Persians, and so obtain from them the money they needed for their survival as a naval power. The idea was born among officers of the Athenian fleet then stationed on Samos and was sent from there to Athens, where it took hold among a group that had long been yearning for an excuse to abolish democracy. The failure in Sicily was not entirely the fault of the democratic form of government, but many conservatives would have agreed with Thucydides' view of the matter: it was the democracy that had pulled Alcibiades out of the command when he was most needed, and it was the democracy that had been unwilling to accept failure from its generals and so had driven them to sink more and more resources in a losing proposition.

For all these reasons, then, the cause of oligarchy gained momentum and in June 411 a new government was established in Athens, known as The Four Hundred, promising to extend power to a wider group of five thousand (a promise they probably never intended to make good). One of the most important of the oligarchic reforms was the elimination of all forms of state pay for public service (except for military service). Such payments had enabled the poor to take part in government, and indeed may have enticed them to do so. The Four Hundred managed to intimidate the people of Athens, so that in the beginning the oligarchy met little resistance. Thucydides was struck by their success:

> It was no marvel that this business succeeded, since it was managed by many intelligent men;[270] but it was a great undertaking, since the Athenian people

269. Athens and the Delian League had liberated these cities from the Persian Empire long before the Peloponnesian War.
270. The man who planned the coup was Antiphon, who was also well known as

took it hard to lose their freedom almost a hundred years after the expulsion of the tyrants. During this time they had not been subject to anyone, and for half of it had grown accustomed to being the rulers of others. [viii.68.4]

Oligarchy and empire

Some Athenians had argued that oligarchy in Athens would be well received in the empire. The counterargument, given by a general named Phrynichus, is of some interest:

> As for the allied cities to whom the conspirators promise oligarchies, because they will be rid of democracy in Athens, Phrynichus said he knew full well that this would neither make those who had already rebelled more likely to return, nor would it strengthen the loyalty of those who remained, because they would not want to be subject to an empire, whether democracy or oligarchy, if they could have their liberty with either form of government. And even those who are called "good and noble men"[271] would, he thought, give them no less trouble than the democracy has done, since those men had devised evil projects into which they had led the people, and then they had themselves made the largest profit from them. Besides, under an oligarchy, allies would be put to death violently without trial; whereas democracy offers a refuge to ordinary people and is a moderating influence on the oligarchs. [viii.48.5–6]

Phrynichus was exactly right: those allies that did accept oligarchy turned soon after to freedom from the Athenian empire. An oligarchy installed in Thasos, for example, rebelled within two months:

> At Thasos the outcome was contrary to what was expected by the Athenians who had installed the oligarchy; and so, in my opinion, it was in many of the other parts of their empire. For as soon as the cities adopted "sensible" policies and felt free from fear in their actions, they moved straightway to

---

a sophist. Thucydides expresses great respect for Antiphon's intelligence. After the restoration of democracy, Antiphon was put on trial for his life. Part of the speech he made in his own defense (much admired by Thucydides) has survived in a papyrus. Antiphon's speech is a striking attempt to use the argument from likelihood (*eikos*) against the plain evidence of the case against him: it is not likely, he claims, that an orator would want to bring down democracy, since that is the political context in which he does best. For a translation, see Gagarin and Woodruff, forthcoming.

271. A favorite expression used by aristocrats to refer to members of their class.

freedom from the superficial "good government"[272] given them by the Athenians, for which they had no respect. [viii.64.5]

Collapse of the oligarchy

The oligarchy in Athens did not fare well. The troops on Samos never accepted it. That year Alcibiades reappeared on the Athenian side of the war. Although the city made no move to reinstate him, the army on Samos welcomed him and elected him general. Then, when they wanted to sail to Athens and put down the oligarchy, Alcibiades talked them out of it, thus averting a civil war that would have been damaging to Athens. Thucydides writes of this as Alcibiades' first good service to Athens.

Meanwhile, the oligarchs were not getting along with each other:

> Most of the Four Hundred fell into the private ambition that is fatal to an oligarchy grown out of a democracy. For at once each of them claimed not merely to be equal to the others, but to be the top man by far. In a democracy, on the other hand, if a man is defeated in an election he bears it better, because he does not think he has been beaten by his equals.[273] [viii.89.3]

And the war continued. With Spartan encouragement, the island of Euboea rebelled in September, and this threw the Athenians into an even greater panic than the loss of the Sicilian expedition had done, as Euboea was the breadbasket of Athens.

The Five Thousand

In the panic that followed the loss of Euboea, the Four Hundred oligarchs were ousted and a new form of government introduced:

> The Athenians . . . immediately called an assembly on the Pnyx, where they had been accustomed to assemble in former times.[274] There they deposed the Four Hundred, and voted to entrust affairs of state to the Five Thou-

272. "'Sensible' policies": *sōphrosunē;* "good government": *eunomia.* Both expressions are associated with oligarchy.
273. This is a troublesome paradox. The idea seems to be that in democracy a good man who is defeated can be consoled by the belief that the people who beat him were his inferiors, as would be true in class terms when an aristocrat is defeated by a common man.
274. The Pnyx is a hill near the Acropolis and, as the regular meeting place of the Assembly, had symbolic importance for the democracy.

8. Aftermath of the Sicilian Expedition

sand—or the number that could afford a hoplite's equipment[275]—and to give no one a salary for holding any public office, on pain of a curse. There were also frequent assemblies after this, in which they elected law-makers and voted in other measures towards a constitution. And now for the first time, at least in my life, the Athenians seemed to have ordered their constitution well: it consisted now of a moderate blending, in the interests of the few and the many. And this was the first thing, after so many misfortunes had occurred, that made the city raise her head again. [viii.97]

We do not know as much as we would like about the Five Thousand, or about why Thucydides thought so well of this form of government. The career of the Five Thousand was short, and may have been only a ploy of the oligarchs to win over the hoplite class to their side. In any case, Thucydides' *History* breaks off shortly after this passage, and we are left to make out the story of the rest of the war from other sources.

The last phase of the war

The story was picked up by Xenophon in his *Hellenica*. After the restoration of democracy in Athens, the city made a valiant effort to restore enough of the empire to stay afloat. The Athenians still had good hopes of defense until the destruction of their fleet at Aegospotami ("Goat River") in 405. When the news of this reached Athens "a wail ran up from Piraeus through the long walls to the city" as the Athenians were struck with the fear that they would be treated as they had treated the Melians and other conquered peoples.[276] After this, Athens was besieged by Sparta and forced to surrender unconditionally in 404.

Sparta did not treat Athens as Athens had feared. The Spartans did not destroy Athens, but merely tore down the long walls between Athens and Piraeus that had secured Athenian access to the sea and took away all but twelve triremes of the Athenian navy. This disabled Athens from waging war for the foreseeable future. At the same time, the Spartans installed an oligarchic regime favorable to themselves, the group known later as the

---

275. Hoplites were the heavily armed infantry that formed the backbone of every fighting force in Greece during this period. Since they were expected to pay for their own weapons and armor, they had to be men of at least moderate means.

276. Xenophon, *Hellenica* ii.2.3. For some of the Athenian atrocities against conquered peoples, see **v.116** (massacre of the Melians), **ii.27** (exile of the people of Aegina), and **iv.57.** (execution of the Aeginetan prisoners), and compare the atrocities committed by the Spartans at Plataea (**iii.68**) and the Corcyreans against their own people (**iv.47-48**).

Thirty Tyrants. These are the authorities Socrates would not serve, as he tells us in the *Apology* of Plato. [277]

What happened next? Democracy was restored in Athens in 403, and the long walls were rebuilt in 393. Some facsimile of the empire rose from the ashes, and Athenian culture bloomed as bright as ever. With the foundation of Plato's Academy about 385, Athens began to become truly the school of Greece. Its population never recovered, however, from the plague and the war. In 431 we believe there were more than forty thousand adult male citizens in Athens; in 317 there were only twenty-one thousand.

Sparta went into an even steeper decline. The Spartans' old ally Thebes turned against them, and their subject peoples in the Peloponnesus rose up against them again and again. Sparta meanwhile lost population at an astounding rate. By the end of the fourth century Sparta was no longer a factor in Greek affairs.

---

277. Socrates was even-handed: he would not support either the democracy or the Thirty Tyrants in the commission of crimes (*Apology* 32b–d).

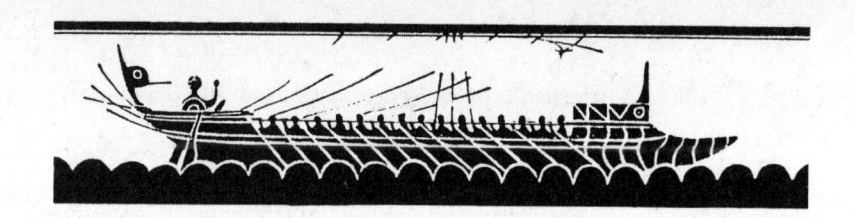

Dates

(All dates are B.C.E.)

c. 594	Solon's reforms in Athens.
c. 560	The Athenians give Pisistratus a bodyguard and this marks the beginning of his first period of rule as a tyrant.
546-5	King Cyrus seizes Asia Minor, including the Asiatic Greeks, for the Persian empire.
527-10	The sons of Pisistratus rule in Athens.
508/7	Democratic institutions begin to evolve in Athens.
499-94	The Asiatic Greeks rebel against the Persian empire.
494	The Persians take Miletus; they kill the men of Miletus, and burn the temple of Apollo at Didyma.
490	The Persian King Darius sends an army against Greece, which is defeated by the Athenians at the battle of Marathon.
482	The Athenians under Themistocles build the great fleet that will defeat the Persian navy at Salamis.
480	The Persian King Xerxes brings a larger army against Greece; battles of Thermopylae and Salamis.
479	Battle of Plataea: the Greek allies defeat the Persian army.
478	Fortification of Athens
477	Foundation of the Delian League

461	Athenian democracy is fully evolved with the reforms of Ephialtes.
c. 461-29	The age of Pericles in Athens
458	The Athenians build the long walls to protect the road to their seaport at the Piraeus.
454	The treasury of the Delian Lague is transferred to Athens.
447-33	Athens builds the Parthenon (the chief temple to the goddess Athena on the Athenian acropolis).
447/6	Athens puts down a rebellion in Euboea.
446/5	Athens and Sparta conclude the Thirty Years' Peace.
432	The 'Megarian Decree' is passed in Athens.
431-21	Peloponnesian War, first phase (Archidamian War)
430	The Plague breaks out in Athens
429	Death of Pericles
427	Surrender of Mytilene to Athens
427	Surrender of Plataea to Sparta and Thebes
427	Civil war (stasis) in Corcyra
425	Capture of 120 Spartan soldiers on Sphacteria
424	Amphipolis revolts against Athens. Thucydides goes into exile.
421-14	Peace of Nicias
416	Slaughter of the Melians
415	Athenian invasion of Sicily
414-04	Peloponnesian War, second phase (Decelean or Ionian War)
413	Destruction of Athenian army and navy outside Syracuse
412	Revolt of Athenian allies
411	Rule by the Four Hundred
411	Thucydides' *History* breaks off.
405	Destruction of the Athenian Navy at the Battle of Aegospotami ("Goat River")
404	Surrender of Athens to the Spartans

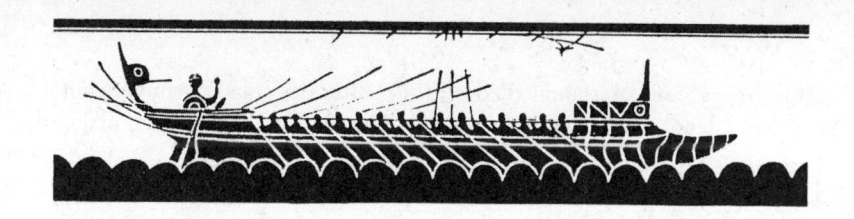

Glossary

This glossary explains the most important Greek words and proper names that occur in the text. References at the end of each entry lead readers to relevant passages in Thucydides.

Aegean Sea, the body of water to the east of Greece, between Greece and what is now Turkey. It is dotted with islands, and was rimmed all around with Greek cities in ancient times.

adikia, "injustice," is consistently rendered that way in this translation, although "wrong" is sometimes more accurate (**i.77, iii.38 ff., 44, 47, v.89**).

advantage, see *sumpheron*.

Alcibiades, an Athenian general and politician who rose to prominence at an early age in about 420. A former disciple of Socrates, he was a man of enormous charm and great wealth. He talked the Athenians into the expedition to Sicily (**vi.17** f.); after he was removed from command and indicted for impiety he fled to Sparta and gave them tips on conducting the war against Athens (**vi.91–92**). He returned to the Athenian side in 411 but was exiled in 406 and died two years later under mysterious circumstances. He is best known to modern readers through a stunning speech he gives at the end of Plato's *Symposium*. Though this is fiction, it reveals a great deal about the historical figure behind it.

Amphipolis, a city in Thrace in northern Greece that was of strategic importance because it guarded access by river to major sources of timber (for shipbuilding) and precious metals. Originally settled by Thracians, it was made a colony of Athens in 437, but was lost to the Spartans in 424. The historian Thucydides held a command in the area at the time of its loss; he was held accountable and exiled (iv.108). After this time it maintained its independence until Philip of Macedon (Alexander's father) took it in 357.

anankē, "necessity" or "compulsion." *Ananke* in Thucydides is usually the subjective necessity felt under the influence of fear (see Introduction, p. xxx). In this translation it is usually translated by "compulsion" or "compels." The word's most famous occurrence is at **i.23**; see also **i.75** and **v.105**.

archē, in Thucydides means "empire" and is translated that way throughout. It can also mean "rule," "reign," and in other contexts "cause," "origin," "beginning," or "first principle." On the Athenian Empire, see especially **i.76, ii.8, ii.36, iii.37 ff., 45, 48, v.89, 97, vi.18, viii.48**.

Archidamus, (**i.80**, ff.) Spartan king during the first phase of the war (the Archidamian War), 431–21.

aretē, good character, often translated by "virtue." In Thucydides it often refers particulary to courage.

Asiatic Greece, the Greek cities located along the coast of Asia Minor (modern Turkey). Most of these were inhabited by Greeks who were known as *Ionians*.

Athenagoras, Syracusan radical democrat (**vi.39**).

Attica, the Athenian homeland (see map)

autonomia, independence, having one's own laws. See Ostwald, 1982. In Thucydides' time autonomy was a relatively new concept. Some allies evidently complained that Athens extended the jurisdiction of her courts into allied states for some types of cases (**i.77**). For some of Athens' enemies autonomy probably meant "retaining a traditional form of government"— i.e., oligarchy. Athens supported democratic changes in many cities belonging to the empire. Such changes would have violated autonomy in the traditional sense, while leaving the people loyal to Athens. This would explain why, when Athens was at her weakest later in the war, she was not entirely abandoned by the allies she was supposed to have subjugated. See p. xiv.

Boeotia, the country bordering on Athens to the west, with its main city at Thebes. Boeotia had shrugged off Athenian attempts at conquest before the war, and during the war was an ally of Sparta.

Chios, an island in the eastern Aegean that remained loyal to Athens until 413, after which it resisted Athens until the end of the war. Chios was one of the very few members of the Delian League that retained its own fleet.

Glossary

civil war, see *stasis*.

Cleon, Athenian politician and demagogue who rose to power after the death of Pericles. He was responsible for the brilliant Athenian success at Sphacteria (425). In this *History*, he figures mainly as the speaker who advocates the death penalty for all male citizens of Mytilene (**iii.36 ff.**).

colonies, city-states founded by older Greek cities. They were usually independent politically, but maintained friendly relations with their parent cities. Greek colonies in Sicily and southern Italy date from the eighth century.

compulsion, see *anankē*.

Corcyra, an island off the west coast of Greece, modern Corfu. Corcyra was a colony of, but in conflict with, Corinth. See p. 16 and **iii.81 ff**.

Corinth, a Dorian city on the isthmus between Athens and the Peloponnesus. Corinth was an important commercial center and a major ally of Sparta.

Cyrus, king of Persia and founder of the Persian empire. He conquered Asia Minor, along with the Greek cities located there, in 546/45.

Darius, king of Persia who put down the Ionian revolt in 494 and proceeded to send by sea an expedition against Greece that was defeated at Marathon in 490.

Delian League, the alliance of Greek city-states led by Athens, formed in 477 in the extended conflict with Persia that followed Greek victories at Salamis and Plataea.

Delos, a tiny island near the center of the Aegean. Sacred to Apollo, and a center of Greek religious life, Delos also became the center of the League established by Athens to continue fighting against the Persian Empire. In 454 the league's treasury was moved to Athens.

demagogue, literally, "leader of the people." Demagogues in Athens exercised influence without holding public office by speaking effectively in the Assembly.

dēmos, literally "people," often means a political group that claims to represent ordinary people. See for example, **ii.65, v.85, vi.39, viii.48**.

Demosthenes, Athenian general who occupied Pylos in 425 and commanded the reenforcements for the Sicilian expedition in 413.

dikaion, rendered "justice" in this translation, although "right" (as opposed to "wrong") is sometimes more accurate. See **iii.39 ff., 44, 47, 82, v.89 ff., 98, 105, 107**.

Diodotus, the Athenian speaker who defended the lives of the Mytileneans (**iii.42** ff.). Nothing more is known of him.

Dorians, a group of Greeks with a distinct cultural tradition marked by the Doric dialect. Spartans, Corinthians, and, indeed, most of the Peloponnesian League were Dorians, as were the Syracusans.

drachma, see *talent*.

eikos, "reasonable expectation." Greek orators frequently built arguments around what was *eikos*, or what could reasonably be expected. I have followed Hobbes in translating the word as "reason." Some modern translators prefer "probability," but this is misleading. Typical uses are at **ii.63, iii.40.4, vi.17–18**.

empire, see *archē*.

ephor, one of five high elected officials in Lacedaemon.

epieikeia, in Thucydides means "fairness" or "sense of fairness" (**iii.40, 48, v.86, 90**).

Epipolae, the strategic height overlooking Syracuse, site of the night battle that turned the tide against the Athenians in 413 (**vii.42, ff.**).

Euboea, the long island off the north coast of Attica. Athenian military and economic strategy depended on retaining control over Euboea, which tended to prefer independence.

Eurymedon, Athenian commander at Corcyra (**iii.81**).

factionalism, see *stasis*.

fairness, see *epieikeia*.

Five Thousand, the more democratic oligarchy that the Four Hundred promised to the Athenians, and which briefly succeeded them. See **viii.97**.

Four Hundred, the oligarchy, named after the size of its executive body, that seized power in Athens and held it for a few months in 411 (**viii.64 ff.**).

Hipparchus. The younger son of the tyrant Pisistratus, killed by Harmodius and Aristogeiton (**vi.54 ff.**).

hoplites, or heavily armed infantry, formed the backbone of Greek armies in this period. As they were expected to pay for their own armor (*hopla*), they had to have some money of their own. Hoplites, in most cases, were moderately well-off citizens.

injustice, see *adikia*.

Ionians, a group of Greeks characterized by a distinct dialect and cultural tradition, and living mainly on or near the coast of Asia Minor, where they came in contact with stimulating non-Greek cultures. Athens was commonly accepted as the original homeland of the Ionians.

isonomia, a system of law or justice that is fair or equal. See the notes on **iii.62** and **iii.82**.

justice, see *dikaion*.

Lacedaemon, the name usually used for Sparta.

Lamachus, Athenian general who was given shared command of the Sicilian expedition with Nicias and Alcibiades in 415 and was killed in 414.

Lesbos, the largest of the islands off the coast of Asia Minor. Its main city was Mytilene.

Marathon, a plain on the coast north of Athens and the site of the battle in which the Athenians and their Plataean allies defeated the Persian army that first invaded Greece in 490.

Megara, a city located between Athens and Corinth and a member of the Peloponnesian League. The Megarian Decree of the Athenians barred Megara from commerce with Athens and her empire, and was one of the causes of the war.

Melos, a Dorian but nonaligned island in the Aegean. In 416/5 the island was seized by Athens and its people destroyed (**v.85–116**).

Messenians, the inhabitants of Messenia, the district of the Peloponnesus west of Sparta. Conquered by Sparta in the eighth and seventh centuries, most of the Messenians were forced to work their own land for Spartan landlords. Something between serfs and share-croppers, they were known as *helots*. A series of uprisings led to the settlement of a group of Messenians at Naupactus, a safe distance from Sparta, in the middle of the fifth century. Messenians fought alongside Athens against Sparta whenever they could, and in 369 finally achieved independence.

metics, resident aliens in Athens.

Miletus, an Ionian city of Asiatic Greece, the main center of Ionian Greek culture before its destruction by the Persians in 494.

Mytilene, capital of the island of Lesbos, and one of the few members of the Delian League to retain its own fleet. It rebelled against the Athenian empire in 428, was defeated in 427, and narrowly missed total destruction (**iii.36–49**). In 412, amid the general revolt of the allies, it rebelled again.

Naupactus, site of a settlement of Messenian enemies of Sparta on the north shore of the Gulf of Corinth. See Messenians.

necessity, see *ananke*.

new learning, the enlightenment of the fifth century in Greece, which grew around the sophists and the teaching of rationalist science and rhetoric. Pericles was associated with the movement, and under his leadership Athens gave the warmest welcome in Greece to the new teachers. Sparta, characteristically, gave the coldest.

Nicias, an Athenian politician and general. His name is given to the peace treaty of 421 between Athens and Sparta. Opposed to the expedition against Sicily (**vi.9** ff.), he was nevertheless made one of its three commanders in 415. He is best known to philosophers through his part in Plato's dialogue on courage, the *Laches*.

oligarchy, literally, "rule by the few." Oligarchs, rich men or aristocrats, held power in most of the cities that were allied with the Spartans. See **i.19, iii.39, 47, 82, v.85, vi.39, viii.48**.

Peloponnesus, the near-island in which Sparta is located. A system of military alliances gave Sparta effective control of most of the Peloponnesus during the period of this war.

people, see *demos*.

Pericles (490–29), leader of Athens during the period of her greatest expansion and most explosive cultural development (**ii.65**).

Phrynichus, a conservative Athenian general (**viii.48**).

Piraeus, the main port of Athens.

Pisistratus, first tyrant of Athens, from about 560 to his death in 527. During his rule and that of his sons, Athens emerged as a military and commercial power in Greece and began its rise to cultural ascendancy (**i.20, vi.54**).

Plataea, small city in Boeotia that distinguished itself by joining Athens and Sparta during the Persian wars. Site of the decisive battle in which Greek allied troops led by Sparta defeated the Persian army (479). Plataea sided with Athens in the wars with Sparta, and was destroyed in 427 (**ii.71–78, iii.20–24, iii.52–68**).

pleonexia, avarice that leads to overreaching.

Pnyx, the hill next to the Acropolis at which the Athenian assembly met.

Potidaea, a colony of Corinth with a strategic position near Macedonia. A member of the Delian League, it rebelled in 432 in protest against a rise in taxes, and was taken after a long siege in the winter of 430. The siege of Potidaea was one of the immediate causes of the war. Socrates served there as a soldier, and his hardiness during that cold winter is reported by Alcibiades in Plato's *Symposium* 219e ff.

Pylos, see Sphacteria.

reason, i.e., what is reasonable, see *eikos*.

Salamis, an island in the gulf offshore from Attica. Site of the naval battle in which the Greek navy defeated the navy of the invading Persians in 480.

Samos, an island off the coast of Asia Minor not far from Miletus. A strong member of the Delian League, Samos tried to quit in 440, but was brought to heel by Pericles. In the second phase of the war, after 412, Samos became a major Athenian naval base.

Solon, Athenian statesman and poet, born about 638. In about 594, at a time of great social unrest, he attempted to preserve a balance in government by instituting moderate popular reforms. These were thought to have paved the way for the development of Athenian democracy a century later.

sōphrosunē, the virtue of being sound-minded, clear-headed, prudent, self-controlled, and moderate; the basis the Spartans claimed for all their virtues (**i.84**). This virtue was also claimed by supporters of oligarchy.

Sphacteria, a tiny island offshore of Pylos on the west coast of the Peloponnesus. In 425 Athenians and Messenians fortified Pylos, and when the Spartans countered with a garrison on Sphacteria, the allies besieged and eventually captured a hundred twenty Spartan soldiers on the island. This was the most dramatic success Athens had in the war.

stasis, the Greek word for civil disturbances ranging from political conflict to all-out civil war. It is translated as "civil war" here, as Thucydides uses the word mainly for violent *stasis*. The word can be used, however, simply for factionalism. See **i.18, ii.65**, and, most important, **iii.81–82** and **vi.17**.

sumpheron, "advantage" or "what is advantageous" (**i.76, ii.39, iii.38, 44, 47, v.90, 98, 106, 107**).

Syracuse, a colony of Corinth and the most prosperous of the Greek cities on the island of Sicily. It was the main target of Athens' ill-fated expedition of 415–413.

talent, a large sum of money amounting to sixty minas, each of which was worth a hundred drachmas. A drachma would pay for one day's labor by a skilled man: a citizen's pay for a day of jury duty was half a drachma (three obols).

Thermopylae a battle in 480 in which a small Spartan force was wiped out in a glorious defense of the pass of Thermopylae against the invading Persian army. The stand of the Spartans against overwhelming numbers gave luster to the reputation of the Spartans for discipline and courage.

Thirty Years' Peace, the treaty that kept a kind of peace between the Athenians and the Lacedaemonians and their respective allies from 446/5 to 432/1, when the Spartans voted to go to war.

trireme, a large Greek warship of the period (**i.13–14**). A trireme carried a crew of two hundred rowers, marines, and officers. They fought by ramming each other at speed or by placing themselves close enough to other vessels that the marines on board could fire off javelins, arrows, or slings.

Tyrant, tyrannos, a sole ruler without the legitimacy of a traditional monarch (**i.17–18, ii.63, iii.37, vi.54**). Rulers called "tyrants" were established in many Greek cities during the seventh and sixth centuries. The word *tyrannos* did not have a pejorative connotation until late in the fifth century.

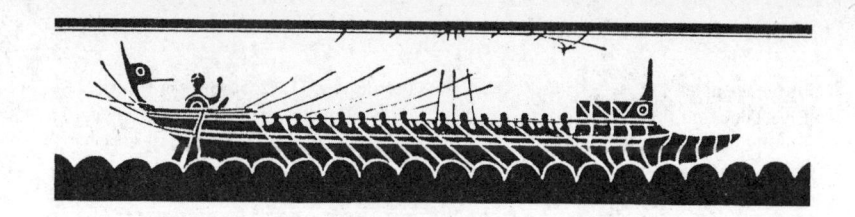

Index

Acanthus, 97
Aegina, 16, 32, 84
Agamemnon, 5
Alcibiades, xviii, xxix, 113, 158; character, 115, 116; about Sicily, 117–20; suspected of impiety, 123, 125; recalled from Sicily, 57 *n.* 128, 156; speaks at Sparta, 127–28
Amphipolis, xi, 100
Antiphon, xi, 156 *n.* 270
archaeology, 2
Archidamus, speech at Sparta, 25–28; invades Attica, 46; besieges Plataea, 62; speeches, 62, 63
Aristogeiton, 12, 126
Athenian Empire (*see also* Delian League), origins, 22, 40, 119; power, 54; popularity, xiv–xv, 37, 74, 115 with *n.* 202; relation to virtues, 43, 55, 70, 74; as tyranny, 55; democracy in, 157–58
Athens (*see also* democracy, education), origins, xvi, 2, 3; constitution, xiii–xiv, 40–41; power, 17, 25, 34, 41, 54, 56; customs, 19, 42–44, 135; Athenian speech at Sparta, 21–25
autonomy (*see also* freedom), 31–32, 34, 99
Boeotia (*see also* Thebes), 8, 82, 83, 85
Brasidas, 24 *n.* 74; speech at Acanthus, 97–99; at Amphipolis, 100
Callicles, xxvii
Carians, 5
Catana, 112, 125, 148 *n.* 255

Chios, 11, 139, 155
civil war, 8, 58, 89–95
Cleon, xviii, xx, 100; as speaker, xxiii, xxix; on Mytilene, 67–71
colonies, 8
Corcyra, 16, 89–95
Corinth, 8, 16; speeches at Sparta, 17–20, 30–31
Coronea, 83, 85
death penalty, 73
Decelea, 127
Delian League (*see also* Athenian Empire), xiv, xvii
Delium, 100
demagogues, xiii
democracy, in Athens, xiii, 40–41, 57; in Delian League, xiv; weaknesses, xxiv, xxv, 154, 156; strengths, xxvi, 124, 138
Demosthenes, 130, 134, 159, 151
Diodotus, 71–76
Dorians, 8, 10
eclipse, 137
education, xv–xvi, xxxii; in Sparta, 27; in Athens, 41–42, 67
Egesta, 111, 116
eikos, 2, 157 *n.* 270
Epidamnus, 16, 36
Epipolae, 129
equality, in democracy, 40, 92; in oligarchy, 82
Euboea, 15, 29, 158

171

Eurymedon, 89, 137
Five Thousand, 158
Four Hundred, 156, 58
freedom, 40, 98, 99, 141
gods, 29, 50, 62, 106, 108, 146
Gylippus, 129
Hagnon, 51
Harmodius, 12, 126
Hermocrates, 124, 144
Herodotus, 12 *n.* 51, 153 *n.* 261
Hipparchus, 12, 126
Hippias, 10 *n.* 48, 126
Homer, 3, 6, 43, 139
Ionians, 9
justice/injustice, xxvi, 23, 29, 63, 79, 106
Lacedaemonians, constitution, xii–xiii, 11, 12; customs, 4, 17–20, 23, 27–28, 106; defenders of Greek liberty, 37; power, 6, 26, 160; vote for war, 29, 130
Lamachus, 113, 129
law, xxix, 41, 49, 67, 73, 82, 93; unwritten law, 41, 80; divine law, 91; law of nature, 106
Marathon, 11, 21, 36
Megara, 16, 31, 35
Minos, 3, 5
Mycenae, 5
Mytilene, xviii, 66, 75
nature, human nature, xxix, 48, 69, 73, 90, 93, 106, 146
naval power, xxviii, 3, 8–10, 34
Nicias, xxiii, xxix, 76, 135, 151; speaks about Sicily, 113–16, 120–22, 130; defends camp, 129; exhorts troops, 146–47; Thucydides' judgment, 152
oligarchy, 92, 125, 154 *n.* 266; equality in, 82; in Athens, 156 (see Four Hundred); in Peloponnesian League, xiv, 11, 115; weaknesses of, 157, 158
oracles, 37, 47, 50, 101, 105
Peace of Nicias, xviii, 101, 114, 130, 152
Peloponnesian League, xiii, 16, 29–33

Pericles, xv, 31, 52, 56–58; war speech, 31–36; Funeral Oration, 39–46; strategy, xvii–xviii, 35, 51, 56–57; last speech, 52–56
Persia, 59, 155
Persian Wars, xvi, 11, 15, 21, 78
Phrynichus, 157
piety, 79–80, 92
Pisistratus, xvi, 126
plague, 46–50, 53, 55
Plataea, xvii, xviii; origin, 82; attack and siege, 36–37, 62–66; speech of the Plataeans, 77–81
Polycrates, 9
Potidaea, 16, 20, 28, 32, 50–51, 61
poverty, 73, 93
Protagoras, xi, xxvii, 31 *n.* 85
punishment, xxvii with *n.* 13, 68, 69, 72–73
Pylos, 100, 109
quarries, 152
Samos, 8, 155
Sicilian expedition, xix, xxv, 57, 111, 124, 153, 155
Sicily, 9–10, 112
Sparta, *see* Lacedaemonians
speeches, authenticity, xxi–xxiv, 13; effectiveness of, xxiv, xxviii, 39, 68, 71–72, 77, 86, 102, 113, 118
Sphacteria, xviii, 100, 152
Sthenilaidas, 28–29
Syracuse, 111, 118, 119, 121, 124, 138
Thebes, 78; speech of the Thebans, 81–86
Themistocles, 9, 22
Thirty Year's Peace, 15, 29
Thucydides, life, x–xi; as general, 100; mentions himself, 1, 47, 61, 101, 159; unity of the *History*, xxv; political theory, xxv–xxxii
Trojan War, 3, 8
tyranny, 8, 10, 125
virtue, 43–45, 85
war, xxix, 25, 27, 33, 53, 90, 105, 120